PROGRAMMING PARADIGMS IN LISP

McGraw-Hill Series in Artificial Intelligence

Allen: *Anatomy of LISP*
Davis and Lenat: *Knowledge-Based Systems in Artificial Intelligence*
Nilsson: *Problem-Solving Methods in Artificial Intelligence*
Rich and Knight: *Artificial Intelligence*
Sangal: *Programming Paradigms in LISP*

Also Available from McGraw-Hill

Schaum's Outline Series in Computers

Most outlines include basic theory, definitions, and hundreds of solved problems and supplementary problems with answers.

Titles on the Current List Include:

Advanced Structured Cobol
Boolean Algebra
Computer Graphics
Computer Science
Computers and Business
Computers and Programming
Data Processing
Data Structures
Digital Principles, 2d edition
Discrete Mathematics
Essential Computer Mathematics
Mathematical Handbook of Formulas & Tables
Matrix Operations
Microprocessor Fundamentals, 2d edition
Programming with Advanced Structured Cobol
Programming with Assembly Language
Programming with Basic, 3d edition
Programming with C
Programming with Fortran
Programming with Pascal
Programming with Structured Cobol

Schaum's Solved Problems Books

Each title in this series is a complete and expert source of solved problems containing thousands of problems with worked out solutions.

Related Titles on the Current List Include:

3000 Solved Problems in Calculus
2500 Solved Problems in Differential Equations
3000 Solved Problems in Linear Algebra
2000 Solved Problems in Numerical Analysis

Available at your College Bookstore. A complete listing of Schaum titles may be obtained by writing to: Schaum Division
McGraw-Hill, Inc.
Princeton Road, S-1
Hightstown, NJ 08520

PROGRAMMING PARADIGMS IN LISP

Rajeev Sangal

Indian Institute of Technology Kanpur, India

McGraw-Hill, Inc.

New York   St. Louis   San Francisco   Auckland   Bogotá   Caracas
Hamburg   Lisbon   London   Madrid   Mexico   Milan   Montreal
New Delhi   Paris   San Juan   São Paulo   Singapore   Sydney   Tokyo   Toronto

This book was set in Times Roman by J. M. Post Graphics, Corp.
The editor was David M. Shapiro;
the production supervisor was Janelle S. Travers.
The cover was designed by Edward Butler.
Project supervision was done by The Total Book.
R. R. Donnelley & Sons Company was printer and binder.

PROGRAMMING PARADIGMS IN LISP

1 2 3 4 5 6 7 8 9 0 DOC DOC 9 5 4 3 2 1 0

ISBN 0-07-054666-5

Library of Congress Cataloging-in-Publication Data

Sangal, Rajeev.
    Programming paradigms in LISP / Rajeev Sangal.
        p.   cm.
    Includes bibliographical references.
    ISBN 0-07-054666-5
    1. LISP (Computer program language)   2. Artificial Intelligence.
I. Title.
QA76.73.L23S26   1991
005.13'3—dc20   90-4506

CONTENTS

PREFACE

This book is about artificial intelligence (AI) programming in LISP. It describes the programming techniques and principles that have arisen chiefly out of work in AI. Not only have they arisen from AI, they continue to be especially applicable to AI. Whenever an AI system is built, they invariably appear in one form or another. Examples include search, pattern matching, unification, backtracking, and inheritance, along with a host of techniques associated with each of them.

This book, however, differs from the few other books that are available on the practice of AI in one important way. It looks at AI programming through the glasses of paradigms. The paradigms affect the way we think about a problem. They help us approach the solution, select the algorithms, and develop and use the tools. They provide a framework in which diverse techniques can be knit together. As a result, the solution to problems can be approached in a more systematic manner. The paradigms that have been covered in this book are logic and rule-based programming, functional programming, data-driven programming, and object-oriented programming.

Each of the paradigms is explained, and its use is illustrated by solving many short examples and some extended examples. The examples are intended to acquaint the reader with the features of a paradigm, where it should be used, what kinds of problems it is suitable for, etc. This is followed by a detailed discussion of how the paradigm can be implemented. Various alternative approaches to implementation are compared. Actual code is given for at least one of the approaches. The code is developed incrementally for pedagogical reasons. First, the core features are implemented; later, the implementation is enhanced, a step at a time, with pedagogy in mind. Each enhancement is discussed with the actual code.

LISP is the language in which the implementations in this book are coded. The choice of LISP was fairly obvious. AI systems are generally large and complex. Their development requires that the implementation language and the support environment provide flexibility, rapid prototyping, and good debugging tools. On these counts, LISP wins over all other languages. It has an interpreter which implies that the debugging facilities would be unmatched by any compiled language. LISP encourages the use of dynamic data structures which lead to the design of a flexible system. There

is a notation for data which allows complex data structures to be viewed at leisure on the screen (or a printout) or created by nimble keystrokes. It permits the user to become a part of the system under development, filling in wherever the programs and data are incomplete. LISP also permits data to be treated as programs and executed, or programs to be treated as data and manipulated (even created) by other programs. Finally, the macro facility allows new languages to be defined and embedded within the LISP system. At times in AI, it is easier or more elegant to first define and implement a suitable language and then to write the solution in it. The history of AI is replete with the development of specialized languages and sublanguages that are tailored to solve a problem. The macro facility has played an indispensable role in the rapid prototyping of such languages.

There will be ample illustrations of the capabilities of LISP in this book. It should remove some of the mystery associated with LISP and reveal how advanced LISP programmers make use of it. This book can be said to be an attempt at describing the AI and LISP folklore developed by myriads of practitioners but unified by means of the paradigms.

There has never been a standard for LISP. However, with the development of COMMON LISP in the 1980s and its acceptance by a large number of system implementors and manufacturers, it has become a de facto standard. This ensures that COMMON LISP programs developed on one type of machine can run with minimal or no changes on another type of machine.

The material in this book can be used in a one-semester course on AI programming or advanced LISP programming with an emphasis on implementations. There are many exercises involving implementations. It is better if students in such a course have a background in programming and data structures so that they will be able to appreciate implementation issues better. The material in the book can be supplemented in various ways. If the students do not know LISP programming but are conversant with programming in another language and with data structures, the initial part of the course may be devoted to teaching elementary LISP, possibly using another book. If more emphasis is to be given to knowledge representation or logic or production systems, for example, suitable additional material can be referred to.

This book is also suitable for self-study by AI and LISP programmers. A mature reader can follow the book easily, reimplementing the systems described and exploring alternative approaches that have been outlined but left as exercises. The reader not only will get an in-depth understanding of the material but also will be equipped with a tool box containing his or her own implementations.

This book does not discuss multiparadigm systems. Such systems, however, can be designed and implemented quite easily by anyone who has mastered this book. Also, it has not been possible to include the COMMON LISP object-oriented system (CLOS). The material in this book was more or less finalized by the summer of 1987, before CLOS appeared.

This book is now in your hands. Enjoy.

ACKNOWLEDGMENTS

This book owes an intellectual debt to Charniak, Riesbeck, and McDermott (1980) because it follows their style of giving actual code and enhancing features incrementally, resulting in impressive systems.

Many people helped in the book-writing project: Harish Karnick, T. V. Prabhakar, and Somenath Biswas read an early draft; Nitin Indurkhya gave extensive comments on an earlier draft; K. S. H. S. R. Bhatta and P. V. Ramesh tested the programs on Domain COMMON LISP; several batches of students who took the courses CS365 Artificial Intelligence Programming and CS450 Principles of Programming Languages at IIT Kanpur contributed in various ways as this was class tested on them; participants in 14-day intensive courses on AI Programming-1 and several other people too numerous to name here gave useful comments; and finally the following referees did a very thorough job of reviewing the manuscript: Maria Gini, University of Minnesota; Wade Hennessey; and Louis Steinberg, Rutgers University. The Department of Computer Science and Engineering at IIT Kanpur provided the stimulating environment in which this book was written. J. P. Mall typed the original manuscript.

My parents and Neeraj and Susmita were constant sources of encouragement. Finally, thanks are due to my wife, Nisha, and daughter Sapna for putting up with long hours and days when I was there but not there.

Rajeev Sangal

PROGRAMMING PARADIGMS IN LISP

PART
1

PRELIMINARIES

CHAPTER

1

REVIEW OF LISP

In the early days, computers were primarily used for doing arithmetic. As a result, many people used to and still think of the computer as a number cruncher: computer memory as a store in which numbers can be stored, and the processor as one which performs arithmetic operations on it. There is another, more important, aspect of computers: computer as a manipulator of symbols.

The language LISP provides us with a flexible yet powerful mechanism for storing and manipulating symbols. Instead of dealing with bit patterns, we deal directly in terms of objects. The atomic objects are symbols and numbers, and they can be grouped together as lists. Examples of atoms are COLOR, LEGS, 4, and 3.2. Examples of lists are

```
(TABLE   BROWN   COLOR)
(TABLE1  (COLOR   BROWN)
         (LEGS   4)
         (HEIGHT   (30   INCH)))
(2   3   5   7   9)
(IF   ((HIGH-PRESSURE    ?X)
       (MOD-CORROSIVE    ?X)
       (HIGH-TEMP        ?X)
       (SEVERE-FOULING    ?X))
THEN (TUBES-SIDE-HEAT-EXCHANGER ?X))
```

Although all the above are lists, they arise in different contexts and are used very differently. The first two appear as descriptions of physical objects, the third one

is a list of five prime numbers, and the last one is a rule regarding selection of heat exchangers. Thus, we will always consider objects in a context and in terms of operations that can be performed on them.

There are many situations where the computer is primarily acting as a symbol processor as opposed to a number cruncher, for example, in compilers, operating systems, expert systems, natural language interfaces, machine translation, knowledge representation and inference, vision, and learning. In each of these, the primary thing is the symbolic representation of the concerned entities and their manipulation. For example, a compiler takes a program in a high-level language, builds its representation internally, and uses it to generate machine code. Similarly, a natural language interface must accept user input in a natural language, say Hindi, understand it, and take appropriate action like transforming it and passing it to the host system.

There are many reasons why LISP has been the dominant language for symbol processing particularly in the area of artificial intelligence. LISP is interactive, has a notation for data structure, is primarily based around a single (dynamic) data structure, allows data to be treated as programs and vice versa, has macro and other facilities using which new languages and features can be implemented easily, etc. These will become clear as we learn and use LISP.

1.1 DATA STRUCTURES

There are many types of data objects in LISP. The most important ones are number, symbol, and list. List is the primary means of structuring data.

Unlike most other programming languages, LISP provides a rich notation for the data objects. This notation is accepted by the LISP system. Following are the important types of data objects and their notation:

1. *Number* (e.g., 3, 8.6, -9). A number is written with an optional $+$ or $-$ sign, followed by a sequence of digits possibly having a decimal point somewhere in the sequence.
2. *Symbol* (e.g., COLOR, XY3). A symbol is a LISP object which is written as a sequence of characters consisting of letters of the alphabet, digits, dashes (-), or special characters ($+$, *, ?, etc.).
3. *List*. An open parenthesis followed by notations for zero or more objects followed by a close parenthesis is the notation for a list. For example,

```
( )
(3  (4  COLOR  RED)  (5  COLOR  BROWN))
((B  (RED  COLOR))  (8  3.2))
```

A list consisting of only the open and close parentheses, (), is called a nil list or empty list. It is also written as NIL. Symbols, numbers, and NIL are called atoms. NIL or () is the only object which is both an atom and a list.

Parentheses play a definite role in defining lists. Unlike arithmetic expressions

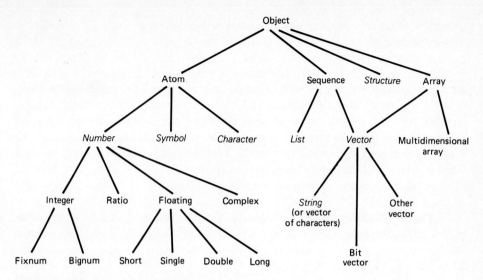

FIGURE 1-1
Important types of data objects in COMMON LISP.

in mathematics where pairs of extra parentheses around a parenthesized expression do not change its meaning, extra parentheses in our notation imply different objects. For example, (PLUS 5 4) and ((PLUS 5 4)) denote different objects. The former is a list of three atoms, while the latter is a list of one object which, in turn, is a list of three atoms.

We will use the term *expression* for the notation for objects. Historically, expressions have been called symbolic expressions or S-expressions (S-exprs). S-exprs have also been used to refer to the object denoted by them when the ambiguity (between the notation and the object it denotes) does not cause any problem.

There are other data types in COMMON LISP like string, character, array, and structure. Figure 1-1 shows the important types of data objects. The objects emphasized in this book are shown in italic.

There are other types of objects like stream, path name, package, read table, and hash table. Most of them serve specialized purposes and will be introduced later.

1.2 PROGRAM STRUCTURE

Programs, like data structures, are also objects. All programs are objects, but only a small subset of all possible objects will qualify to be programs.

When we evaluate an object (or execute a program), we get a new object. We can think of evaluation in terms of a function called EVAL that maps objects to objects:

```
EVAL: object → object
```

When EVAL is applied to an object that is not a program, it results in an error. An object that is evaluated is also called a *form*.

Before we can define evaluation we need the notion of binding. We can *bind* a symbol to an arbitrary object. The bound symbol is said to *possess a value*. For example, we can bind the symbol COLORS to the object (RED GREEN BLUE), in which case, the symbol COLORS is said to have the value (RED GREEN BLUE). When a symbol is bound, its earlier binding if any is not lost irretrievably. It is saved and is normally restored after due time. For example, when a function call is made, bindings of appropriate symbols are saved. They are restored on return from the call. This will be discussed further later in the chapter.

Evaluation can be defined for the following terms:

1. A number evaluates to itself. For example, 5 evaluates to 5, and -3.2 evaluates to -3.2. We write it as

   ```
   5 =>   5
   -3.2 =>   -3.2
   ```

   where $=>$ represents evaluation.

2. A symbol evaluates to its binding or value. For example, if COLOR has the value 3, it evaluates to 3, i.e.,

   ```
   COLOR => 3
   ```

   If COLOR has the value RED,

   ```
   COLOR => RED
   ```

   and so on. If the symbol being evaluated is unbound, its evaluation results in an error. In other words, function EVAL is not defined on unbound symbols.

   Symbols T and NIL evaluate to themselves and cannot be bound by the user. (Symbols whose name begins with the character : are called *keywords* and also evaluate to themselves.)

3. A list of the form

   ```
   (<function-name> <parm1> ... <parmN>)
   ```

   where <function-name> is an atom and is the name of a function, and <parm1> to <parmN> are arbitrary forms, is a function application. It is evaluated as follows: First each of the *parameters,* <parm1> to <parmN>, is evaluated, and then the named function <function-name> is applied to the *arguments* (i.e., to the result

of evaluation of the parameters).[1] For example, with PLUS or + being the standard addition function:

```
(+ 5.3 8) =>    13.3
(+  (+ 5 8) 9) => 22
```

Similarly if X is bound to 23,

```
(+ X 4.5) =>    27.5
```

TIMES or * is the standard multiplication function.

If the number of arguments or the type of arguments does not match that required for a function, an error results.

4. A list of the form

```
(<special-word> <parm1> ... <parmN>)
```

where <special-word> is a special symbol, is called a special form. It evaluates depending on the <special-word>. The parameters may or may not be evaluated, again depending on the <special-word>. There are a number of built-in special forms provided in LISP. For example, QUOTE takes one parameter and the entire expression evaluates to the parameter

```
(QUOTE (1 3 5)) => (1 3 5)
(QUOTE (+ 8 9)) => (+ 8 9)
```

As the second example illustrates, QUOTE blocks the application of + to its arguments. The result is the list (+ 8 9), not 17. In due course, we will introduce more special words.

The following abbreviation is used with QUOTE: (QUOTE <S-expr>) is written as '<S-expr>. Thus,

```
'(1 3 5)
```

---

[1]The rule that the parameters must be evaluated before the function is applied is the usual rule for function application in other programming languages. Only the syntax is different. In other languages, we write function application as

```
<function-name> (<parm1>, ... , <parmN>)
```

The reason for the particular syntax in LISP is that it makes programs and data structures look similar — a great convenience while manipulating programs as data or evaluating data as programs.

is an abbreviation for

```
(QUOTE (1 3 5))
```

One of the reasons why we need QUOTE in LISP is because unlike in other languages, constants and variables, or list data and forms, do not look different in LISP. A symbol expression can behave both as a constant or a variable. A quoted symbol expression is like a constant, while an unquoted symbol expression is like a variable. Similarly, a list expression can be constant data or a function application depending on whether it is quoted or not. Thus, '(+ 8 9) is data, while (+ 8 9) is a function application.

5. If a list is of the form

```
(<nonatom> <parm1> ... <parmN>)
```

where the <nonatom> is a lambda expression, it is evaluated as follows: Each of the parameters is evaluated yielding the arguments, and the lambda expression is applied to the arguments.

Normally, the LISP interpreter reads the S-expr typed by the user, produces an object, evaluates it, and prints the S-expr for the resulting object. This is called the top level or the read-eval-print loop of the LISP interpreter. Thus, for example, if the user types the digit

```
5
```

the interpreter reads it as the number 5, evaluates it to 5, and prints it back as

```
5
```

Similarly, if the user types

```
(+ 5 8)
```

it will be printed back as

```
13
```

Evaluation of a form is done using the rules defined above. Also, since the evaluation is done and the result printed right away, LISP encourages a highly interactive style of programming.[2]

---

[2]Unlike Pascal or other compiled languages there is no long intermediate step of compilation that needs to be performed before a program can be executed.

1.3   DEFINITION OF FUNCTIONS

Suppose we wanted to have a method for computing the sum of the squares of two arbitrary numbers. We could define a function named SUMSQ as follows in mathematics:

$$\text{sumsq } (x,\ y) = x * x + y * y$$

If we were using the prefix notation, we would write it as,

$$\text{sumsq } (x,\ y) = \text{plus}(\text{times}(x,\ x),\ \text{times}(y,\ y))$$
$$= +(*(x,\ x),\ *(y,\ y))$$

The corresponding LISP definition is

```
(DEFUN   SUMSQ   (X Y)
   (+ (* X X) (* Y Y)))
```

SUMSQ could be applied to the arguments as needed, for example,

```
(SUMSQ 2 3) => 13
```

Functions are defined using the following syntax:[3]

```
(DEFUN <function-name> <parameter-list> <b1> ... <bm>)
```

Where <function-name> is a symbol that gives the name of the function being defined, <parameter-list> is a list of distinct symbols which are called the *formal parameters*, and the forms <b1> to <bm> constitute the body. In the last example, SUMSQ is the name of the function, X and Y are formal parameters, and (+ (* X X) (* Y Y)) is the body of the function.

The function application is performed as follows: The formal parameters are bound to the respective arguments, and then the forms in the body are evaluated. The function application evaluates to whatever the last form in the body evaluates to.

To evaluate (SUMSQ 2 3) in the example, we first evaluate the parameters 2 and 3, respectively. They evaluate to themselves; and the arguments are 2 and 3, respectively. The formal parameter X gets bound to 2, and Y gets bound to 3. Now we evaluate the form in the body, resulting in 13:

```
(+ (* X X)
   (* Y Y)) => 13.
```

---

[3]In some LISPs, DE or DEFINE instead of DEFUN is used to define functions.

The bindings of the symbols that are formal parameters remain in effect only while the body of the function is being evaluated. After the body of the function is evaluated, the current bindings of the formal parameters are removed and the atoms get back their earlier bindings. For example, let X be bound to 7 and Y be unbound when the function SUMSQ is applied to arguments 2 and 3. While the body of the function SUMSQ is being evaluated, X and Y would be bound to 2 and 3, respectively. However, after the function application is over, X would be bound to 7 and Y would be unbound, as earlier.

Applying a function is also termed making a *function call*. The result of the application is termed *returning a value* from the call. Thus, evaluation of (SUMSQ 2 3) is referred to as making a function call on SUMSQ and returning 13.

For conditional evaluation, COND can be used: COND is followed by zero or more clauses; each clause is a list of one or more forms. The first form in a clause is called a test.

```
(COND   (<test1>   <S-expr>  ...  <S-expr>)
        (<test2>   <S-expr>  ...  <S-expr>)

        ...

        (<testn>   <S-expr>  ...  <S-expr>))
```

The COND form[4] is evaluated by the following rule: Evaluate the first test in the first clause. If it evaluates to true, remaining forms, if any, in the clause are evaluated, and the COND form evaluates to the value of the last form in the clause. If the test evaluates to false, the same thing is repeated with the second clause, and so on. If all the clauses are exhausted without any of the tests evaluating to true, the COND form evaluates to ().

If a clause contains only one form, it serves as a test, and if it evaluates to non-NIL, it is the value of the COND form as well (being the last and the only form in the clause). If a clause contains more than one form after the test, the forms are evaluated for their side effects. Only the value of the last form in a clause gives the value of the conditional expression.

Now, the question is what is true and what is false. In LISP, NIL stands for false, everything else is true.

The following is an example of a COND form. If the value of X is zero, the following returns a symbol; otherwise it returns a number:

```
(COND [(= X 0) 'INFINITY]
      [T (/ A X)])
```

Note that square brackets have been written instead of parentheses for the sake of readability. While typing the above into your LISP system, use parentheses (unless

---

[4]A form whose first element is an atom <f> will be called an <f> form. Hence the term COND form.

your LISP implementation accepts square brackets). Whenever square brackets are used in this or other forms in this book, the above must be kept in mind.

Exercise 1.1 Define a function ADD8 that adds 8 to its argument.

Exercise 1.2 Define a function AVERAGE3 that takes three numbers as its arguments and returns their average.

1.4   PRIMITIVE OPERATIONS ON OBJECTS

Let us now look at some of the primitive or built-in operations on objects. First, let us focus on manipulation of lists.

CAR and CDR are the basic functions for extracting parts of a list. Both take a list as their argument. CAR returns the first element (also called the head) of its argument list, and CDR returns the rest of the elements minus the first (also called the tail) of its argument list. When applied to the null list, (), both return (). For example, if L is bound to (C D E F G) then

```
(CAR L) => C
(CDR L) => (D E F G)
```

Sequences of application of CARs and CDRs can be abbreviated as follows: CAR of a CDR of an object can be replaced by the function CADR and so on. For example,

```
(CAR (CDR S)) = (CADR S)
(CDR (CAR (CAR S))) = (CDAAR S)
```

Such replacements can be done up to a sequence of length four.

CONS is the constructor of lists. Given an object and a list object as its two arguments, it returns a list whose head is the first argument and whose tail is the second argument. For example,

```
(CONS 'C '(D E F G)) => (C D E F G)
(CONS 'B L) => (B C D E F G)
(CONS 'B ()) => (B)
```

When the second argument of CONS is an atom, a dotted pair (a generalization of list) is produced.

```
(CONS 'A 'B) => (A . B)
```

This is actually the fundamental data structure for lists. It will be described in the next chapter. The following holds true of any nonnull S:

```
(CONS (CAR S) (CDR S)) = S
```

There are other useful functions for constructing lists. Although they can be defined using CONS, they are built in because of their frequent use. LIST takes one or more arguments and returns their list:

```
(LIST 'A 'B 'C) => (A B C)
(LIST '(A D) '(B C)) => ((A D) (B C))
```

APPEND takes one or more lists as its arguments and returns a list containing the elements of the argument lists:

```
(APPEND '(A D) '(B C)) => (A  D B   C)
(APPEND '(1 2)  '()  '(3)) => (1 2   3)
```

There are a number of functions (called predicates) that return true or false when applied to objects. NULL and ATOM take an object as their argument; the former returns true if the argument is (), the latter returns true if the argument is an atom.

```
(NULL '()) => T
(NULL '(A B)) => NIL
(ATOM 'L) => T
(ATOM 5) => T
```

Similarly, NUMBERP returns true if the argument is a number, and CONSP returns true if the argument is a nonnull list.

To test for equality of two objects the following predicates are available: EQUAL returns true if its arguments are structurally equal (i.e., their S-expr notations are the same). EQ is true of two equal symbols or, in general, of two identical objects (i.e., objects whose internal representations are the same). EQL is true of its arguments whenever either EQ is true of them or they are two equal numbers of the same type.

```
(EQUAL '(A B C) '(A B C)) => T
(EQUAL 'A 'A) => T
(EQ 'A 'A) => T
(EQ 5 5) => T or NIL
(EQL 5 5) => T
```

If L and M are both bound to (A B C),

```
(EQUAL L M) => T
(EQ L M) => T or NIL
```

In the last example, the result depends on the internal representations of the values of L and M. (This will be discussed in Chap. 2.)

1.5 SOME EXAMPLES

In this section, some examples are given to illustrate the various concepts described so far. The first example illustrates recursive definitions of functions; the second example discusses representation of sets.

1.5.1 Recursive Functions

While evaluating the body of a function, the function might be applied again, and so on. In other words, a function can call itself. Such a function is called *recursive*.

  If in trying to solve a given problem we can reduce it to one or more problems that are similar but smaller in size than the original, it is ideal for a recursive program. The reduction process is continued until the problem is reduced in size for which the solution is known. For example, if the problem is to reach the second story from the first, we can reduce it to the known problem of stepping on the first step of the staircase, and the simpler problem of reaching the second story from the new position. This reduction procedure repeated enough times will take us to the second floor provided we know when to stop.

  As an example let us consider LEN, a function that finds the length of a list. On being applied to a list, it evaluates to a number equal to the number of elements in the list. For example,

```
(LEN  '(8 9))  =>  2
(LEN  '((8 7)))  =>  1
(LEN  '(8 7 (3 4)))  =>  3
```

The following is its definition,

```
(DEFUN LEN (L)
    (COND  [(NULL L)  0]
           [T (+ 1 (LEN (CDR L)))] ))
```

The definition of the recursive function LEN is based on two simple observations:

1. Length of the null list is 0.
2. Length of a nonnull list is one more than the length of its tail.

The second observation allows us to write the recursive step because we have reduced the problem of finding the length of a list to finding the length of the tail of the list. The first observation allows us to terminate recursion.

  The recursive calls are shown below by the trace of sequence of function calls. The function calls are preceded by a right arrow, $\rightarrow$, and the returns by a left arrow, $\leftarrow$. The nested calls are indicated by indenting the right arrow, and the left arrow for a return is indented by the same amount as its matching function call.

```
-> apply LEN to (10 20)
  -> apply LEN to (20)
    -> apply LEN to ()
    <- 0
  <- 1
<- 2
```

1.5.2 Simple Sets

A *set* is an unordered collection or aggregate of objects without any duplicates. The objects might be atomic (they cannot be decomposed further) or composite (other sets). Let us call a set containing only atoms a *simple set*.

A simple set can be represented by a list of atoms with no atom occurring more than once. The empty set is represented by a null list. Examples of simple sets are

```
(A B XYZ 3)
(THE FAT MAN)
```

The order of elements in a list representing a set is unimportant. (THE FAT MAN) and (THE MAN FAT) both represent the same set. In defining set operations, we will make use of a list function called MEMBER, which takes an element and a list and returns true if the element occurs in the list.

Now we define a function called SET-UNION that returns the union of two simple sets S1 and S2. If S1 is the empty set, then the union with S2 is S2. Otherwise, if the first element of S1 is a member of S2, then we make a recursive call on SET-UNION with the tail of S1 and S2. The first element of S1 is not included in the resulting set so as to avoid duplicates. On the other hand, if the first element of S1 is not a member of S2, it must be included in the resulting set as shown below.

```
(DEFUN SET-UNION (S1 S2)
   (COND [(NULL S1) S2]
         [(MEMBER (CAR S1) S2)
          (SET-UNION (CDR S1) S2)]
         [T (CONS (CAR S1)
                  (SET-UNION (CDR S1) S2))]))
```

Similarly, for intersection of two simple sets we have SET-INTERSECTION. If S1 is the empty set, then the result is the empty set as there are no elements common to S1 and S2. The rest is straightforward.

```
(DEFUN SET-INTERSECTION (S1 S2)
   (COND [(NULL S1) ()]
         [(MEMBER (CAR S1) S2)
          (CONS (CAR S1)
                (SET-INTERSECTION (CDR S1) S2 ))]
         [T (SET-INTERSECTION (CDR S1) S2)]))
```

UNION and INTERSECTION are primitives in COMMON LISP.

Exercise 1.3 SET-DIFF computes the difference between two sets as follows: It takes two simple sets as arguments and produces a new simple set that contains all the elements of the first argument except those that are elements of the second. Thus, (SET-DIFF '(1 3 4 8) '(3 6)) => (1 4 8). Define SET-DIFF.

Exercise 1.4 Let simple number sets be sets that consist of numbers. They are called ordered if the numbers in the set are in some order, say ascending order. Redefine SET-UNION and SET-INTERSECTION for ordered simple number sets, making use of the ordering to perform the operations more efficiently.

The *cartesian product* of two sets is a set of all possible distinct pairs, whose first elements are members of the first set and whose second elements are members of the second set. For example, the cartesian product of (1 3 5) and (A X) is ((1 A) (3 A) (5 A) (1 X) (3 X) (5 X)).

```
(DEFUN CART-PROD (S1 S2)
   (COND [(NULL S1) ()]
         [T (APPEND (ELEM-PROD (CAR S1) S2)
                    (CART-PROD (CDR S1) S2) )]))
(DEFUN ELEM-PROD (E S)
;;; Take an element E and a set S and return a set
;;; of pairs in which the first elements are equal to E
;;; and the second elements are members of S.
   (COND [(NULL S) ()]
         [T (CONS (LIST E (CAR S))
                  (ELEM-PROD E (CDR S)) )]))
```

For example,

```
(ELEM-PROD 5 '(3 4 6)) => ((5 3) (5 4) (5 6))
```

Note the use of ; in the above definition. A semicolon indicates the beginning of a comment that extends to the end of the line. These lines are only for the human reader and are ignored by the LISP interpreter.

1.6 LOCAL VARIABLES

There are times when we wish to store a temporary result. This may be necessary, for example, to avoid making a function call twice. Consider the definition of a function SUMPROD given below that takes a list of numbers and returns the sum and product of the numbers. Thus,

```
(SUMPROD '(2 3 4)) => (9 24)
```

where

```
(DEFUN SUMPROD (L)
   (COND [(NULL L) '(0 1)]
         [T (LIST (+ (CAR L) (CAR (SUMPROD (CDR L))))
                  (* (CAR L) (CADR (SUMPROD (CDR L)))))]))
```

On examining the body of SUMPROD we find that it makes two recursive calls with exactly the same arguments. We show below the LET construct which allows us to avoid doing so.

The syntax of a LET form[5] is as follows:

```
(LET ([<var1> <expr1>]
          ...
      [<varn> <exprn>])
   <s1> ... <sm>)
```

Its evaluation is carried out as follows: First, all the expressions <expri> are evaluated one by one, and then the atoms <vari>, which are also called local variables, are bound to the result of evaluation of the respective <expri>s. Next, the expressions in the body are evaluated sequentially from <s1> to <sm>, and the value of the last expression is the result of evaluating the LET form. After the evaluation of the LET form is over, the bindings of the local variables disappear. (There is a LET* form that behaves like LET except that after each <expri> is evaluated, its value is bound to <vari>.)

SUMPROD is redefined below using LET. In the LET form a local variable X is bound to the result of making a recursive function call on SUMPROD. X is now used twice in the body of the LET form without making duplicate function calls.

```
(DEFUN SUMPROD (L)
   (COND [(NULL L) '(0 1)]
         [T (LET ([X (SUMPROD (CDR L))])
              (LIST (+ (CAR L) (CAR X))
                    (* (CAR L) (CADR X))))]))
```

Another way to achieve the same effect is to introduce additional parameters where they will act as variables in which the temporary or intermediate result is *accumulated*. An example for SUMPROD is as follows:

```
(DEFUN SUMPROD (L)
   (SUMPROD-AUX L 0 1))
```

---

[5]Note that the square brackets are purely for readability, as mentioned earlier. Parentheses must be keyed in while typing this into your LISP system.

```
(DEFUN SUMPROD-AUX (REM-LIST SUM-SO-FAR PROD-SO-FAR)
   (COND [(NULL REM-LIST) (LIST SUM-SO-FAR PROD-SO-FAR)]
         [T (SUMPROD-AUX
                (CDR REM-LIST)
                (+ (CAR REM-LIST) SUM-SO-FAR)
                (* (CAR REM-LIST) PROD-SO-FAR))]))
```

The additional parameters serve as local variables.

The definition of SUMPROD-AUX is tail recursive because no operation is performed by the function on the result of any of its recursive calls (in this case only one). Tail recursion is converted to iteration by the LISP system and is thus handled very efficiently.

> **Exercise 1.5** Define a function FIB that computes the nth element of the Fibonacci series given n as its argument. The nth element of the Fibonacci series is given by the following recursive relations:
>
> $$\text{fib}(n) = \frac{1 \qquad\qquad\qquad\qquad\qquad \text{if } n = 1 \text{ or } 2}{\text{fib}(n - 1) + \text{fib}(n - 2) \; \text{if } n > 2}$$

> **Exercise 1.6** Write a more efficient version of FIB that makes only one recursive call using (a) additional parameters and (b) LET and local variables. [*Hint*: In both parts you will have to define an auxiliary function, say FIB-AUX. In part (a) FIB-AUX should have two additional parameters having the value of two recently computed elements of the Fibonacci series. In part (b) FIB-AUX should return a list of two elements of the Fibonacci series.]

1.7 LAMBDA EXPRESSIONS AND VARIABLES

1.7.1 Lambda Expressions and APPLY

A lambda expression is a function without a name. The following is its form:

```
(LAMBDA <formal-parameters> <s1> ... <sn>)
```

where <formal-parameters> is a list of distinct symbols, and the body consists of the forms <s1> to <sn>. For example, the following is a lambda expression:

```
(LAMBDA (X Y)
   (+ (* X X) (* Y Y) ))
```

A lambda expression can be applied to its arguments similar to functions. Its formal parameters are bound to the arguments, the forms in the body are evaluated one after the other, and the value of the last form in the body is returned. For example,

if the lambda expression defined above is applied to arguments 3 and 4, the formal parameter X is bound to 3, and Y to 4; with these bindings the form in the body evaluates to 25.

A function called APPLY is provided in LISP that allows us to apply functions or lambda expressions. APPLY takes two parameters, each of which is evaluated yielding the arguments. The first argument, which must be a function name or a lambda expression, is applied to its second argument. (If a function name or a lambda expression has to be quoted, it is preferable to use #' rather than '. This is discussed later.) For example,

```
(APPLY #'+ '(3 4))        => 7
(APPLY #'SUMSQ (3 4))  => 25
(APPLY #'(LAMBDA (X Y) (+ (* X X) (* Y Y)))
       '(3 4))            => 25
```

Lambda expressions can also be applied using FUNCALL. It is like APPLY except the arguments are passed as normal instead of putting them in a list. For example,

```
(FUNCALL #'+ 3 4)      => 7
(FUNCALL #'SUMSQ 3 4) => 25
(FUNCALL #'(LAMBDA (X Y) (+ (* X X) (* Y Y)))
         3 4)          => 25
```

Another method of applying a lambda expression is by writing it as an application as mentioned earlier:

```
((LAMBDA (X Y) (+ (* X X) (* Y Y)))
    3 4)     => 25
```

Exercise 1.7 Define a function GEN-ADDN that takes a number n as its argument and returns a lambda expression that when applied to a number, adds n to it.

Exercise 1.8 Show how a lambda expression bound to Z below can be applied to 8:

```
(LET ([Z (GEN-ADDN 3)])
    ...)
```

From now on whenever we use the term function, we will include functions that have names as well as lambda expressions.

1.7.2   Backquote Facility

The following function generates a sum-of-squares function that uses the specified functions for taking the sum and the square:

```
(DEFUN GEN-SUMSQ (SUMFN SQFN)
   (LIST 'LAMBDA '(X Y)
         (LIST SUMFN (LIST SQFN X)
                     (LIST SQFN Y) )))
```

There is a special form called *backquote* that is useful in building expressions, given the templates. It can facilitate the writing of GEN-SUMSQ and other similar functions.

Just as a quoted expression evaluates to itself,

```
'<expr> => <expr>
```

similarly, a backquoted expression evaluates to the expression but with one difference: Those subexpressions that are preceded by a , or ,@ are evaluated and substituted appropriately before returning the result. For example, if B is bound to (1 2) then

```
`(A B C)      => (A B C)
`(A ,B C)     => (A (1 2) C)
`(A ,@ B C)   => (A 1 2 C)
`(A B ,B ,@B C) => (A B (1 2) 1 2 C)
```

As the examples indicate, a form following a , is evaluated and the result is substituted. A form following a ,@ is evaluated and splice-substituted. For splice substitution, the result of the evaluation must be a list. The list is substituted instead of the form, after which the parentheses are removed. Thus, we see that by using a backquote, a template containing fixed and changeable parts can be defined.

Using a backquote, GEN-SUMSQ becomes:[6]

```
(DEFUN GEN-SUMSQ (SUMFN SQFN)
 `(LAMBDA (X Y)
     (,SUMFN (,SQFN X) (,SQFN Y))))
```

Exercise 1.9 Let a complex number be represented by a list of length 2. Define +COM-PLEX and *COMPLEX that respectively take the sum and product of two complex numbers:

```
(+COMPLEX '(5 3) '(2 8)) => (7 11)
(*COMPLEX '(5 3) '(2 8)) => (-14 46)
```

Use these to generate a lambda expression that takes the sum of the squares of two complex numbers.

---

[6]We will soon see that the preferred method of returning a function is to use lexical closure rather than constructing functions on the fly. It is the more efficient of the two.

1.7.3   Free and Bound Variables

Variables are those symbols in a construct or form that may get bound or get evaluated when the form gets evaluated.

   Bound or *local* variables with respect to a function are the symbols that appear as its formal parameters (i.e., appear in the parameter list in the function definition). For example, in SUMSQ, X and Y are bound variables. Similarly, bound variables for a LET form are its local variables. Loosely speaking, *free* variables are those variables in the respective constructs (e.g., in the function definition or LET form) that are not bound.

   We have already seen how the bound variables get their values during execution in each of the two constructs. The question is, How do the free variables get their values? To answer the question let us first look at global variables and then define the concepts of scope and extent.

1.7.4   Global Variables

If we want to have a *global* variable that is accessible from a number of functions, all we have to do is to declare (rather proclaim) the variable as global and leave it free in each of the functions. For example, a global variable called *DB* can be accessed in functions F1 and F2 as follows:

```
(DEFVAR *DB* '((ON A B) (ON B C)))
(DEFUN F1 (X)    ... *DB* ...)
(DEFUN F2 (X Y)    ... *DB* ...)
```

   The DEFVAR form is used for proclaiming that a variable is global. Optionally, it can also provide the initial value as in the above example.

   Global variables are special variables and not lexical. Special variables are discussed in the next section.

1.7.5   Scope and Extent of Variables

Scope refers to the region of program text within which a variable can be referred to (and hence within which its binding is available when the program is executed). *Extent* refers to the interval of time during which the variable and its binding can be referenced.

   The scope is said to be *static* or *lexical* if the scope of variables is the region of program text which is textually within the establishing construct. For example, in

```
(DEFUN SUMSQ (X Y) (+ (* X X) (* Y Y)))
```

variables X and Y and their bindings can be referred to only from within the body of the program and not from anywhere else. Hence they are statically scoped. As opposed to this, there is *indefinite* scope in which case the variable and its bindings can be referenced from anywhere.

The extent is called *dynamic* if the variable and its bindings come into existence when the construct begins to be evaluated and cease to exist when the evaluation is over. As opposed to this, we have *indefinite* extent which means that the variable and its bindings continue to exist indefinitely.

Normally, COMMON LISP has static scope and indefinite extent.[7] Variables in COMMON LISP can be made to have indefinite scope and dynamic extent by declaring them to be *special*. These variables are also said to be *dynamic*. In the example below, both normal and special variables coexist. INCR-STEP-SQ has a normal free variable STEP (in the LET form) and a special free variable N.

```
(DEFUN INCR-STEP-SQ (STEP)
   (DECLARE (SPECIAL N))
   (LET ((X (SQUARE STEP)))
      (+ N X)))
(DEFUN F (N DELTA)
   (DECLARE (SPECIAL N))
   ...
   (INCR-STEP-SQ DELTA)
   ...)
```

Since STEP is a normal variable, it is statically scoped. It takes its value from the establishing construct, namely, the formal parameter of the function F in the current call. N on the other hand has indefinite scope and dynamic extent. It takes its value from the most recent creation, which in general depends on who has called INCR-STEP-SQ. When F calls INCR-STEP-SQ, the free variable N takes its value from the formal parameter in F. The binding of N disappears after F returns.

Finally, let us talk about closures. When we take the *closure* of a lambda expression, we get back an object (also called a closure) containing the lambda expression together with the prevailing environment (that is, the set of bindings). When such a closure is applied, the lambda expression gets applied under the environment contained in the closure. As a result, the free variables, if any, in the lambda expression take their values from the original environment at the time the closure was taken. Syntax for taking closure is

```
(FUNCTION <lambda expression>)
```

or abbreviated as

```
#'<lambda expression>
```

---

[7]In the SUMSQ example above, the bindings of X and Y continue to exist forever (at least as far as we are concerned) except they cannot be referenced after return because of reasons of scope. (We will see other examples using closures where it will be possible to reference the bindings after return.)

COMMON LISP supports lexical closure; in other words, the environment of the normal variables (not special variables) is put in the closure.

We have already used #' to quote functions. But since they did not have any free variables, the purpose at that time was simply to indicate (to the compiler or a human reader) that what follows is a function. Here is an example, GEN-SUMSQ, in which it is used for taking lexical closure.

```
(DEFUN GEN-SUMSQ (SUMFN SQFN)
  #'(LAMBDA (X Y)
      (FUNCALL SUMFN (FUNCALL SQFN X)
                     (FUNCALL SQFN Y))))
```

Such a closure might be used as follows:

```
(DEFUN F (M N)
   ...
   (LET ((SUMSQ (GEN-SUMSQ #'+COMPLEX
                           #'SQ-COMPLEX)))
     (FUNCALL SUMSQ M N))
   ...   )
```

The indefinite extent for normal variables, SUMFN and SQFN, assures us that their bindings continue to exist even after the function GEN-SUMSQ has returned. Hence they are available when SUMSQ is applied.

1.8 PROPERTY LISTS

Properties can be attached to atoms. There are two functions that allow properties to be stored and retrieved: SETF and GET. When the SETF form

```
(SETF (GET 'LION 'LEGS) 4)
```

is evaluated, the value 4 is associated with the atom LION under the attribute LEGS. This property can be retrieved by providing the atom and the attribute to the function GET:

```
(GET 'LION 'LEGS) => 4
```

The following, then, are the forms for storing and retrieving properties, respectively:

```
(SETF (GET <atom> <attr>) <value>)
(GET <atom> <attr>)
```

Each of the parameters <atom>, <attr>, and <value> is evaluated, before anything is stored or retrieved. (The <atom> must evaluate to a symbol, while <attr> should normally evaluate to a symbol.)

For a given atom and attribute only a single value can be stored, in other words, the relationship is functional. If for the same atom and attribute we store two different values, the first value will be overwritten. For example, if we evaluate the following two expressions,

```
(SETF (GET 'LION 'FOUND-IN) 'AFRICA) => AFRICA
(SETF (GET 'LION 'FOUND-IN) 'INDIA)  => INDIA
```

the effect of only the second one remains.[8]

```
(GET 'LION 'FOUND-IN) => INDIA
```

GET returns () if the named attribute is not present in the property list for an atom. If on the other hand the attribute is present and its value is (), again () will be returned. Normally, the user should take care that the above ambiguity does not pose any problems in his or her application.[9]

Properties provide an extremely convenient mechanism for associating information with symbols. They are efficient as long as any given symbol has only a small number of properties at any given time. The attributes and values are stored as pairs on a linear list stored in the symbol representation.

With a symbol, three kinds of things can be associated: a value, a function definition, and properties. The function definition and properties are global. In other words, they have indefinite scope and indefinite extent. The scoping rules for values bound to a symbol are more involved as already given earlier.

1.9 MAPPING FUNCTIONS AND ITERATION

When the same function is to be performed repeatedly on different parts of a list, recursion can be used. However, mapping functions can also be applied resulting in

---

[8]In earlier dialects of LISP, PUTPROP was used to store the properties. For example, instead of

```
(SETF (GET 'LION 'FOUND-IN) 'INDIA)
```

we would have written

```
(PUTPROP 'LION 'INDIA 'FOUND-IN)
```

[9]COMMON LISP allows an optional third argument with GET which is returned if the attribute is not found.

a more elegant solution. Two mapping functions are introduced here: MAPCAR and MAPC.

MAPCAR takes a function as its first argument and a number of lists of equal length as its remaining arguments. There should be as many lists as the arity of the function in its first argument. MAPCAR applies the function to the heads of the lists, then repeats the above with the heads of the tails of the lists, and so on until the lists are null. The results of the applications are accumulated in a list. For example,

```
(MAPCAR #'1+ '(5 9 13))
   => (6 10 14)
(MAPCAR #'+ '(1 2 3) '(10 20 30))
   => (11 22 33)
```

MAPC behaves similar to MAPCAR except that it does not accumulate any result. It returns NIL.

Iteration is the technical name given to performing an operation repeatedly (on possibly different items) without using recursion. Besides the mapping functions, there are DO and DO* constructs that allow us to specify iterative solutions.

Before discussing them further we need to discuss the notion of assignment. We have seen that when an atom is bound, a value is associated with it. The earlier value if any is not destroyed but saved. Assignment sets the value of a variable which irretrievably destroys the variable's value. For example, in

```
(SETQ X 3)
(SETQ X 5)
```

after the first form is evaluated, the value of the variable X is set to 3. After the second statement is executed, the value of X is set to 5. The earlier value of 3 is gone forever. (SETF can also be used here instead of SETQ.) As is clear from the example, the first parameter of SETQ must be a symbol that is not evaluated and the second parameter is a form that is evaluated, the result of which is assigned to the symbol.

Most block-structured languages like Pascal have an iterative construct called the until loop. It has the following form:

```
X := INIT;
UNTIL P(X) DO X := F(X);
RETURN (X);
```

A predicate P is applied to the value of a variable X, and if the result is false, the value of X is changed to the value of F(X) and the loop is repeated. If the result of P(X) is true, the loop terminates and the value of X is returned.

Using the DO construct we can write the above as

```
(DO ([X INIT])      ;Local var and initialization
   ((P X) X)        ;Termination test and value to be
                    ;   returned
  (SETQ X (F X)))   ;Body of loop
```

in which X is initialized to INIT, followed by a termination test, and body of the loop. The iteration continues until (P X) is true, and then the value of X is returned. DO has the following syntax:

```
(DO (<var-spec-1>
       ...
     <var-spec-n>)
    <termination-clause>
  <b1>
  ...
  <bm> )
```

The first parameter is a list of variable specifications <var-spec-i>, the second parameter is a termination clause, after which there are zero or more S-exprs <bi> called the body. A <var-spec-i> is of the following form:

```
[<var-i>  <init-i>  <step-i>]
```

where <step-i> or both <init-i> and <step-i> are optional. Each of the <var-i>s is the bound or local variable of DO. Its scope is the DO form. When the DO form is entered, a bound variable gets an initial value by evaluating <init-i>, if present. After each iteration, each of the <step-i>s is evaluated and the <var-i>s are set to the value. If there is more than one bound variable (i > 1), the bound variables get values in parallel. In other words, first the initial values or the step expressions are evaluated and then the assignments are made.

The form of the <termination-clause> is as follows:

```
(<test> <s1> ... <sp>)
```

In each iteration, including the first, the <test> is evaluated. If it yields NIL, the iteration continues. If, on the other hand, it yields true, the iteration terminates and each of the <si>s are evaluated, and the value of <sp> is returned. If there are no S-exprs following the <test>, NIL is returned.

<b1> to <bm>, possibly empty, constitute the body of the iteration and are evaluated in sequence. They may contain a RETURN form which causes the DO to be exited immediately. Factorial function defined below illustrates the use of DO. It has COUNT and RES as its bound variables. COUNT is initialized to 0 and incremented by 1 in every iteration. RES stores the result of multiplication so far.

```
(DEFUN FACT (N)
   (DO ([COUNT 1 (+ 1 COUNT)]
        [RES 1 (* RES COUNT)])
       ((= N COUNT) (* RES COUNT))))
```

DO* is similar to DO except that the assignment of the bound variables occurs sequentially rather than in parallel.

Exercise 1.10 Define LEN using DO.

Exercise 1.11 Define SET-UNION, SET-INTERSECTION, and SET-DIFF using DO.

FURTHER READINGS

There are a number of books introducing COMMON LISP to the beginner. Among them are Brooks (1985), Winston and Horn (1988), and Wilensky (1987). The reader not familiar with COMMON LISP should go through one of them before continuing past the first two chapters.

The reference manual and language specification for COMMON LISP is contained in Steele (1984).

CHAPTER
2

REVIEW OF ADVANCED LISP

In this chapter, we will look at the representation of objects in computer memory and at some other features like macros, reading and writing, structures, and nonlocal exits.

2.1 REPRESENTATION OF LISTS

Let us now examine the representation of objects in computer memory. We will first take a look at the representation of lists and then at the representation of atoms.

A nonnull list is represented by cons cells. A single cons cell consists of two pointers: one for the head and the other for the tail. We show a cons cell by means of a box below. NIL is a special pointer, but for better readability we will draw a diagonal in the position meant for the pointer. As an example, the representation of list (3) is shown in Fig. 2-1 and list ((3 4)) is given in Fig.2-2.

The cons cells are realized in a computer by memory locations, and pointers are nothing but addresses of the memory locations. The pointer to NIL could simply be a special address. A cons cell consists of one or more memory locations that are large enough to store two addresses.

This representation suggests the relative speeds of different operations. CAR of a list accesses the cons cell given to it and returns its first pointer, similarly for CDR. CONS allocates a free (unused) cons cell and stores the two argument pointers in it. Operations CAR, CDR, ATOM, EQ, NULL, etc., are very fast and take about an equal amount of time. CONS is a little more expensive because a free cons cell has to be identified and allocated. However, if we include the time needed for garbage collection per cons cell (i.e., in freeing cons cells that have been allocated but are no longer accessible), CONS turns out to be much more expensive.

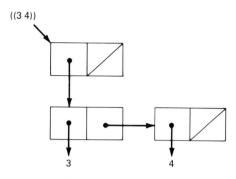

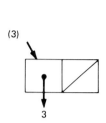

FIGURE 2-1   **FIGURE 2-2**

Exercise 2.1 Show the representation of the following:

```
(1 (8 9) 5)
((3))
(1 (8 9) ((3)))
((TABLE (COLOR BROWN)) (CHAIR (SIZE 20)))
((TABLE (COLOR BROWN)) (CHAIR (COLOR BROWN)))
```

2.1.1   Dotted Pair

There is another notation called *dotted pair* for writing nonatomic objects. In this notation, the head and tail of a list object are separated by a . and enclosed in a pair of parentheses. Thus, the list (3) is written as

```
(3 . ())
```

showing the head and the tail explicitly. Similarly, the list (2 3) is written as

```
(2 . (3 . ()))
```

This notation is strictly more powerful than the list notation we used earlier. When the tail of a list is an atom other than NIL, we can write it in the dot notation but not in the list notation:

```
(CONS 'A 'B) => (A . B)
(CONS '(A . B) 'C) => ((A . B) . C)
```

The representation of the dot notation is in terms of cons cells. As usual, a cons cell consists of two pointers. In case the tail is an atom, the second pointer points to the tail that happens to be an atom. In other words, our representation is capable of representing objects with atomic tails. See Fig. 2-3.

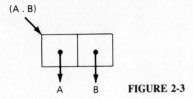

FIGURE 2-3

We adopt an intermediate notation called dotted list notation (as part of S-expr notation) in the rest of the book. We will write a given list object in the normal list notation if it contains an atomic tail other than NIL. Whenever there is an atomic tail, we will prefix it with a dot. For example,

```
((A . (B . ())) . C)
```

will be written as

```
((A B) . C)
```

In other words, list notation is written wherever possible. Dots are used only when necessary.

Exercise 2.2 Write the following in dotted pair notation:

```
(1 2 (3 4))
(1 2 ((3 4)))
((1) 2 ((3 4)))
(1 2 (3 . 4))
```

2.1.2   Destructive Updates

The functions we have seen so far do not allow us to modify an existing list structure. CONS only adds a new cons cell, but leaves the already allocated cons cells unchanged. (SETQ alters the value of variables, but it does not alter an existing list structure.) Using RPLACA and RPLACD we can make destructive updates to a cons cell. RPLACA takes two arguments: a nonnull list (represented as a cons cell) and an arbitrary object. It destructively changes the head of its first argument such that the first pointer in the cons cell points to the object in its second argument. For example, if X is bound to (1 2), then

```
(RPLACA X 3) => (3 2)
```

and the value of X is changed to (3 2). Figure 2-4 shows the cons cells (a) before and (b) after performing RPLACA.

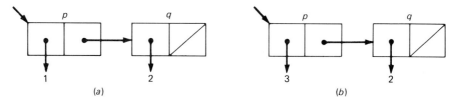

FIGURE 2-4

RPLACD is similar except that the tail of the first argument is changed. For example, if X is bound to (1 2),

```
(RPLACD X '(4 5)) => (1 4 5)
```

and the value of X becomes (1 4 5).

SETF allows us to combine the above two operations into one:

```
(RPLACA L S) = (SETF (CAR L) S)
(RPLACD L S) = (SETF (CDR L) S)
```

Actually, SETF generalizes to sequences of CARs and CDRs as well:

```
(RPLACA (CxxxR L) S) = (SETF (CAxxxR L) S)
(RPLACD (CxxxR L) S) = (SETF (CDxxxR L) S)
```

Exercise 2.3 Suppose we want to add elements at the end of a list. Can you use destructive updates to speed up the operation?

Exercise 2.4 Can you make the last exercise more efficient by keeping a pointer to the last cons cell of the list to be updated?

2.2 REPRESENTATION OF SYMBOLS

Symbols have a unique mapping from their notation (or print name) to the object in memory. For two or more occurrences of a symbol notation, we get back the same object. In contrast, identical-looking S-exprs for lists or numbers do not necessarily represent the same object in memory. For example, if we write the atomic S-expr A, it denotes a unique object. On the other hand if we write the S-expr (1 2) twice, the two S-exprs might not denote the same list object in memory.

We are now in a position to discuss EQ introduced in Sec. 1.4. It takes two objects as arguments and tests for equality of pointers to their representation. Thus,

```
(EQ 'A 'A) => T
```

since the two occurrences of the object A are represented by the same memory structure (and hence by the same pointers). On the other hand,

```
(EQ (CONS 'A 'A) (CONS 'A 'A)) => NIL
```

because the two occurrences of list structure (A . A) are represented by two different memory structures. EQ will yield true for two lists only if their memory structures are the same. For example if X is bound to (1 2), then

```
(EQ X X) => T
```

or if X and Y are bound to lists with the same memory structures by perhaps the following two statements

```
(SETQ X '(1 2))
(SETQ Y X)
```

then

```
(EQ X Y) => T
```

COMMON LISP uses packages to provide mappings from the print names of symbols to their representations. At any time, there is a current package which provides a mapping from the print name of a symbol to its object representation. A package indexes symbol objects from their print names. There is only one current package at a time.

There are at least four packages in COMMON LISP: system, LISP, keyword, and user. More can be created. The user package is current by default. A symbol (say A) belonging to a package other than the current, say, system can be referred to by prefixing the print name with the name of the package (SYS:A). Consult Steele (1984) for more details.

The packages are consulted at read time. Once the print name of a symbol is read, we have access to the symbol object.

Since symbols have unique memory structure, attachment of properties, function definitions, and value to a symbol can be done by storing appropriate pointers in its unique structure. They can be accessed quite simply through the unique structure.

It is possible to have *uninterned* symbols, that is, symbols that have not been entered in any package. As an example, GENSYM is a function that generates an uninterned symbol every time it is called. An uninterned symbol, if used, should be handled with care because its representation cannot be obtained from its print name.

2.3 FUNCTIONS WITH OPTIONAL AND OTHER PARAMETERS

So far we have seen functions that take a fixed number of parameters. Optional parameters are needed in many situations. Let us take an example to set the stage. We want to define a function called EXPONENTIATE that normally takes a single argument and produces e raised to the power of its argument (where e is the base of the natural logarithm). Thus,

```
(EXPONENTIATE 3) = e³ = 20.086
```

If it is given an additional argument, however, it raises the first argument to the power of its second argument. For example,

```
(EXPONENTIATE 5 3) = 5³ = 125
```

This is how we define the two versions of EXPONENTIATE that take one and two arguments, respectively.

```
(DEFUN EXPONENTIATE1 (N)
    (EXPT 2.718218 N))

(DEFUN EXPONENTIATE2 (BASE POWER)
    (EXPT BASE POWER))
```

To combine the two we write as follows using optional parameters:

```
(DEFUN EXPONENTIATE (P1 &OPTIONAL P2)
    (COND [(NULL P2) (EXPT 2.7182818 P1)]
          [T (EXPT P1 P2)]))
```

The syntax for defining functions with optional parameters is very similar to that for ordinary functions.

```
(DEFUN  <function-name> <parm-list>  <b1> ... <bm>)
```

It only differs in the specification of <parm-list>. The <parm-list> consists of a list of formal parameters (possibly zero) for the required arguments. They are followed by a special keyword &OPTIONAL (where '&' indicates that it is not a formal parameter but a keyword) followed by a list of formal parameters for optional arguments. We will call them required formal parameters and optional formal parameters, respectively.

When a function defined as above is applied, its actual parameters are evaluated yielding arguments. The required formal parameters are bound to an equal number of arguments in left-to-right order. Of the remaining arguments, they are bound to the

optional formal parameters. If some optional formal parameters still remain unbound, they are bound to (). It is an error for the number of arguments to be less than the required parameters and more than the required plus optional ones. For example,

```
(DEFUN TEST-OPT (R1 R2 &OPTIONAL S1 S2)
   (LIST R1 R2 S1 S2))

(TEST-OPT 1 2 3 4) => (1 2 3 4)
(TEST-OPT 1 2 3)   => (1 2 3 ())
(TEST-OPT 1 2)     => (1 2 () ())
(TEST-OPT 1)           => error
(TEST-OPT 1 2 3 4 5) => error
```

If it is not known a priori how many arguments a function might take, another keyword called &REST can be used in <parm-list>. It must be followed by exactly one formal parameter. This formal parameter is bound to a list of all the arguments (possibly empty) that remain after the binding of the required formal parameters.[1] For example,

```
(DEFUN TEST-REST (R1 R2 &REST S)
   (LIST R1 R2 S))

(TEST-REST 1 2 3 4 5) => (1 2 (3 4 5))
(TEST-REST 1 2 3)     => (1 2 (3))
(TEST-REST 1 2)       => (1 2 ())
(TEST-REST 1)         => error
```

The keywords &OPTIONAL and &REST can both occur together in a <parm-list> in a function definition. The former must appear before the latter. When such a function is applied, first the required formal parameters are bound, next the optional formal parameters are bound, and finally the formal parameter after &REST is bound to the list of remaining arguments.

In the functions defined so far, the arguments are passed by position. At times, it is convenient to have functions that take arguments by keywords rather than by position. They are useful when a function takes a large number of parameters (which makes it difficult to remember them by position) and only a few of them are supplied in a typical call, others being taken by default. For example, the SORT function takes as its two required arguments a list to be sorted and the predicate to be used for comparing elements of the list. In addition, it takes a keyword parameter called :KEY for the function to be used for retrieving the key from the elements in the list. (The

---

[1]In earlier dialects of LISP, an equivalent capability was provided with a slightly different syntax using special functions called LEXPRS.

default is the identity function.) The key part of the elements is compared for ordering them. Definition of SORT will look as follows:

```
(DEFUN SORT (L PRED &KEY (KEY #'IDENTITY)) ... )
```

It can be called with and without the keyword parameters, respectively, as follows:

```
(SORT L  #'< :KEY #'CAR)
(SORT M #'<)
```

In the latter case, IDENTITY is used to get the key.

Another useful function called ASSOC takes an object and an association list (that is, a list of sublists), and if the object occurs as the first element of any sublist, it returns the sublist. Otherwise, it returns nil. For example, if L is equal to

```
((A 1) (B 2) (C CC 3) (B 20)):

(ASSOC 'B L)  =>  (B 2)
(ASSOC 'D L)  =>  NIL
```

To search on the CADR of the sublists instead of CAR, we can make use of the keyword parameter :KEY as follows:

```
(ASSOC 'CC L :KEY #'CADR)  =>  (C CC 3)
```

Normally to check for equality of the search argument with the appropriate part of the association list, ASSOC makes use of the EQL test. A different test can be specified using the keyword :TEST.

Exercise 2.5 Define OUR-APPEND that like the built-in function APPEND takes zero or more argument lists and appends them togther.

Exercise 2.6 Define OUR-LIST that is similar to LIST, using iteration (with DO or DO*).

Exercise 2.7 Define INCREMENT that takes a number n and an optional increment size s. It returns $(n + 1)$ if there is only one argument; otherwise it returns $(n + s)$.

2.4 DEFINING STRUCTURES

Frequently, a need arises to represent an entity by means of a data structure. For example, a node in a nonnull binary tree has three parts: a value, a left subtree, and a right subtree. This could be represented by a list of length 3:

```
(<value> <left-tree> <right-tree>)
```

Parts of a node can be accessed by means of CAR, CADR, and CADDR selector functions. It is desirable, however, to use mnemonic names for the selector functions. The same is true for the constructor function. All this is accomplished automatically by means of DEFSTRUCT, a structure-defining facility. For example, on evaluating

```
(DEFSTRUCT NODE VAL LEFT RIGHT)
```

appropriate selector and constructor functions are generated for the structure NODE. The constructor uses keywords, and the selector names are names of the structure followed by - and the field names. For example,

```
(SETQ T1 (MAKE-NODE :VAL 1 :LEFT NIL :RIGHT NIL))
     => #S(1 NIL NIL)
(SETQ T3 (MAKE-NODE :LEFT NIL :VAL 3 :RIGHT NIL))
     => #S(3 NIL NIL)
(SETQ T2 (MAKE-NODE :LEFT T1 :VAL 2 :RIGHT T3))
     => #S(2 #S(1 NIL NIL) #S(3 NIL NIL))
(NODE-VAL T2) => 2
(NODE-RIGHT T2) => #S(3 NIL NIL)
```

The constructor is a keyword constructor. SETF can also be used with the selectors:

```
(SETF (NODE-VAL T2) 2.5)   => 2.5
T2 => #S(2.5 ... )
```

There are a large number of options that can be specified with the name of the structure and its field names. The examples below illustrate some commonly occurring options.

1. For generating a constructor which takes parameters by position:

```
(DEFSTRUCT (NODE (:CONSTRUCTOR MAKE-TREE
                              (VAL LEFT RIGHT)))
          VAL LEFT RIGHT)
```

Now MAKE-TREE takes arguments not by keywords but by position.

2. For ensuring that the structure is represented as a list:

```
(DEFSTRUCT (NODE (:TYPE LIST))
          VAL LEFT RIGHT)
```

Otherwise an implementation is free to choose any representation. Normally, a representation is chosen that allows any component to be accessed equally fast.

3. For generating a tag with each instance of the structure represented as a list:

```
(DEFSTRUCT (NODE (:TYPE LIST) (:NAMED))
           VAL LEFT RIGHT)
```

Tags are always generated when :TYPE option is not specified.

4. For generating selector names without prefixing them with NODE-:

```
(DEFSTRUCT (NODE (:CONCNAME NIL))
           VAL LEFT RIGHT)
```

The options above can be combined as well.

2.5   ARRAYS AND STRINGS

An array object can be created by the MAKE-ARRAY function with rank and dimensions specified as arguments. The following

```
(MAKE-ARRAY '(<dim-1> ... <dim-n>))
```

creates an n-dimensional array with the ith dimension ranging from 0 to <dim-i>. It takes an optional keyword argument specifying the element type using the keyword :ELEMENT-TYPE. An element of the array can be accessed using AREF as follows:

```
(AREF <array> <index-1> ... <index-n>)
```

SETF can be used for storing into the array.

For example, A is bound to a three-dimensional array:

```
(SETQ A (MAKE-ARRAY '(8 5 4)))
```

We can store in it as follows:

```
(SETF (AREF A 3 1 2) 33)
```

It can be accessed by

```
(AREF A 3 1 2) => 33
```

A string is a vector, or one-dimensional array, whose elements are of type character. Either MAKE-ARRAY or a function called MAKE-STRING can be used. Thus, we can write

```
(SETQ B (MAKE-STRING 4))
```

or

```
(SETQ B (MAKE-ARRAY '(4) :ELEMENT-TYPE 'CHAR))
```

To store the string "LISP", we write:

```
(SETF (AREF B 1) #\L)
(SETF (AREF B 2) #\I)
(SETF (AREF B 3) #\S)
(SETF (AREF B 4) #\P)
```

or equivalently,

```
(SETF B "LISP")
```

2.6 MACROS

Macros are useful in defining functions that evaluate only some of their parameters. This results in a very important capability, that of defining new syntax or embedding new languages in LISP.

The syntax for defining macros is similar to that for defining functions:

```
(DEFMACRO <name> <formals> <b1> ... <bm>)
```

Its semantics are quite different, however. When a macro call

```
(<name> <p1> ... <pn>)
```

is encountered, this is what is done: The parameters $<p1>$ to $<pn>$ are not evaluated. The formal parameters in $<formals>$ are bound to the parameters $<p1>$ to $<pn>$, respectively. Now, forms in the body of the macro are evaluated. This is called the first evaluation or the macro *expansion*. After this, the bindings of the formal parameters disappear and the result of the macro expansion is evaluated again (called the second evaluation) yielding the result of the macro call.

Consider for example, a function that pushes an element on a stack. It takes two parameters, the first one on evaluation yields the element to be pushed, and the second one is (without evaluation) the name of the stack. If ANIMALS is a stack (initially bound to NIL) and the value of N is an animal name, say LION, then

```
(PUSH N ANIMALS)
```

pushes LION on the stack ANIMALS. If the stack is represented as a list, an equivalent effect is obtained by evaluating

```
(SETQ ANIMALS (CONS  N ANIMALS))
```

Clearly, the PUSH macro should expand as above. Therefore, we write

```
(DEFMACRO PUSH (ELEM STACK)
  `(SETQ ,STACK (CONS ,ELEM ,STACK)))
```

After macro expansion of a call on PUSH, we obtain the appropriate SETQ form which on evaluation yields the answer.

The following should be kept in mind while defining macros:

1. First determine what the macro call should expand into; then write the macro definition keeping in mind the expansion.
2. After the macro expansion, the result should not contain any occurrence of the formal parameters of the macro. This is because the bindings disappear after the expansion.
3. If a parameter in the macro call is to be evaluated, such an evaluation should take place after the macro expansion is over. For example, in PUSH we avoided evaluating the first parameter [by writing, say (EVAL ELEM)] during the macro expansion. This is important because the evaluation should take place in the original environment of the macro call.

Exercise 2.8 What is wrong with the following?

```
(DEFMACRO PUSH (N ST)
  `(SETQ ,ST (CONS `,(EVAL N) ,ST)))
```

[*Hint*: What happens when you try evaluating the call: (PUSH N ANIMALS)?]

Exercise 2.9 Define a macro called RECORD which is like DEFSTRUCT except that it produces a constructor that takes parameters by position. For example,

```
(RECORD NODE VAL LEFT RIGHT)
```

is equivalent to

```
(DEFSTRUCT (NODE (:CONSTRUCTOR MAKE-NODE
                              (VAL LEFT RIGHT)))
           VAL LEFT RIGHT)
```

(*Note*: You will need string manipulation capability for doing the above. Consult the LISP manual.)

There is one more reason for defining macros. The macro expansion can be substituted in-line yielding efficient code. For example, if a generated selector NODE-KEY is a macro

```
(DEFMACRO NODE-KEY (L) `(CADR ,L))
```

then the expansion of a macro call, (NODE-KEY S), say, is (CADR S). If the latter
is substituted in-line (whether in interpreted code or compiled code), a call on the
selector function is saved; only a direct call to CADR needs to be made. Typically,
this substitution can be controlled by the user by setting appropriate flags. Some useful
functions in this regard are given below.

MACRO-FUNCTION takes a symbol as its argument and returns the macro
definition, if one exists for it. MACROEXPAND takes a form and expands the macro
call, repeatedly if necessary, until the expansion is not a macro call.

The formal parameters in a macro definition can contain &OPTIONAL and
&REST keywords as described for functions with optional arguments. They may also
contain &WHOLE which is useful for controlling in-line substitution.

2.7   READING AND WRITING

A function called READ is used in the read-eval-print loop of LISP to read an S-expr
from the terminal. It reads an S-expr, character by character, and converts it into an
appropriate object using cons cells and atoms, etc. The same function can be used by
the user explicitly to perform reads. For example, if a function F defined as

```
(DEFUN F (N)
   (- N (READ))))
```

is applied

```
(F 8)
```

and given the input

```
3
```

then we get

```
5
```

When the body of F is evaluated, READ is applied. It reads the input typed by the
user, 3 in the present case, and the body evaluates to 5. Similarly,

```
(SETQ X (READ))
(CAR Y)
```

will cause X to be set to the object denoted by S-expr (CAR Y). First, (SETQ X
(READ)) is read as part of the read-eval-print loop. Second, in trying to evaluate it,
(READ) is evaluated which reads the next S-expr typed by the user, i.e., (CAR Y).

(CAR Y) is not read as part of the read-eval-print loop and hence is not evaluated. X gets set to (CAR Y) because of SETQ. Finally, the value of X is printed because of the read-eval-print loop.

The function READ-CHAR applied without any parameters reads the next character typed by the user, including a blank. In other words, READ-CHAR reads one character and returns it. PEEK-CHAR applied without any parameters returns the next character in the input to be read. It does not consume the character, however. On performing READ-CHAR after PEEK-CHAR, the same character will be read.

There is a function called PRIN1 that evaluates its single parameter and prints the result on the screen. For example, (PRIN1 5) causes 5 to be displayed and (PRIN1 (CONS '1 '(2 3))) causes (1 2 3) to be displayed on the screen. It is used by the read-eval-print loop of LISP. It can also be used by the user.

There is another function called PRINT that is like PRIN1 except before printing its argument, it outputs a new line and afterward outputs a blank space. Both PRIN1 and PRINT return their argument.

PRINC is like PRIN1 except it strips the beginning and ending double quotes around a string and does not put \ before special characters. For example,

```
(PRINC "This is good")  -prints->  This is good
(PRINC 'A\ B)  -prints->  A B
```

unlike PRIN1:

```
(PRIN1 "This is good") -prints->  "This is good"          )dÄ
(PRIN1 'A\ B) -prints->  A\ B
```

If we read (using READ) what is printed by PRINT or PRIN1, we will get back an EQUAL memory structure. The same does not hold for PRINC, which is meant for producing output for people. Another function called PPRINT (or PP in some LISPs) pretty-prints function definitions, values of variables, etc., by indenting them appropriately.

Reading and writing from files and the terminal is done in a uniform manner. We associate with files and the terminal an object called an input-output (I/O) stream. These streams serve as sources or sinks of data. When the LISP system is loaded, a stream corresponding to the terminal is created. It is assigned to the variable *TERMINAL-IO*. All input and output from the terminal is done using it. For performing I/O from a file, first we must create a stream and then use it to perform the desired I/O.

An I/O stream can be created using OPEN. Its syntax is as follows:

```
(OPEN <filename> :DIRECTION <direction>)
```

It takes <filename> and <direction> as its arguments and returns a stream that is connected to the specified file. The <direction> must be one of :INPUT, :OUTPUT, or :IO and specifies whether the file is to be read, written, or both. For example,

```
(SETQ LL
      (OPEN 'LEXICON :DIRECTION :INPUT))
```

creates a stream for reading the file LEXICON and assigns it to LL. Similarly, the following creates a stream for output,

```
(SETQ SS (OPEN 'STORY :DIRECTION :OUTPUT))
```

and assigns it to SS. Once a stream is created, it can be used for I/O by including it as an additional (optional) argument to the functions for reading and writing (e.g., READ, READ-CHAR, PRINT).

There are also facilities for defining what are called read macros. When a character that is defined as a read macro is read by the READ function, the read macro is applied immediately. The result of the application is deemed to have been read instead of the character, after which the normal read-eval-print loop is carried to completion. Thus, an evaluation takes place while the input is being read; the normal, eval-print part of the loop is resumed later.

The syntax of read macros is given by

```
(SET-MACRO-CHARACTER <single-char> <function> <boolean>)
```

where <single-char> is the name of the read macro. When <single-char> is read during the read-eval-print loop or any other time structured reading is taking place (i.e., using READ but not with READ-CHAR, etc.), the <function> is applied and the result is considered to be read instead of the characters actually read. If <boolean> is true, the <single-char> in the middle of a symbol name is not considered as a read macro. The last argument is optional and NIL by default.

The <function> must take two arguments: the name of the stream from which reading is taking place and the read macro character.

As an example, consider the substitution of pronouns with the following simple rule: Whenever a $ is read, it is substituted by the value of the variable *ADJ*. Thus, if *ADJ* is bound to FAT, then

```
(THE $ MAN FELL IN WATER)
```

will be expanded during reading as

```
(THE FAT MAN FELL IN WATER)
```

The read macro to accomplish this is as follows:

```
(SET-MACRO-CHARACTER #\$   #'(LAMBDA (STREAM CHAR) *ADJ*))
```

Exercise 2.10 Define a read macro for $ that substitutes $ by the value of *SUBJ*, *OBJ*, or *IND-OBJ* depending on whether the value of a variable called *TYPE* is *SUBJ*, *OBJ*, or *IND-OBJ*, respectively.

Exercise 2.11 Define a read macro for ? such that ?X is read as ($VAR X).

2.8 NONLOCAL EXITS

While discussing DO form, we saw that RETURN could be used to exit the DO immediately. This is an example of more general constructs for exiting from within a block of code. Two special forms provide this facility: BLOCK and RETURN-FROM. The symbol BLOCK is followed by a symbol called the <name> followed by forms:

```
(BLOCK <name> <s1> ... <sn>)
```

Normally, the forms are evaluated from left to right, and the value of the last form returned. If, however, any of the forms

```
(RETURN-FROM <name> <s>)
```

is executed, <s> is evaluated and the enclosing block with the given <name> is exited. This may cause exit from many levels of textually nested blocks. The <name> is not evaluated, and it has lexical scope and dynamic extent.

All function definitions have an implicit block which has the same name as the function name.

The block mechanism described above works only for lexical nonlocal exits. There is another mechanism for dynamic nonlocal exits: CATCH and THROW.

In the evaluation of the CATCH form

```
(CATCH <tag> <s1> ... <sn>)
```

<tag> is evaluated (usually resulting in a symbol), after which the remaining forms are evaluated and the value of the last form is returned. If, however, a THROW form

```
(THROW <tag> <s>)
```

is evaluated, <tag> is evaluated followed by <s>. Then the CATCH form with the same tag is exited. The CATCH form need not lexically enclose the THROW form. Appropriate search is made on the function calls to locate the dynamically enclosing CATCH form.

Exercise 2.12 Write a function PARSE-EXPR that takes an arithmetic expression and

converts it from infix notation to prefix notation. Use CATCH and THROW to exit in case of an error.

FURTHER READINGS

COMMON LISP has a large number of features. Those not discussed here include control constructs such as UNWIND-PROTECT, returning multiple values, operations on different types of numbers, hash tables, and error signaling. The best single reference is Steele (1984).

CHAPTER
3

SEARCH

A large number of problems, particularly those that are the concern of artificial intelligence (AI), can be modeled in terms of a state space search. That is why we have chosen it to illustrate LISP programming. The state space consists of states and operators that allow us to go from one state to other related states. A state could be viewed as a snapshot of conditions on the problem at some stage of solution or simply as a candidate solution. To solve a problem, its space is searched until a desired or an acceptable state (called a goal state) is reached, if one exists. The search begins by examining a given initial state and proceeds to its related states using the operators, and so on.

Consider the problem of finding the molecular structure of a compound given its chemical composition and spectrum. It can be formulated in terms of a search of the space of all possible molecular structures, and the goal state is one which satisfies the composition and spectrum. It can also be formulated as the space of possible molecular structures for the given composition. Now the goal state is one which satisfies the given spectrum. What state space to consider for a problem is largely dependent on our knowledge and properties of the domain. In the example above, the second formulation has a smaller state space, but we can use it only if we know how to generate all possible structures with the given composition.

In the next section we will look at tree and graph search strategies that are uninformed (that is, do not use domain knowledge). In Sec. 3.2, informed search that

incorporates domain knowledge using heuristics is described. In Secs. 3.3 and 3.4, search for paths leading to the goal state is looked at. AND-OR graphs are presented in Sec. 3.5.

In the searches discussed in this chapter, it is assumed that three domain dependent functions are available:

SUCCESSORS(N). Given a node or state N, it returns a list of nodes that are successors of (or are adjacent or related to) N.

GOALP(N). Returns true if N is a goal node.

BADP(N). Returns true if node N is a bad node, that is, cannot lead to a goal state.

The search algorithms call the above three functions, but they themselves are independent of the domain.

Usually in AI, the entire state space is not explicitly represented in computer memory; the states are generated during the search. However, the algorithms work independent of whether the state space is explicitly represented or not. It is the task of the SUCCESSORS function to either generate a list of states or access them in an existing data structure, as the case may be.

3.1 TREE AND GRAPH SEARCH

We begin the discussion with tree search. Let us assume that the state space is structured as a tree. When we go from one state to another, we never come across a state that has already been visited.

3.1.1 Depth-first and Breadth-first Search

To understand the depth-first tree search, let us take the example of a binary tree. Figure 3-1 illustrates the orders in which nodes will be traversed when we perform the depth-first and breadth-first searches.

To perform a search in a tree-structured state space, we use the function given below. It makes use of a list called OPEN in which are placed the nodes to be examined (initially containing a single node—the root node). The first node in OPEN is examined: If it is a goal node, the search is over; otherwise it is replaced by its successors.

```
(DEFUN SEARCH-DF (START)
  (DO ((OPEN (LIST START)
             (APPEND (REMOVE-IF #'BADP
                                (SUCCESSORS (CAR OPEN)))
                     (CDR OPEN))))
      ((NULL OPEN)) ;Failure to find goal
    (COND [(GOALP (CAR OPEN)) (RETURN (CAR OPEN))])))
```

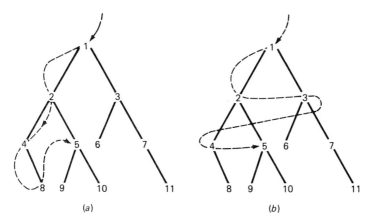

FIGURE 3-1
Order of traversal in tree search: (*a*) depth-first search; (*b*) breadth-first search.

The bad nodes are removed using REMOVE-IF as soon as they are generated, and they are not put in OPEN.

The above does a depth-first search. It is a simple matter to change it to do a breadth-first search by appending the nonbad successors at the end of the OPEN list. Thus, in a depth-first search OPEN is used like a stack (in a LIFO manner), while in a breadth-first search it is used like a queue (in a FIFO manner).

The OPEN list, at any time, contains the set of nodes that are yet to be examined. After a node in the OPEN list is examined, it is replaced by its successors. For example, in the tree given earlier, when the node with value 5 is reached (i.e., it is the first element in OPEN), the OPEN list will contain nodes with the following values in the depth-first and breadth-first searches, respectively:

(5 3)

and,

(5 6 7 8)

Viewed differently, OPEN contains the frontier nodes in the tree traversal. The frontier nodes are marked by dotted lines in Fig. 3-2 for depth-first and breadth-first searches when node 5 is examined.

Nodes above the dotted line have been generated and examined, nodes on the dotted line have been generated and placed on OPEN but are waiting to be examined, and nodes below the dotted line have yet to be generated and examined.

Exercise 3.1 Write the tail recursive version of SEARCH-DF.

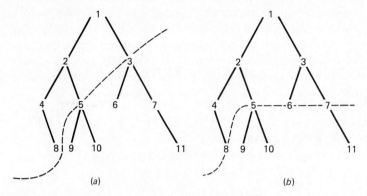

FIGURE 3-2
A frontier in tree search: (*a*) depth-first search; (*b*) breadth-first search.

3.1.2 An Example—Four-Queens Problem

As an example, consider the four-queens problem. On a chessboard consisting of 4 × 4 squares, the problem is to place four queens such that no two queens attack each other. Two queens attack each other if they are on the same row, column, or diagonal. The same row or column test follows from the data structure; the diagonal test is also straightforward. All squares whose row and column numbers add up to the same value lie on the same northeast-southwest (NE-SW) diagonals, while those with the same difference from their row to column number are on the same northwest-southeast (NW-SE) diagonals. (See Fig. 3-3.)

To solve the four-queens problem we need to define the appropriate SUCCESSORS, BADP, and GOALP functions. But first we must select a suitable representation for nodes, that is, for boards. Since no two queens must be in the same column, the data structure we choose to represent a board is a list of numbers, each number representing the row number of a queen for a different column. An empty list denotes an empty board; otherwise the first number denotes the row number for the queen in

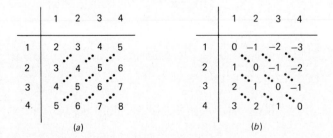

FIGURE 3-3
Diagonals on a chessboard: (*a*) NE-SW diagonals (row + column); (*b*) NW-SE diagonals (row − column).

column 1, second number for queen in column 2, and so on. Initially, the board is empty, and a queen is to be placed in the first column in any of the rows, thus leading to four possible successors. In successors to each of them, a queen can be placed in any of the four rows on the second column, and so on. SUCCESSORS checks whether all four queens have been placed on the board, and if not, it generates four successors in which a queen is placed on a different row in the next available column.

```
(DEFUN SUCCESSORS (BOARD)
   (COND [(EQL 4 (LENGTH BOARD)) ()]
         [T (MAPCAR #'(LAMBDA (N) (APPEND BOARD (LIST N)))
                    *POSITIONS*)]))
```

where *POSITIONS* is a global variable whose value is a list of numbers from 1 to 4

```
(DEFVAR *POSITIONS* '(1 2 3 4))   ;Rows on the chessboard.
```

BADP checks to see that on a given board no two queens attack each other. In case they do, that board is rejected and its successors are not explored. NO-DUPLICATES checks whether a given list is a set.

```
(DEFUN BADP (BOARD)
   (NOT (AND
          ;; Test for two queens on the same row
          (NO-DUPLICATES BOARD)
          ;; Test for two queens on the
          ;;   same NE-SW diagonals
          (NO-DUPLICATES (MAPCAR #'+
                                 *POSITIONS*
                                 BOARD))
          ;; Test for NW-SE diagonals
          (NO-DUPLICATES (MAPCAR #'-
                                 *POSITIONS*
                                 BOARD)))))
```

```
(DEFUN NO-DUPLICATES (S)
   (COND [(NULL S) T]
         [(MEMBER (CAR L) (CDR L)) NIL]
         [T (NO-DUPLICATES (CDR L))]))
```

A goal node is reached if all the queens have been placed (such that no two queens attack each other),

```
(DEFUN GOALP (BOARD)
   (EQL 4 (LENGTH BOARD)))
```

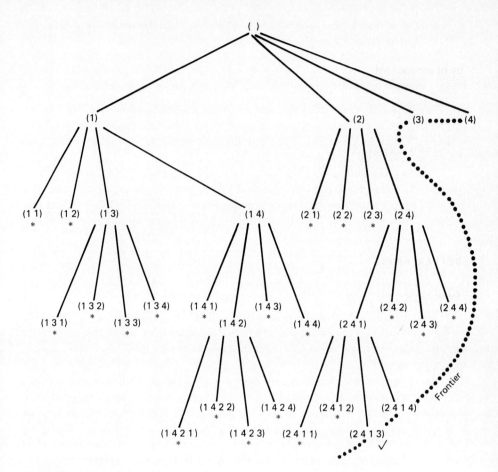

FIGURE 3-4
Tree search for four-queens problem.

Now, to perform a depth-first search starting from an empty board, we write:

```
(SEARCH-DF ())
```

The tree that is traversed when a goal configuration (2 4 1 3) is found is given in Fig. 3-4 (where bad nodes are marked by * below them and a goal node by √).

Exercise 3.2 Show the frontiers when the tree in Fig. 3-1 is being traversed and the node with value 6 is to be examined next. Show for both depth-first and breadth-first searches.

Exercise 3.3 Show a trace of the four-queens solution using a breadth-first search.

Exercise 3.4 Modify the functions given earlier for solving the four-queens problem to

make them work for an *n*-queens problem where *n* can take any value. Use them to solve an eight-queens problem. Show the traversal.

3.1.3   Graph Search

So far we have only considered tree search. While traversing nodes in a tree, we are assured that we will always come across new nodes; old nodes will not be produced by the SUCCESSORS function. In many problem domains the state space is structured as a graph. There we must deal with graphs.

Actually, the state space might not have any or might have more than one natural structure. It is the SUCCESSORS function that defines (at times, even imposes) a structure. For example, in the four-queens problem, a SUCCESSORS function that produces permutations of (1 2 3 4) by exchanging adjacent numbers in a list representing the queens causes the resulting state space to be a general graph instead of a tree. If we use the function defined in the last section, the state space is structured as a tree. Therefore, a more accurate statement is that for a given state space, a SUCCESSORS function that imposes a tree structure might be difficult to define, and there we must deal with general graphs.

While traversing nodes generated by the SUCCESSORS function in a graph, we must test whether they have already been encountered. A check can be made at the time nodes generated by SUCCESSORS are to be put in OPEN. Such nodes, then, are not put in OPEN.

There are two basic methods for determining whether we have come across a node. The first method is applicable when each state in the state space is represented uniquely in memory. Whenever a node is encountered, it is marked so that later on if we come across the same node we will find it marked. Thus, before processing the first node in OPEN, we should check whether it is marked. Marks can be put on a node by including an additional boolean flag in the node record structure.

In the second method, a list called CLOSED, say, is maintained which contains all those nodes that have been encountered. Before processing a new node, we must check to make sure that it is not in CLOSED.

Using the second method above, a depth-first search on a graph is carried out by SEARCH-GRAPH-DF.

```
(DEFUN SEARCH-GRAPH-DF (START)
  (DO ([OPEN (LIST START)
             (APPEND (REMOVE-BAD-PREV-VISITED
                       (SUCCESSORS (CAR OPEN))
                       #'BADP CLOSED)
                     (CDR OPEN))]
       [CLOSED () (CONS (CAR OPEN) CLOSED)])
      ((NULL OPEN)) ;Search failed
    (COND [(GOALP (CAR OPEN)) ;Search successful
           (RETURN (CAR OPEN))])))
```

```
(DEFUN REMOVE-BAD-PREV-VISITED (L BADPRED CLOSED)
;;; Returns a list of those nodes in L that are not bad
;;; and are not in the CLOSED list.
(COND [(NULL L) L]
      [(OR (FUNCALL BADPRED (CAR L))
           (MEMBER (CAR L) CLOSED :TEST #'EQUAL))
        (REMOVE-BAD-PREV-VISITED
           (CDR L) BADPRED CLOSED)]
      [T (CONS (CAR L)
               (REMOVE-BAD-PREV-VISITED
                  (CDR L) BADPRED CLOSED))]))
```

In the implementation above, CLOSED is a list. As a result, the membership test is expensive. It can be speeded up by doing appropriate kinds of indexing or building discrimination nets. These data structures are discussed in detail later (Chaps. 6 and 7).

If we have a SUCCESSORS function that imposes a graph structure on a state space, we can modify it such that it results in a tree structure. The modification is as follows: After generating the list of successors as in the original function, delete those nodes that are present in CLOSED. However, before returning the new list of nodes, append it to CLOSED. This new SUCCESSORS function will never produce a node that has already been placed in CLOSED, thus resulting in a tree structure. This approach is undesirable because it removes the clean separation between the search and the SUCCESSORS functions. CLOSED, a part of the search function, is manipulated by the SUCCESSORS function.

Exercise 3.5 Write a function SUCCESSORS1 that converts a graph-generating function to a tree-generating function.

Exercise 3.6 There are k types of coins of value v_1 to v_k, respectively. There are n_1 coins of the first type, n_2 of the second type, and so on. You have to select some of these coins such that the total value is V. Frame this problem as a state-space search. Define appropriate SUCCESSORS, GOALP, and BADP functions. [*Hint*: Let $(n_1, n_2, \ldots n_k)$ represent the initial selection of coins where n_1 coins of the first type, n_2 coins of the second type, etc., are selected. The SUCCESSORS function generates k successor nodes each with one different type of coin less than the predecessor.]

Take as an example the search of the graph in Fig. 3-5 (where the bad node is marked by * and goal node by $\sqrt{}$). First, we choose a representation: Nodes are represented by the atoms by which they are labeled. Edges are stored using property lists for the sake of convenience. If a node N has directed edges to k different nodes, then the list of nodes is stored on the property ARCS of the atom N. The graph of Fig. 3-5 is represented as

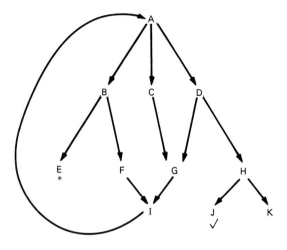

FIGURE 3-5
An example graph.

```
(SETF (GET 'A 'ARCS) '(B C D))
(SETF (GET 'B 'ARCS) '(E F))
(SETF (GET 'F 'ARCS) '(I))
(SETF (GET 'C 'ARCS) '(G))
(SETF (GET 'G 'ARCS) '(I))
(SETF (GET 'D 'ARCS) '(G H))
(SETF (GET 'H 'ARCS) '(J K))
(SETF (GET 'I 'ARCS) '(A))
```

If E is a bad node and J is a goal node, these facts can be incorporated in the functions BADP and GOALP, respectively. SUCCESSORS is straightforward.

```
(DEFUN SUCCESSORS (NODE) (GET NODE 'ARCS))
(DEFUN BADP (NODE) (EQL NODE 'E))
(DEFUN GOALP (NODE) (EQL NODE 'J))
```

Exercise 3.7 Search the graph in Fig. 3-5 starting from (*a*) node A, and (*b*) node I.

3.1.4   Finding Multiple Goal Nodes

In some state spaces there is more than one goal state, and we might be interested in some or all of them. For example, in the four-queens problem we might want to know all the different solution configurations of queens, to analyze the underlying structure of solutions. Or, for example, given chemical composition and spectra, we might be interested in finding all the molecular structures that satisfy the data. (It is meaningful to talk about finding all goal states only when the number of goal states is finite and it is possible to find the states by traversing a finite part of the search space.)

First, we will consider a function that operates on each goal state, and then another that returns a list of goal states. The second solution provides greater flexibility

because each of the goal states can be operated upon individually, or any of them can be operated upon after making a comparative study, etc.

To perform an operation OP on each of the goal states, the change needed to be made on the search routines is simple. Instead of returning when the first goal state is found, we operate on it and continue the search. For example, the last expression in the DO form in SEARCH-DF or SEARCH-GRAPH-DF can be replaced by

```
(COND [(GOALP (CAR OPEN))
       ;; Operate on goal. Continue traversal.
       (OP (CAR OPEN))])
```

To return a list of goal states, the search routines must be changed to accumulate the goal states in a list. For example, RESULT is used to accumulate the goal states in the following tree search:

```
(DEFUN TRAVERSE-DF (START)
 (DO ((OPEN (LIST START)
            (APPEND (SUCCESSORS (CAR OPEN)) (CDR OPEN)))
      (RESULT ()))
     ((NULL OPEN) RESULT) ;Search over. Return RESULT.
     (COND [(GOALP (CAR OPEN))
            ;; A goal found. Put in RESULT
            (SETQ RESULT (CONS (CAR OPEN) RESULT))])))
```

Exercise 3.8 Write the tail recursive versions of TRAVERSE-DF.

Exercise 3.9 So far we have seen that for searching in a particular state space, we must define the functions named SUCCESSORS, GOALP, and BADP. This can cause problems if we are searching more than one state space at a time. Redefine SEARCH-DF so that instead of having to name the functions as above, they can be passed as arguments.

3.2   BEST-FIRST SEARCH

In the last section, we examined a number of search methods. All the methods, however, searched the space by using a static strategy (e.g., breadth-first or depth-first search). They did not make use of any information regarding the state space or the concerned domain, e.g., likelihood of reaching a goal state from a given state. In this chapter, we introduce heuristic functions that give us an estimate of "goodness" of a state. These estimates will be used in conducting a search which does not follow any fixed predetermined order.

A small next step is to allow not just depth-first or breadth-first searches, but one in which the most promising node of the frontier (i.e., from the nodes in OPEN) is expanded first. This is called best-first search, and it opens up a whole new world—that of heuristic search. An evaluation function is used to determine the rating of the

nodes in OPEN; it is called a *heuristic* function. This rating is used to decide what node of the frontier to examine and expand next.

SEARCH-BEST defined below does the best-first search. Similar to earlier searches it uses an OPEN list. Every entry in OPEN consists of two items: a node and the cost estimate of reaching a goal from it (as determined by a function called HEURISTIC). For efficiency reasons, OPEN is kept sorted on the rating. (Can you explain why?) Since its first entry is examined and expanded in each iteration, the best node is selected every time, resulting in a best-first search.

```
(DEFSTRUCT (ENTRY (:CONSTRUCTOR MAKE-ENTRY (NODE COST-EST))
                  (:CONC-NAME ()))
           NODE
           COST-EST)
(DEFUN SEARCH-BEST (START)
  (DO ((OPEN (LIST (MAKE-ENTRY START 0))
             (MERGE 'LIST      ;Merge the two lists:
                               ; tail of OPEN and
                               ; sorted good successors
                    (CDR OPEN)
                    (SORT (EVAL-HEUR-FORM-ENTRIES
                           #'HEURISTIC
                           (REMOVE-IF
                            #'BADP
                            (SUCCESSORS
                             (NODE (CAR OPEN)))))
                          #'<
                          :KEY #'COST-EST)
                    #'<
                    :KEY #'COST-EST)))
      ((NULL OPEN)) ;Failure
    (COND [(GOALP (CAR OPEN)) (RETURN (CAR OPEN))])))

(DEFUN EVAL-HEUR-FORM-ENTRIES (H L)
;;; Take a list L of nodes and generate a list of node and
;;; rating pairs using H as the heuristic function.
  (COND [(NULL L) ()]
        [T (CONS (MAKE-ENTRY (CAR L)
                             (FUNCALL H (CAR L)))
                 (EVAL-HEUR-FORM-ENTRIES H (CDR L)))]))
```

The above can be extended easily to deal with graphs rather than trees.

Exercise 3.10 Test the SEARCH-BEST function on the tree shown in Fig. 3-6. The numbers on the nodes are their ratings. Define HEURISTIC appropriately.

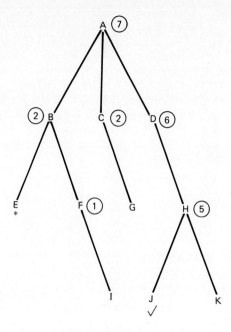

FIGURE 3-6

Exercise 3.11 Define SEARCH-GRAPH-BEST that performs a best-first graph search. (*Hint*: Introduce ratings in SEARCH-GRAPH-DF defined earlier and keep OPEN sorted.)

Exercise 3.12 In a hill-climbing method, the successors of a node are sorted based on their rating and added in front of the OPEN queue. The whole queue is not sorted. Thus, it is a depth-first search in which we make a local choice about the order in which to try the successors. Clearly, this method would suffer if it makes a wrong choice at any point, because then it will have to explore a wrong subtree fully before coming to the right one. If the wrong tree is infinite or very large, such a thing may be fatal for the search. This algorithm, however, can be implemented quite efficiently.

Define SEARCH-HILL that implements the hill-climbing search.

Exercise 3.13 Can you think of a heuristic to guide your search for a set of coins so that their total value is V, as described in Exercise 3.6?

Exercise 3.14 Cryptarithmetic problems have been studied extensively to determine how people solve problems [Newell (1972)]. These involve an addition or a subtraction of sequences of letters. The problem is to assign a distinct decimal digit to each of the letters in such a way that on substitution the arithmetic is correct. For example, in

$$
\begin{array}{r}
\text{SEND} \\
+ \text{ MORE} \\
\hline
\text{MONEY}
\end{array}
$$

a suitable assignment must be found for the letters S, E, N, D, M, O, R, Y.

Formulate the cryptarithmetic problem as a search problem. Solve it as an uninformed search.

Can you think of a heuristic for speeding up the solution? What else would you like to incorporate for improving search efficiency?

Exercise 3.15 (Difficult) While solving the cryptarithmetic problem, it is convenient to think in terms of constraints placed on values of letters. A state is a set of constraints. For example, on examining the result of addition in the problem given in the previous exercise, we can conclude that M is equal to 0 or 1, because the carry cannot be greater than 1 when adding two numbers. Thus the state is

We might further conclude that O is either equal to $(S + M)$ or $(S + M + 1)$. Thus, there are two successor states:

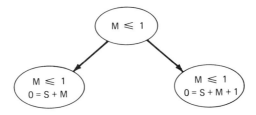

This is an example of a search getting reduced by the domain knowledge, which in the present case means knowledge of the properties of integer addition.

Model the state by a set of constraints. Define appropriate GOALP, BADP, and SUCCESSORS functions. The quality of your solution will depend upon how good a SUCCESSORS function you can define.

3.3   SEARCH FOR A SOLUTION PATH

So far, the problem has been to find a goal node starting from the start node in a state space. The path that was taken in traveling from the start node to a goal node was unimportant, except for efficiency reasons. For many problems, however, the path taken to reach a goal node is more important than the goal itself.

Consider as an example the eight-puzzle: There are eight tiles and an empty space in a two-dimensional rectangular frame. The tiles are labeled uniquely by numbers from 1 to 8 as shown in Fig. 3-7. A tile can move into the space if it is left, right, above, or below the space; when a tile moves into the space, its original position becomes the space. The problem is to reach the goal state given in Fig. 3-7 starting from an arbitrary initial state by a sequence of moves of tiles.

We consider a configuration of the tiles as a state in the state space. Successors of a state are all those states that can be reached by any of the moves of tiles. Some

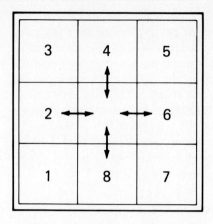

FIGURE 3-7
Eight-puzzle goal state (four possible moves marked by arrows).

example successors are given in Fig. 3-8. Clearly, the goal state is known beforehand; the important thing is the sequence of moves that lead to it. The sequence of moves corresponds to the path followed in the graph by the search function to arrive at the goal.

The graph search function that stores the path information along with the nodes (or states) is given below. It returns the first path leading to a goal. To accomplish

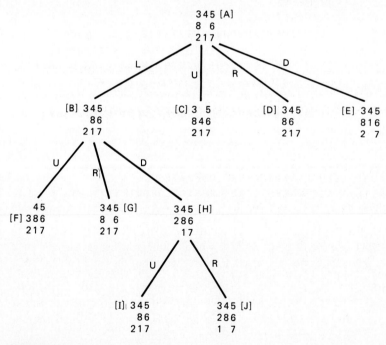

FIGURE 3-8
Examples of successors in eight-puzzle.

this, each of the entries in the OPEN and CLOSED lists is an edge rather than a node. Edges are represented by a pair: the first node in the pair is the node to be processed as usual, while the second is its predecessor. For the root node, NIL is stored instead of the predecessor in the pair. While checking whether the first entry in OPEN has been encountered before, we should take care to test for equality of the first element of the pair (in the first entry) in OPEN with the first elements of entries in CLOSED. If a match is found, it shows that the node in OPEN has been encountered before via another path. The functions GOALP, SUCCESSORS, and BADP are independent of whether the path is to be determined or not. When the successors of a node are generated, pairs are created by the path search function before storing them in OPEN. Similarly, GOALP and BADP are called with a node and not a pair.

```
(DEFSTRUCT (ENTRY (:CONSTRUCTOR MAKE-ENTRY (NODE PREDEC)))
           NODE
           PREDEC)


(DEFUN SEARCHPATH-BF (START)
;;; Very similar to SEARCH-DF except now OPEN and CLOSED
;;; lists contain edges.
  (DO ((OPEN (LIST (MAKE-ENTRY START ()))
             (APPEND
              (CDR OPEN)
              (FORM-PAIRS
                (REMOVE-BAD-PREV-VISITED2 ;The "good"
                                          ; successors
                  (SUCCESSORS (ENTRY-NODE (CAR OPEN)))
                  #'BADP
                  CLOSED)
                (ENTRY-NODE (CAR OPEN)) ;The predecessor
                )))
       (CLOSED () (CONS (CAR OPEN) CLOSED)))
      ((NULL OPEN)) ;Search failed
    (COND [(GOALP (ENTRY-NODE (CAR OPEN)))
           (RETURN (GET-PATH (CAR OPEN) CLOSED))])))
```

REMOVE-BAD-PREV-VISITED2 is like REMOVE-BAD-PREV-VISITED except that now CLOSED is a list of pairs. Hence, while testing whether an element of L has been visited previously, we must check the first element of the pairs on CLOSED.

```
(DEFUN REMOVE-BAD-PREV-VISITED2 (L BADPRED CLOSED)
;;; Similar to REMOVE-BAD-PREV-VISITED except CLOSED is
;;; a list of edges. Uses below ASSOC rather than MEMBER.
  (COND [(NULL L) ()]
```

```
[(OR (FUNCALL BADPRED (CAR L))
     (ASSOC (CAR L) CLOSED :TEST #'EQUAL))
  (REMOVE-BAD-PREV-VISITED2 (CDR L) BADPRED CLOSED)]
 [T (CONS (CAR L)
          (REMOVE-BAD-PREV-VISITED2
                (CDR L) BADPRED CLOSED))]))
```

GET-PATH constructs a sequence of states defining the path, and FORM-PAIRS makes a list of edges.

```
(DEFUN FORM-PAIRS (L PREDEC)
;;; PREDEC = a node or state.
;;; L = list of its successors.
;;; Returns a list of pairs each consisting of
;;;   a different element from L as the successor
;;;   and PREDEC as the predecessor.
   (COND [(NULL L) ()]
         [T (CONS (MAKE-ENTRY (CAR L) PREDEC)
                  (FORM-PAIRS (CDR L) PREDEC))]))

(DEFUN GET-PATH (PAIR CLOSED)
;;; Constructs the path (that is, a sequence of nodes)
;;;   given the last edge PAIR and a set of edges in CLOSED.
   (COND [(NULL PAIR) ()]
         [T (CONS (ENTRY-NODE PAIR)
                  (GET-PATH (ASSOC (ENTRY-PREDEC PAIR)
                                   CLOSED
                                   :TEST #'EQUAL)
                            CLOSED))]))
```

If the search function above is applied after defining SUCCESSORS, GOALP, and BADP for the eight-puzzle on the initial node labeled A, given in Fig. 3-8, then the following will be the OPEN and CLOSED lists after B is expanded:

```
CLOSED: ((B A) (A ()))
OPEN:   ((C A) (D A) (E A) (F B) (G B) (H B))
```

Using these we can reconstruct the paths traversed. For example, to find the path to reach node F, we would retrieve the entry (F B) and then the entries (B A) and (A ()), and construct (F B A) as the path (last node first).

A depth-first search can be defined analogous to a breadth-first search.

Exercise 3.16 Find a solution path for the graph in Fig. 3-5 when the start node is A.

To solve the eight-puzzle, we need to choose an appropriate representation. If

we represent each row of the eight-puzzle by a list of terms, with the space represented by *, then the following is an example representation:

```
  4 5
3 8 6
2 1 7
```

is represented as:

```
((* 4 5) (3 8 6) (2 1 7))
```

The goal state is represented by

```
((3 4 5) (2 * 6) (1 8 7))
```

> **Exercise 3.17** Define the SUCCESSORS, BADP, and GOALP functions for the state space for an eight-puzzle using the representation of the state given above.

> **Exercise 3.18** Choose another representation for the eight-puzzle (say, using arrays) and define SUCCESSORS, BADP, and GOALP.

A new kind of problem, determining a path to a goal node, has been introduced in this section. In a way, such problems can always be reformulated in terms of the old problem of finding a goal node. However, it usually results in an unnatural, clumsy, and difficult solution. For example, the eight-puzzle can be reformulated as follows: Each state consists of a start configuration of the eight-puzzle, a sequence of moves, and an end configuration. The sequence of moves is such that it takes us from the start configuration to the end configuration in the state. Thus, the sequence of moves has been made part of the state. Successors of a state consist of the same start configuration, a new sequence of moves having one additional move after the old one, and the new end configuration. The initial state consists of the given initial configuration, a null sequence of moves, and the end configuration which is the same as the initial configuration. Finally, a goal state is one in which the end configuration is the desired goal configuration of eight-puzzle.

What has been done is nothing extraordinary. The sequence of moves has been encoded as part of the state. We will prefer searching for a path explicitly rather than encoding it as part of the state.

3.3.1   Least-cost Path

The function defined above terminates execution on finding the first path to a goal node during a search. At times, there is a need to retrieve the path with the least cost. Of course, there should be a way of computing the cost of a path. The cost of a path is the sum of the costs of its edges where the cost of each edge is nonnegative and known. (We shall assume that the SUCCESSORS function applied to node n produces

a list of pairs, each pair consisting of a successor node *m* and the cost of the edge from *n* to *m*.)

As an example of the above, we have the problem of computing the minimum road distance between two cities, when the names of cities and road distances between them is given. Similarly, in the eight-puzzle, if a solution that takes a minimum number of moves is required, all we have to do is to assign the same cost, say 1, to all the moves, and find the least-cost path.

The main concern earlier, in finding a goal, was to reduce the search time. Here, the major concern is to reduce the cost of the path even if it means putting extra effort into the search. Clearly, in the road map example, spending extra time in analyzing the map (search) is well worth the effort because actual traveling time will be reduced (least-cost path).

The following three changes need to be made to SEARCHPATH-BF defined above:

1. In the entries in the OPEN and CLOSED lists, the cost of the path found so far ought to be stored in addition to the node and its predecessor.
2. While checking that the node in the first entry in OPEN does not occur as a node in any of the entries in CLOSED, we need to do the following: If a match is found, it shows that the node has been encountered earlier via another path. Here, the cost of the old path to that of the new one must be compared. If the cost of the new one is lesser, the old one can be removed; otherwise the new one ought to be removed.
3. The OPEN list ought to be kept sorted by cost so that every time we select the first entry, it is the lowest-cost one.

Let each entry on the OPEN and CLOSED lists be defined as follows:

```
(DEFSTRUCT (ENTRY (:CONSTRUCTOR MAKE-ENTRY
                              (NODE COST PREDEC)))
          NODE COST PREDEC)

(DEFUN SEARCHPATH-LEAST (START)
  (DO ((OPEN (LIST (MAKE-ENTRY START 0 ())))
              ;;In each iteration sort the successors
              ;;and merge with tail of OPEN using
              ;;ENTRY-COST as the key.
              (MERGE 'LIST
                      (SORT (PROCESS-SUCCESSORS
                              (SUCCESSORS
                                (ENTRY-NODE (CAR OPEN)))
                              (ENTRY-NODE (CAR OPEN))
                              (ENTRY-COST (CAR OPEN))
                              CLOSED)
```

```lisp
                                    #'<
                             :KEY #'ENTRY-COST)
                  (CDR OPEN)
                  #'<
                    :KEY #'ENTRY-COST))
      (CLOSED () (CONS (CAR OPEN) CLOSED)))
    ((NULL OPEN))
    (COND [(GOALP (ENTRY-NODE (CAR OPEN)))
          (RETURN (GET-PATH (CAR OPEN) CLOSED))]))))


(DEFUN PROCESS-SUCCESSORS (L PREDEC COST CLOSED)
;;; L is a list of pairs: successor node and cost of an
;;; edge. This removes those pairs in L that are bad. If
;;; a node in L is also on CLOSED with a higher cost, the
;;; cost in CLOSED is updated. Costs of its successors
;;; are also updated.
;;;   Finally a list of ENTRYs is returned, each ENTRY
;;; consisting of a good node in L together with its new
;;; cost and predecessor PREDEC.
  (COND [(NULL L) ()]
        [(BADP (ENTRY-NODE (CAR L))) ;Drop (CAR L).
         (PROCESS-SUCCESSORS (CDR L) PREDEC COST CLOSED)]
        [T (LET ((X (ASSOC (ENTRY-NODE (CAR L))
                           CLOSED
                           :TEST #'EQUAL
                           :KEY #'ENTRY-NODE)))
             (COND [(NULL X)             ;(CAR L) is neither
                                         ; bad nor on CLOSED.
                    (CONS (MAKE-ENTRY
                            (ENTRY-NODE (CAR L))
                            (+ COST (ENTRY-COST (CAR L)))
                            PREDEC)
                          (PROCESS-SUCCESSORS
                            (CDR L) PREDEC COST CLOSED))]
                   [(< (ENTRY-COST X)
                       (+ COST (ENTRY-COST (CAR L))))
                    ;; Earlier path on CLOSED is cheaper
                    ;;   than the current path. Drop (CAR L).
                    (PROCESS-SUCCESSORS
                      (CDR L) PREDEC COST CLOSED)]
                   [T ;; Earlier path is costlier. Put
                      ;;   current path on the list to be
                      ;;   returned.
                    (CONS (MAKE-ENTRY
```

```
            (ENTRY-NODE (CAR L))
            (+ COST (ENTRY-COST (CAR L)))
            PREDEC)
        (PROCESS-SUCCESSORS
          (CDR L) PREDEC
          COST CLOSED))])))])))
```

As usual GOALP, BADP, and SUCCESSORS must be defined depending on the state space.

Take as an example, the same graph as in Fig. 3-5 except now there is a cost associated with every edge (see Fig. 3-9). The following are, without explanation, the representation of the graph and the requisite functions.

```
(SETF (GET 'A 'ARCS) '((B 3) (C 9) (D 12)))
(SETF (GET 'B 'ARCS) '((E 2) (F 4)))
(SETF (GET 'F 'ARCS) '((I 1)))
(SETF (GET 'C 'ARCS) '((G 1)))
(SETF (GET 'G 'ARCS) '((I 3)))
(SETF (GET 'D 'ARCS) '((G 1) (H 2)))
(SETF (GET 'H 'ARCS) '((J 5) (K 2)))
(SETF (GET 'I 'ARCS) '((A 1)))

(DEFUN SUCCESSORS (NODE) (GET NODE 'ARCS))
(DEFUN GOALP (N) (EQL N 'J))
(DEFUN BADP (N) (EQL N 'E))
```

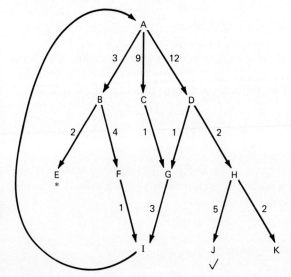

FIGURE 3-9
Graph as in Fig. 3-5 with cost of edges.

Exercise 3.19 For the weighted graph given if Fig. 3-9, find the least-cost path.

Exercise 3.20 Define the appropriate functions needed to find the least number of moves to solve the eight-puzzle.

Exercise 3.21 Define the appropriate functions needed to find the shortest road distance between two cities. Select an appropriate representation for the road map.

Exercise 3.22 Define a SEARCHPATHS function that returns all possible paths from a start node to a goal node.

3.4 HEURISTIC SEARCH FOR THE LEAST-COST PATH

In this section, the least-cost path search algorithm will make use of heuristics to estimate the cost of the path from a given node to a goal node. This will allow us to speed up the search for the least-cost path, provided the heuristic is good.

To incorporate heuristics, we keep two numbers with every node in OPEN: The first one gives the cost of reaching the node from the start node, and the second one is the estimate of the cost of reaching a goal node from there. Thus, if for a node n we have

$f^*(n)$ = cost of the least-cost path from the start node to the goal node that passes through n

$g^*(n)$ = cost of the least-cost path from the start node to n

$h^*(n)$ = cost of the least-cost path from node n to a goal node

then it follows that

$$f^*(n) = g^*(n) + h^*(n)$$

For a node n in OPEN, we only have estimates $g(n)$ for $g^*(n)$, and $h(n)$ for $h^*(n)$. $g(n)$ is the actual cost of reaching n and hence it is larger than or equal to the least-cost path to n. For an estimate of h^* we rely upon some heuristic function h. Thus, we have

$$f(n) = g(n) + h(n)$$

where $f(n)$ estimates $f^*(n)$.[1]

For example, if we have the graph given in Fig. 3-10 [with numbers on edges showing the cost, and numbers on nodes (in circles) showing the h values], then the following holds for X when the search begins:

$$f(X) = 0 + 2 = 2$$

---

[1]Note that the lesser the value of h, the better the node. This is the opposite of that used in a best-first search where the higher the value of the function, the better the node.

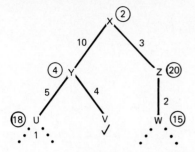

FIGURE 3-10

On expanding X, the following is true of Y and Z, the successors of X:

$$f(Y) = 10 + 4 = 14$$

$$f(Z) = 3 + 20 = 23$$

Y would be chosen for expansion because its f value is the smaller of the two (though its g value is not). If heuristics were not used, Z would have been chosen for expansion.

An algorithm called the A* algorithm that uses $f(n)$ to select among the nodes in OPEN is given below. It can be proved that the A* algorithm finds the least-cost path (i.e., is admissible), if the heuristic function underestimates the cost [Nilsson (1980)]:

$$h(n) \le h^*(n)$$

If h(n) is equal to 0, it reduces to an uninformed search.

```
(DEFSTRUCT (ENTRY (:CONSTRUCTOR MAKE-ENTRY
                              (NODE G H PREDEC)))
           NODE  G  H  PREDEC)


(DEFUN SEARCH-A* (START)
;;; Similar to SEARCH-PATH-LEAST except f value
;;;   instead of h value is used for sorting.
(DO ((OPEN (LIST (MAKE-ENTRY START 0 0 ())))
          (MERGE
            'LIST
            (CDR OPEN)
            (SORT
              (PROCESS-ENTRYS
                (SUCCESSORS (ENTRY-NODE (CAR OPEN)))
                (ENTRY-NODE (CAR OPEN))
                (ENTRY-G (CAR OPEN))
                CLOSED)
             #'ENTRY-LESSTHAN)
           #'ENTRY-LESSTHAN))
     (CLOSED () (CONS (CAR OPEN) CLOSED)))
```

```
                ((NULL OPEN))
      (COND [(GOALP (ENTRY-NODE (CAR OPEN)))
              (RETURN (GET-PATH (CAR OPEN) CLOSED))])))


(DEFUN ENTRY-LESSTHAN (E1 E2)
     (< (+ (ENTRY-G E1) (ENTRY-H E1))
        (+ (ENTRY-G E2) (ENTRY-H E2))))
```

GET-PATH is the same as in Sec. 3.3. PROCESS-ENTRYS takes a list of successor nodes, removes those that are "bad" or already encountered, and returns a list of ENTRYs for the remaining nodes. (Compare with PROCESS-SUCCESSORS in Sec. 3.3.)

```
(DEFUN PROCESS-ENTRYS (L PREDEC COST CLOSED)
;;;   L is a list of pairs, each pair consisting of a
;;;   successor node and cost of an edge.
;;;   It removes those pairs in L that are bad.
;;;   If a node in L is also on CLOSED with a lower cost,
;;;   the node is dropped.
;;;   Finally, a list of ENTRYs is returned, each ENTRY
;;;   consisting of a good node in L together with its new
;;;   cost and predecessor PREDEC.
   (COND
      [(NULL L) NIL]
      [(BADP (ENTRY-NODE (CAR L)))
       (PROCESS-ENTRYS
           (CDR L) PREDEC COST CLOSED)]
      [T (LET ((X (ASSOC (ENTRY-NODE (CAR L))
                     CLOSED
                     :TEST #'EQUAL
                     :KEY #'ENTRY-NODE)))
          (COND [(NULL X)
                 (CONS (MAKE-ENTRY
                       (ENTRY-NODE (CAR L))
                       (+ COST (ENTRY-G (CAR L)))
                       (FUNCALL #'HEURISTIC
                              (ENTRY-NODE (CAR L)))
                       PREDEC)
                     (PROCESS-ENTRYS
                         (CDR L) PREDEC COST CLOSED))]
                [(< (ENTRY-G X)
```

```
      (+ COST (ENTRY-G (CAR L))))
   (PROCESS-ENTRYS
            (CDR L) PREDEC COST CLOSED))]
   [T (CONS (MAKE-ENTRY
            (ENTRY-NODE (CAR L))
            (+ COST (ENTRY-G (CAR L)))
            (FUNCALL #'HEURISTIC
                     (ENTRY-NODE (CAR L)))
            PREDEC)
       (PROCESS-ENTRYS
            (CDR L) PREDEC COST CLOSED))])))])))
```

Consider the example of finding the shortest road distance between two given cities. Suppose we know (or can compute) the aerial distance between the cities. This can be used as the heuristic function which always underestimates the road distance. The A* algorithm is then guaranteed to give us the solution.

Exercise 3.23 Define SUCCESSORS, GOALP, BADP, etc., for solving the shortest road distance problem. Compare with the solution of the same problem in Exercise 3.21.

Exercise 3.24 Solve the eight-puzzle to find a solution that takes the minimum number of moves. (*Hint*: Assume that the cost of making a move is 1.)

Exercise 3.25 Search the graph shown in Fig. 3-11 (same as in Fig. 3-9) with the ratings for nodes marked in circles.

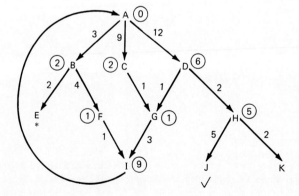

FIGURE 3-11

3.5 AND-OR GRAPH SEARCH

Frequently, it is convenient to decompose a given problem into smaller problems (called subproblems) and solve each one of them separately. For example, to prepare ingredients for cooking soup (task 1) we have to prepare the vegetables (task 2) and grind the spices (task 3), and depending on whether we want eggplant soup or carrot soup we may have to either mash eggplant (task 4) and boil tomato (task 5), or cut carrot (task 6). Thus, task 1 is decomposed into tasks 2 and 3, and to accomplish task 2 we have a choice of either performing tasks 4 and 5 or task 6. This is shown in Fig. 3-12. Nodes [2] and [3] (representing tasks 2 and 3, respectively) are AND nodes, similar to nodes [4] and [5]. Another way of stating the same thing is that node [1] has an AND arc to nodes [2] and [3], and node [2] has an AND arc to nodes [4] and [5] and an OR arc to node [6].[2]

In solving the problem, we will have to traverse the AND-OR tree (or AND-OR graph, as the case may be). Clearly, it is a more complex structure than the one encountered earlier. Successors of a node can be AND nodes, OR nodes, or a mixture of the two. An AND-OR tree is said to be a representation for problem reduction. Although there are obvious connections, a node here should not be confused with a node or a state in a state-space representation. A node here represents a problem. However, two nodes may represent two entirely different problems. The leaf nodes represent primitive problems which cannot be decomposed further.

The solution to an AND-OR graph is a path from the root node to leaf nodes (which includes AND arcs) such that solving the nodes in it solves the problem. A solution path to the problem represented by the graph in Fig. 3-12 contains nodes [1] to [5]. An alternative solution path contains nodes [1], [2], [3], and [6].

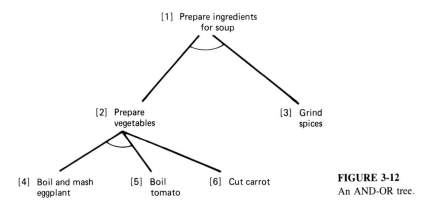

FIGURE 3-12
An AND-OR tree.

---

[2]More formally, the AND-OR graph is a hypergraph in which there is a hyperarc from a node to its AND successors. These hyper arcs are called connectors. Each k-connector is from a parent node to its k AND successors. An ordinary graph is a special case of a hypergraph containing only one-connectors. In Fig. 3-12, for example, there is a two-connector from node [2] to nodes [4] and [5], and a one-connector from [2] to [6].

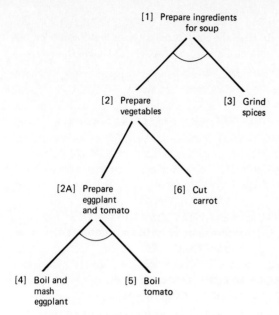

FIGURE 3-13
An AND-OR tree with nodes having only one kind of successor.

An AND-OR graph can be converted to a simpler AND-OR graph in which every node has only one kind of successor—either AND nodes or OR nodes. This is done by introducing an additional node for every set of AND successors of a node that has mixed successors. The AND successors are now made the successors of the new node. The AND-OR tree in Fig. 3-12 can be reduced to that shown in Fig. 3-13 by introducing an additional node [2A].

Let us now look at an algorithm for solving the AND-OR tree. As before, we assume that the SUCCESSORS function yields the successors of a node. If any of the successors is a set of AND nodes, it is represented by a tagged list:

```
($AND <n1> ... <nk>)
```

For example, the successors of node [2] in Fig. 3-12 are represented by

```
(($AND [4] [5]) [6])
```

where nodes [4], [5], and [6] are represented appropriately. Similarly, BADP determines whether a given node or any of its descendents can be solved. Instead of GOALP it is more appropriate to use the name SOLUTIONP. Its purpose is similar; given a node, it determines whether it is a solution node (i.e., denotes a problem that we know how to solve).

SEARCH-ANDOR-DF does a depth-first search. As before, there is an OPEN list that contains nodes yet to be examined, except now an entry in OPEN might be a set of AND nodes (represented as a list tagged by $AND). In each iteration, the

head of OPEN is examined and operated on as usual, but if it is a set of AND nodes, SEARCH-AND-DF is called. SEARCH-AND-DF returns a set of solution nodes, all of which together constitute the solution. Finally, SEARCH-ANDOR-DF returns a solution node (or more appropriately, a solution graph).

```
(DEFUN SEARCH-ANDOR-DF (N)
;;; N is the initial node. Its AND-OR tree is searched.
    (DO ((OPEN (LIST N)))
        ((NULL OPEN))
        (COND [(AND-P (CAR OPEN))
               (LET ((RES (SEARCH-AND-DF
                           (CDR (CAR OPEN)))
                          ;Call with the list of
                          ; AND-nodes after removing
                          ; the tag.
                                        ))
                    (COND [RES (RETURN RES)] ;Success
                          [T (SETQ OPEN (CDR OPEN))]))]
              [(BADP (CAR OPEN)) (SETQ OPEN (CDR OPEN))]
              [(SOLUTIONP (CAR OPEN)) (RETURN (CAR OPEN))]
              [T (SETQ OPEN (APPEND (SUCCESSORS (CAR OPEN))
                                    (CDR OPEN)))])))
```

```
(DEFUN SEARCH-AND-DF (L)
    (DO ((ANDLIST L (CDR ANDLIST))
         (RES () (CONS TEMP RES))
         (TEMP))
        ((NULL ANDLIST) (CONS '$AND RES))
        (SETQ TEMP (SEARCH-ANDOR-DF (CAR ANDLIST)))
        (COND [(NULL TEMP) (RETURN ())])))
```

```
(DEFUN AND-P (L)
    (AND (NOT (ATOM L)) (EQL '$AND (CAR L)) ))
```

Heuristics can be introduced in searching for the least-cost solution in AND-OR graphs. The resulting algorithm is called an AO* algorithm. For details consult Nilsson (1980) or Rich (1983).

Exercise 3.26 Trace the application of SEARCH-ANDOR-DF on the AND-OR trees in Fig. 3-14, where bad nodes are marked by a *. Choose an appropriate representation for the above trees.

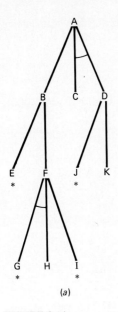 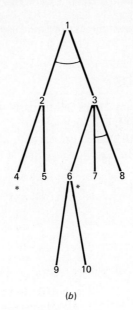

(a)   (b)

FIGURE 3-14

Exercise 3.27 Define a depth-first AND-OR graph search algorithm, and test it on the graph in Fig. 3-15. (*Hint*: You will have to manipulate CLOSED, a list similar to that in Sec. 3.2. If you decide to have functions roughly corresponding to the tree-search functions SEARCH-ANDOR-DF and SEARCH-AND-DF, CLOSED must be passed as an argument and its new value returned.)

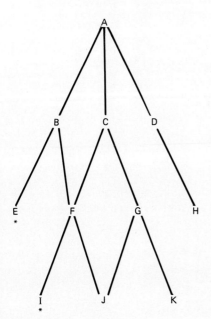

FIGURE 3-15

Exercise 3.28 Implement the AO* algorithm which searches for the least-cost solution in an AND-OR graph. Consult Nilsson (1980) for details of the algorithm.

FURTHER READINGS

Search is discussed in many books. Particularly good references are Nilsson (1980), Horowitz and Sahni (1978), and Rich (1983).

Heuristics have been studied extensively, and there is now a developed theory of heuristic algorithms. See Pearl (1984), and Nilsson (1980).

PART
2

LOGIC AND RULE-BASED PROGRAMMING

CHAPTER
4

PATTERN MATCHING

Pattern matching occurs very frequently in AI. It occurs in theorem proving, planning, game playing, natural language processing, vision, in fact, in all areas of AI. For example, we might be faced with a board position in the game of checkers, and we may have to compare it against known types of positions to decide the next move. Similarly, while processing a verb in a sentence in Hindi, we might compare it with stored patterns for different senses of the verb in order to select the correct sense. In yet another situation, given a geometric figure and a pair of patterns, we might be asked to match the figure with the first pattern and produce another figure that is analogous to the figure in the same way as the second pattern is to the first.

Pattern matching is called macromatching when we are given two "large" things and asked to answer whether they are similar. Here, generally, we are not looking for an exact match but only a similarity match. In micromatching, on the other hand, we are looking for an exact match between two "small" things. In this and subsequent chapters, we will be concerned with the latter.

Translated in LISP terms, pattern matching is a process by which we compare two objects to see whether they are alike.

In this chapter we will progressively define more powerful pattern matchers. Central to all the matchers is the idea of a wild card or a variable in a pattern that matches or is equal to anything. Sections 4.3 and 4.6 show example applications in which the pattern matchers are used for querying a database and in generating a response to the natural language input, respectively.

In the next chapter, we will see how a generalized sort of pattern matching forms the heart of a logic programming system. The subsequent chapters show how these can be used for building systems that carry out inference.

4.1 A SIMPLE PATTERN MATCHER

A *pattern* is an object which might contain zero or more occurrences of the *wild card* written as the atom "?". A *data item* is an object which has no occurrences of the wild card. A pattern *matches* a data item if on replacing each of the wild cards by an appropriate object, we get an object EQUAL to the data item. For example, the following two match

Pattern: (EQU (COLOR TABLE) ?)
Data item: (EQU (COLOR TABLE) RED)

because on substituting ? in the pattern by RED we get the data item. Clearly, a pattern is capable of matching many different data items. For example, the following two also match:

Pattern: (EQU (COLOR TABLE) ?)
Data item: (EQU (COLOR TABLE) (COLOR CHAIR))

and so do the following:

Pattern: (EQU (COLOR ?) ?)
Data item: (EQU (COLOR TABLE) RED)

but the pattern below does not match the two data items written below it:

Pattern: (EQU (COLOR TABLE) ?)
Data item: (EQU (COLOR CHAIR) BROWN)
Data item: (EQU (COLOR TABLE) RED BROWN)

A pattern without any wild card matches the object to which it is equal.

Pattern: (COLOR TABLE BLUE)
Data item: (COLOR TABLE BLUE)

We will define a function MATCH1 that takes a pattern and a data item and returns true if they match. Conceptually, its definition is similar to that of the familiar function EQUAL that tests for equality of two objects. Therefore, let us first look at the definition of EQUAL:

```
(DEFUN OUR-EQUAL (S1 S2)
    (COND [(AND (ATOM S1) (ATOM S2)) (EQL S1 S2)]
          [(OR (ATOM S1) (ATOM S2)) NIL]
          [T (AND (OUR-EQUAL (CAR S1) (CAR S2))
                  (OUR-EQUAL (CDR S1) (CDR S2)))]))
```

MATCH1 is similar to OUR-EQUAL except that if the first argument is ?, it matches the data item irrespective of what the item is. As the first COND clause shows, if PAT is a variable, MATCH1 returns true no matter what the item is.

```
(DEFUN MATCH1 (PAT ITEM)
    (COND [(IS-? PAT) T]
          [(AND (ATOM PAT) (ATOM ITEM)) (EQL PAT ITEM)]
          [(OR (ATOM PAT) (ATOM ITEM)) NIL]
          [T (AND (MATCH1 (CAR PAT) (CAR ITEM))
                  (MATCH1 (CDR PAT) (CDR ITEM)))]))

(DEFUN IS-? (S) (EQL S '?))
```

4.2   A PATTERN MATCHER WITH VARIABLES

Let us now consider more powerful pattern matching. The wild cards in a pattern are named. Wild cards having the same name can only be replaced by equal objects. For example, the pattern given below matches item 1 but not item 2.

Pattern: (TRAVEL (SOURCE ?X) (DEST ?X) (DIST ?Y))
Item 1: (TRAVEL (SOURCE DELHI) (DEST DELHI) (DIST 100))
Item 2: (TRAVEL (SOURCE DELHI) (DEST KANPUR)(DIST 400))

The pattern fails to match item 2 because in item 2 there are two different objects, namely, DELHI and KANPUR, in the positions which correspond to the named wild card ?X. Thus, it violates the condition that two wild cards with the same name must match equal objects.

We call named wild cards *variables*. On matching item 1, the value of variable ?X is DELHI and the value of ?Y is 100. Values of variables which when substituted in a pattern, yield the data item are called bindings of the variables for the match.[1] A set of bindings is called a substitution and will be represented by an association list. In the example above when the pattern matches item 1, ?X is bound to DELHI and ?Y to 100. The association list in this case is written as

((?X DELHI) (?Y 100))

If variables in a pattern are all different, it is like having unnamed wild cards.

MATCH2 defined below is a matcher for patterns with variables. It takes three arguments: a pattern to be matched, a data item which is compared with the pattern,

---

[1]Not to be confused with the bindings of LISP variables that are maintained by the LISP interpreter.

and a list of bindings so far. Initially, the list of bindings is (), but slowly as the matching progresses and variables get bound, the association list grows. MATCH2 returns $FAIL if the match is unsuccessful, and it returns the association list if the match is successful. If the () association list is returned, it indicates that a match has occurred but no variables got bound (because there were none in the pattern).

MATCH2 works much like MATCH1 except that we must keep track of the bindings of variables and make sure that a new binding of a variable does not conflict with one already present. This is accomplished by CHECK-ADD-BINDING. Similarly when we accomplish the matching of the head of the pattern with the head of the data item, then we must use the new association list while trying to match the tails (as shown in the last COND clause).

```
(DEFUN MATCH2 (PAT ITEM ALIST)
;;; Returns the association list if
;;; match successful else returns $FAIL
    (COND [(FAIL-P ALIST) ALIST]
          [(IS-VAR PAT)
           ;;PAT is a variable. It matches ITEM provided
           ;;(1) it does not have a value earlier, or
           ;;(2) its earlier value is same as ITEM.
           (CHECK-ADD-BINDING PAT ITEM ALIST)]
          [(AND (ATOM PAT) (ATOM ITEM))
           (COND [(EQL PAT ITEM) ALIST]
                 [T '$FAIL])]
          [(OR (ATOM PAT) (ATOM ITEM)) '$FAIL]
          [T (MATCH2 (CDR PAT)
                     (CDR ITEM)
                     (MATCH2 (CAR PAT)
                             (CAR ITEM)
                             ALIST))]))
```

```
(DEFUN FAIL-P (L) (EQL '$FAIL L))
```

CHECK-ADD-BINDING and other associated functions are given below:

```
(DEFUN CHECK-ADD-BINDING (VAR VAL ALIST)
;;;Returns $FAIL if VAR has a binding on ALIST other
;;;than VAL, else adds the association (VAR VAL)
;;;on the association list and returns it.
    (LET ((OLD-BINDING (ASSOC VAR ALIST)))
        (COND [(NULL OLD-BINDING)
               ;; Return the new association list
```

```
         (CONS (LIST VAR VAL) ALIST)]
         [(EQUAL (CADR OLD-BINDING) VAL)
         ;; Old binding same as the value
         ALIST]
         [T '$FAIL])))

(DEFUN IS-VAR (V)
  (COND [(ATOM V) (EQL (ELT (SYMBOL-NAME V) 0) #\?)]
        [T NIL]))
```

Exercise 4.1 Does the pattern

```
(COLORS . ?X)
```

match the following item

```
(COLORS RED GREEN BLUE)
```

If yes, then what is the binding of variable "?X"? Does MATCH2 work correctly?

For efficiency reasons, we define ? as a read macro so that ?X, for example, is converted into ($VAR X) at the time it is read.[2] CHECK-ADD-BINDING and IS-VAR change accordingly.

```
(SET-MACRO-CHARACTER #\?
    #'(LAMBDA (STREAM CHAR) (LIST '$VAR (READ STREAM)))
    T)

(DEFUN IS-VAR(V) (AND (NOT (ATOM V)) (EQL (CAR V) '$VAR)))

(DEFUN NAME-OF (V) (CADR V))

(DEFUN CHECK-ADD-BINDING (VAR VAL ALIST)
    (LET ((OLD-BINDING (ASSOC (NAME-OF VAR) ALIST)))
        (COND [(NULL OLD-BINDING)
                (CONS (LIST (NAME-OF VAR) VAL) ALIST)]
               [(EQUAL (CADR OLD-BINDING) VAL) ALIST]
               [T '$FAIL])))
```

---

[2]In most earlier LISPs, symbols had to be exploded to check whether there was a certain first character. There the inefficiencies would be simply unacceptable, and the approach described here would be essential.

In summary, variables in a pattern allow us to specify conditions (e.g., equality of matches) that were not possible earlier in wild-card patterns. They also permit a convenient way of referring to the matched elements (via variable names).

4.3 AN EXAMPLE—QUERYING A DATABASE

Pattern matching can be used to retrieve data from a database. The database consists of a set of data items.[3]

Let us take as an example a database of family relationships. Let the following data items be part of it.

```
(PARENT RAM JAMIR)
(PARENT JAMIR SAMIR)
(PARENT SAMIR ANITA)
(PARENT SARAH JAMIR)
(PARENT SARAH MOHAN)
(PARENT RAM MOHAN)
(PARENT MOHAN SHEILA)
(PARENT MOHAN KUSUM)
```

In this database (PARENT RAM JAMIR) means that RAM is a parent of JAMIR, and so on for other items. The database represents the family tree shown in Fig. 4-1. Now, following are some sample queries each consisting of a pattern and their respective responses:

1. Is RAM a parent of JAMIR?

```
> (PARENT RAM JAMIR)
( )
```

Hence, the answer is true with a NIL association list.

2. Who are the children of RAM?

```
> (PARENT RAM ?X)
?X = JAMIR
?X = MOHAN
```

There are two answers to the query.

---

[3]In the next two chapters we will remove this restriction and allow the database to consist of rules that contain patterns as well as data items.

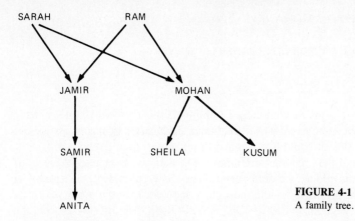

FIGURE 4-1
A family tree.

3. Who are the parents of JAMIR?

```
> (PARENT ?X JAMIR)
?X = RAM
?X = SARAH
```

We cannot query more complex relationships with the pattern as a query. A simple extension, however, allows us to go further: We allow our query to consist of a set of patterns, all of which must match (with common bindings of variables, if any, occurring in the patterns) to get an answer. For example,

4. Who are the grandchildren of RAM?

```
> (AND (PARENT RAM ?X) (PARENT ?X ?Y))
?X = JAMIR,    ?Y = SAMIR
?X = MOHAN,    ?Y = SHEILA
?X = MOHAN,    ?Y = KUSUM
```

For each pair of values for ?X, ?Y the query pattern matches some data items in the database. Since we are interested in the value of ?Y, each value of ?Y is an answer.

5. Who are the grandparents of SAMIR?

```
> (AND (PARENT ?X ?Y) (PARENT ?Y SAMIR))
?X = RAM,     ?Y = JAMIR
?X = SARAH,   ?Y = JAMIR
```

6. Who are the grandparents of MOHAN?

```
> (AND (PARENT ?X ?Y) (PARENT ?Y MOHAN))
NIL
```

7. Who are the brothers of MOHAN?

```
> (AND (PARENT ?X MOHAN) (PARENT ?X ?Y))
?X = RAM,     ?Y = JAMIR
?X = RAM,     ?Y = MOHAN
```

In the above, MOHAN is his own brother. To eliminate this possibility, we will have to assert that ?Y is not equal to MOHAN. Although our query language in its present form does not allow this, it could be extended to include it. (See Exercise 4.4.)

   We take a look at the implementation next. The database is represented as a list of items bound to the global variable *DB*. The query processor makes use of MATCH2. The major task is to handle more than one match for the query.

   QUERY-PROCESSOR and SIMP-QUERY-PROCESSOR together process the query. QUERY-PROCESSOR takes a possible AND query, breaks the query into simple queries (without AND), and calls SIMP-QUERY-PROCESSOR for each simple query appropriately. SIMP-QUERY-PROCESSOR takes a pattern (a query without AND), a list of items yet to be matched in the database, and an association list. It returns a list of association lists, one for each match in the database. NIL indicates that there is no match. For example, if we apply SIMP-QUERY-PROCESSOR to the following arguments

```
(PARENT ?X ?Y),
((PARENT RAM JAMIR) (PARENT RAM MOHAN)
       (PARENT MOHAN SHEILA)),
((?X RAM))
```

that is, the query is (PARENT ?X ?Y) with ?X bound to RAM, then two matches occur and for each match we get an association list:

```
((((?Y JAMIR) (?X RAM))
 (((?Y MOHAN) (?X RAM)))
```

   Now QUERY-PROCESSOR is straightforward. If the query given to it is simple (i.e., is a pattern), it calls SIMP-QUERY-PROCESSOR with the query. Otherwise, it calls SIMP-QUERY-PROCESSOR for each pattern in the query with appropriate association lists. Thus, if the query consists of n simple queries, say Q_1 to Q_n, then Q_1 is matched first resulting in association lists A_{11} to A_{1m}, say. Now, Q_2 is matched with items in the database with each of the association lists A_{11} to A_{1m}, yielding say A_{21} to A_{2p}. This process continues until Q_n is matched. If any of the Q_i's yields (), i.e., no match occurs, the end result is (). Figure 4-2 illustrates this process pictorially, where the incoming arrow to Q_i indicates the list of association lists for which Q_1 to $Q_{(i-1)}$ match with the database, and the outgoing arrow from Q_i indicates the association lists for which Q_i as well matches the database. The incoming arrow into Q_1 shows a list containing a () association list indicating that there are no bindings for any variable.

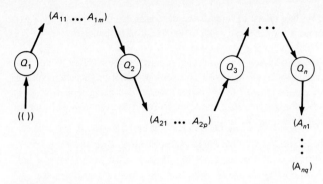

FIGURE 4-2
QUERY-PROCESSOR applied to the query (AND Q_1 . . . Q_n).

```
(DEFVAR *DB*  ...  )
(DEFUN QUERY-PROCESSOR (QUERY)
   (COND
     [(NOT (EQL 'AND (CAR QUERY)))
      (SIMP-QUERY-PROCESSOR QUERY *DB* NIL)]
     [T (DO ((REM-QUERY (CDR QUERY) (CDR REM-QUERY))
             (ALISTS '(NIL)))
            ((NULL REM-QUERY) ALISTS)
         (SETQ ALISTS
               (MAPCAN #'(LAMBDA (ALIST)
                           (SIMP-QUERY-PROCESSOR
                             (CAR REM-QUERY)
                             *DB* ALIST))
                       ALISTS)))]))


(DEFUN SIMP-QUERY-PROCESSOR (SIMP-QUERY DB ALIST)
   (COND [(NULL DB) NIL]
         [T (LET ((MLIST (MATCH2 SIMP-QUERY (CAR DB) ALIST)))
             (COND [(FAIL-P MLIST)
                    (SIMP-QUERY-PROCESSOR
                      SIMP-QUERY (CDR DB) ALIST)]
                   [T ;;MLIST is new association list.
                    (CONS MLIST
                          (SIMP-QUERY-PROCESSOR
                            SIMP-QUERY (CDR DB)
                            ALIST))])])))
```

Exercise 4.2 Think of other operators besides AND, and implement them to enrich your query language.

Exercise 4.3 Can you write a query to find all the descendants of a person, say RAM? Enrich your set of operators so that these kinds of queries can be handled.

Exercise 4.4 There is merit in having computational predicates like NOT-EQU and EQU besides the database predicates like PARENT. The computational predicates have to be computed (by means of an associated LISP function) rather than being looked up in the database. Can you think of a scheme to achieve this? Test your solution with query 7 above in which a person should not be his own brother.

Exercise 4.5 Write an iterative version of SIMP-QUERY-PROCESSOR.

4.4   A SPLICE PATTERN MATCHER

Let us now consider more general kinds of variables which match not just one but an arbitrary number of objects. To simplify the presentation we will first allow wild cards and then variables (or named wild cards), just as we did earlier for simple variables.

We introduce two additional kinds of wild cards besides '?'. ?* matches zero or more objects and ?+ matches one or more objects. For example, the pattern below matches data items 1 and 2 but not 3.

```
Pattern: (TABLE (COLOR ?+) ?*)
Item 1: (TABLE (COLOR RED BROWN))
Item 2: (TABLE (COLOR RED BROWN) (SIZE SMALL))
Item 3: (TABLE (COLOR))
```

When the pattern matches item 1, ?+ matches two objects RED and BROWN, and ?* matches nothing. The pattern fails to match item 3 because ?+ matches nothing which is not permitted.

More formally, a pattern matches a data item if on substituting arbitrary objects instead of ? in the pattern, splice-substituting arbitrary lists for ?*, and splice-substituting nonnull lists for ?+, we get the data item. (By splice-substituting a ?* variable we mean that it is replaced by a list and then the enclosing parentheses of the list are removed.) For example, if we splice-substitute (RED BROWN) for ?+ and () for ?* in the pattern above, we get item 1. Hence, the pattern matches item 1.

MATCH-GENERAL1 determines whether a given pattern with ?, ?*, and ?+ wild cards matches a given data item. Like MATCH1 it has two formal parameters PAT and ITEM. When PAT is a list with ?* as its head, MATCH-GENERAL1 tries two cases:

1. ?* matches nothing in the item. [Hence, the next match attempted is between (CDR PAT) and ITEM.]
2. ?* matches the head of the item and possibly more. [Hence, the next match attempted is between PAT and (CDR ITEM). This can only be done if the item is nonnull.]

When PAT is a list with ? + as its head, the first element of ITEM is consumed and the ? + is changed to ?*. (Why?)

```
(DEFUN MATCH-GENERAL1 (PAT ITEM)
    (COND [(IS-WILDCARD PAT) T]
          [(ATOM PAT)
           (COND [(ATOM ITEM) (EQL ITEM PAT)] [T NIL])]
          [(IS-?* (CAR PAT))
           (COND [(MATCH-GENERAL1 (CDR PAT) ITEM)
                  ;;Case 1 in text above
                  T]
                 [(NOT (NULL ITEM))
                  ;;Item should be nonnull for case 2.
                  (MATCH-GENERAL1 PAT (CDR ITEM))])]
          [(IS-?+ (CAR PAT))
           (COND [(NULL ITEM) NIL]
                 [T (MATCH-GENERAL1
                        (CONS '?* (CDR PAT))
                        (CDR ITEM))])]
          [T (AND (MATCH-GENERAL1 (CAR PAT) (CAR ITEM))
                  (MATCH-GENERAL1 (CDR PAT) (CDR ITEM)))]))

(DEFUN IS-? (V) (EQL V '?))
(DEFUN IS-?+ (V) (EQL V '?+))
(DEFUN IS-?* (V) (EQL V '?*))
(DEFUN IS-WILDCARD (V) (OR (IS-? V) (IS-?+ V) (IS-?* V)))
```

MATCH-GENERAL1 explores an AND-OR tree. For example, matching the pattern with item 2 given earlier in this section proceeds as shown in Fig. 4-3. The AND successors are marked by connectors, failure nodes are marked by *, and success leaf nodes are marked by tick marks.

Variables can be introduced in such patterns similar to before. An example illustrates this. Pattern

```
((TABLE (COLOR ?+X)) (CHAIR (COLOR ?+X)))
```

matches

```
((TABLE (COLOR RED BROWN)) (CHAIR (COLOR RED BROWN)))
```

but not

```
((TABLE (COLOR RED BROWN)) (CHAIR (COLOR GREEN RED)))
```

MATCH-GENERAL1 applied to

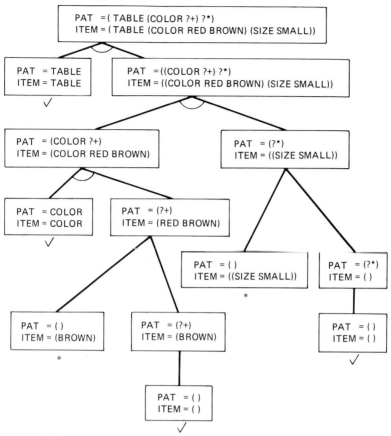

FIGURE 4-3
AND-OR tree generated by recursive calls.

If we splice-substitute (RED BROWN) for X in the pattern above, we get the first item. As before, a variable must have the same value for all its occurrences. An important point is that the variable must have a single value independent of how it is to be substituted in its occurrences. For example, the following item

```
(DISTRIBUTE-1 (AGENT BOY-1)
              (OBJECT (BIG RED FLOWER))
              (RECIPIENT (BOY-1)))
```

matches the pattern

```
(?ACT   (AGENT ?*Y)
        (OBJECT (?*Z FLOWER))
        (RECIPIENT ?Y))
```

because if we substitute for the following bindings

```
ACT = DISTRIBUTE-1
  Y = (BOY-1)
  Z = (BIG RED)
```

in the pattern, we get the item. Note that Y is splice-substituted at one point and plain-substituted at the other.

We first define a read macro for ? as before. It constructs the following form for a variable:

```
(<vartag> <name>)
```

where <vartag> indicates that it is a variable and its type <name> indicates the names of the variable. Following are some examples:

Notation	Form after reading
?Y	($VAR Y)
?*Y	($VAR* Y)
?+Y	($VAR+ Y)

```
(SET-MACRO-CHARACTER #\? #'PP-? T)
(DEFUN PP-? (STREAM CHAR)
      (COND [(EQL (PEEK-CHAR NIL STREAM) #\*)
             (READ-CHAR STREAM) (LIST '$VAR* (READ STREAM))]
            [(EQL (PEEK-CHAR NIL STREAM) #\+)
             (READ-CHAR STREAM)
             (LIST '$VAR+ (READ STREAM))]
            [T (LIST '$VAR (READ STREAM))]))
```

Predicates for testing of variables have to be redefined:

```
(DEFUN IS-? (V) (AND (NOT (ATOM V)) (EQL '$VAR (CAR V))))

(DEFUN IS-?* (V) (AND (NOT (ATOM V))
                      (EQL '$VAR* (CAR V))))

(DEFUN IS-?+ (V) (AND (NOT (ATOM V))
                      (EQL '$VAR+ (CAR V))))
```

NAME-OF retains its earlier definition.

Now we are ready to define the matcher. Just like MATCH2 it takes a pattern, an item, and a list of bindings (or an association list) as its arguments and returns an association list if the match is successful and returns $FAIL if the match is not successful. The matcher called MATCH-GENERAL2 is shown below. It is similar to MATCH2 except when it has to match a ?* or ?+ variable. Then it calls TRY-MATCHES that repeatedly includes more elements of items in matching the variable until a match is found.

```
(DEFUN MATCH-GENERAL2 (PAT ITEM ALIST)
    (COND [(FAIL-P ALIST) ALIST]
          [(IS-? PAT) (CHECK-ADD-BINDING PAT ITEM ALIST)]
          [(ATOM PAT)
           (COND [(EQL PAT ITEM) ALIST] [T '$FAIL])]
          [(AND (NOT (NULL ITEM)) (ATOM ITEM)) '$FAIL]
          [(IS-?* (CAR PAT))
           (TRY-MATCHES (CDR PAT)
                        ITEM (CAR PAT)
                        NIL ALIST)]
          [(IS-?+ (CAR PAT))
           (COND [(NULL ITEM) '$FAIL]
           [T (TRY-MATCHES (CDR PAT)
                           (CDR ITEM)
                           (CAR PAT)
                           (LIST (CAR ITEM))
                           ALIST)])]

          [T (MATCH-GENERAL2
                (CDR PAT)
                (CDR ITEM)
                (MATCH-GENERAL2
                (CAR PAT) (CAR ITEM) ALIST))]))


(DEFUN TRY-MATCHES (PAT ITEM VAR VAL ALIST)
;;; This routine is called when a ?* or ?+ is encountered
;;; in the head of PAT. As many elements as
;;; needed may be removed from ITEM and placed on VAL,
;;; but after that the PAT must match the remaining part
;;; of ITEM.
    (LET ((MLIST (CHECK-ADD-BINDING VAR VAL ALIST)))
        (COND [(NOT (FAIL-P MLIST))
               (LET ((NEWMLIST (MATCH-GENERAL2 PAT ITEM
                                               MLIST)))
                 (COND [(NOT (FAIL-P NEWMLIST)) NEWMLIST]
```

```
                  [T (TRY-NEXT-POSS PAT ITEM VAR
                          VAL ALIST)])))]
             [T (TRY-NEXT-POSS PAT ITEM VAR VAL ALIST)])))


(DEFUN TRY-NEXT-POSS (PAT ITEM VAR VAL ALIST)
;;; Includes one more element from ITEM into VAL
;;; and tries the next possible match.
    (COND [(NULL ITEM) '$FAIL]
          [(ATOM ITEM) '$FAIL]
          [T (TRY-MATCHES PAT (CDR ITEM)
                          VAR (NCONC VAL (LIST (CAR ITEM)))
                          ALIST)]))
```

Exercise 4.6 TRY-MATCHES continues trying to match a ?* variable by including more elements even if the named variable already has such a value that the match is not possible. For example, if the following are the pattern and the item, respectively,

```
(?ACT (AGENT   ?Y)
      (OBJECT   (?*Z   DOTS))
      (RECIPIENT  ?*Y))

(TAKE-1  (AGENT   (BOY-1  BOY-2  BOY-3))
         (OBJECT  (BIG RED DOTS))
         (RECIPIENT  BOY-4  BOY-5  BOY-6))
```

and MATCH-GENERAL2 is applied, then the variable Y gets bound to (BOY-1 BOY-2 BOY-3) the first time it is encountered. Later on in trying to match ?*Y with (BOY-4 BOY-5 BOY-6) all possibilities are tried even though it can be determined that none of the possibilities will succeed.

Modify TRY-MATCHES such that it does not go through all possibilities when unnecessary. (*Hint*: You will have to match the prefix of the binding in ALIST with VAL.)

Exercise 4.7 Is the search in MATCH-GENERAL2 depth-first or breadth-first? Redefine MATCH-GENERAL2 to make the search best-first. Assume you have a function for ordering the alternatives. (*Hint*: See Sec. 3.2 for best-first search.)

Exercise 4.8 More general restrictions on variables can be imposed by allowing arbitrary predicates to be placed on variables. For example, the following expression

```
(?? X P1 P2 ... Pn)
```

stands for variable X that matches exactly one object that satisfies one-place predicates P1 to Pn. Define MATCH-MOST-GENERAL that is capable of handling these.

4.5 SUBSTITUTING VALUES
OF VARIABLES

There are times when variables in a pattern have to be substituted by their values. In this section we will see how.

First, let us consider simple variables, that is, variables whose values are substituted without splicing. A substitution function that makes a copy of the pattern with variables substituted is straightforward. It is called SUBST-VARS here.

```
(DEFUN SUBST-VARS (PAT ALIST)
;;; Creates a copy of the pattern PAT with
;;; variables substituted as given by ALIST
   (COND [(IS-VAR PAT)
          (LET ([BINDING (ASSOC (NAME-OF PAT) ALIST)])
             (COND [(NULL BINDING) PAT] ;No substitution.
                   [T (CADR BINDING)]))]
         [(ATOM PAT) PAT]
         [T (CONS (SUBST-VARS (CAR PAT) ALIST)
                  (SUBST-VARS (CDR PAT) ALIST))]))
```

If we want to substitute in-place (without copying) by destructively modifying the pattern, we have to use SETF (or RPLACA and RPLACD). We must remember, however, that to change in-place we must remain one level higher than the variable. It is shown below as DSUBST-VARS.

```
(DEFUN DSUBST-VARS (PAT ALIST)
;;; Destructive update of variables in PAT
;;; by their values as given by ALIST
   (COND
      [(ATOM PAT) PAT]
      [(IS-VAR (CAR PAT))
       (LET ([BINDING (ASSOC (NAME-OF (CAR PAT)) ALIST)])
          (COND [(NULL BINDING)
                 ;;Variable not bound. No substitution.
                 (DSUBST-VARS (CDR PAT) ALIST)
                 PAT]
                [T (SETF (CAR PAT) (CADR BINDING))
                   (DSUBST-VARS (CDR PAT) ALIST)
                   PAT]))]
      [T (DSUBST-VARS (CAR PAT) ALIST)
         (DSUBST-VARS (CDR PAT) ALIST)
         PAT]))
```

Exercise 4.9 DSUBST-VARS does not work correctly when the tail of the pattern happens to be a variable, for example in (GIVE-1 . ?Y). Why? How will you correct it?

Next we define SUBST-VARS-GENERAL that takes a pattern with variables of all types and an association list and substitutes the values of variables in the pattern, splicing the value wherever so indicated.

```
(DEFUN SUBST-VARS-GENERAL (PAT ALIST)
 ;;; Similar to SUBST-VARS except that generalized
 ;;; variables ?* and ?+ might occur in PAT
  (COND
   [(IS-VAR PAT)
    (LET ([BINDING (ASSOC (NAME-OF PAT) ALIST)])
     (COND [(NULL BINDING)
            (ERROR-MSG
             "Unbound variable - SUBST-VARS-GENERAL"
             PAT)]
           [T (CADR BINDING)]))]
   [(ATOM PAT) PAT]
   [(OR (IS-?* (CAR PAT)) (IS-?+ (CAR PAT)))
    (APPEND (SUBST-VARS-GENERAL (CAR PAT) ALIST)
            (SUBST-VARS-GENERAL (CDR PAT) ALIST))]
   [T (CONS (SUBST-VARS-GENERAL (CAR PAT) ALIST)
            (SUBST-VARS-GENERAL (CDR PAT) ALIST))]))

(DEFUN ERROR-MSG (STR ELEM)
  (PRINC "Error: ") (PRIN1 STR) (PRIN1 ELEM) ELEM)
```

Exercise 4.10 Modify SUBST-VARS-GENERAL so that in case a variable in PAT is not bound, it remains as such in the result. No error message is issued. (*Note*: Be careful.)

Exercise 4.11 Define DSUBST-VARS-GENERAL to be like SUBST-VARS-GENERAL except it makes in-line substitutions by destructively modifying the pattern.

4.6 AN EXAMPLE—DOCTOR PROGRAM

ELIZA (also called DOCTOR) is a much celebrated program that apparently behaves like a psychiatrist. A user communicates with the program in English. The program does pattern matching with the sentence typed by the user, and using the patterns, it generates a sentence for the user. The generated sentence appears to be profound, and it appears that the program is engaging in dialogue like a psychiatrist. For example, when the user types

```
(MY FRIEND MADE ME COME HERE)
```

the response generated might be

```
(YOUR FRIEND MADE YOU COME HERE)
```

or when the user types

```
(I THINK YOU HATE ME)
```

the response might be

```
(WHAT MAKES YOU THINK I HATE YOU)
```

However, the program only provides an illusion of being a psychiatrist. It does not even "understand" what the user is saying, much less do an analysis of the mental state of the user. Nevertheless, the dialogue carried out by the program is very impressive. The illusion about its psychotherapy is easily maintained over at least one session. In this section, we will build ELIZA's sister SITA, also a psychiatrist, and in the process see the power of pattern matching.

The database of SITA consists of a set of transformations where each transformation is a pair consisting of an input pattern and an output pattern. The input pattern is matched against the input sentence, and if the match succeeds, the output pattern is used to generate a response. Two example transformations are given below. They match the inputs in the sample dialogue shown earlier.

```
((?*1 MY ?*2 ME ?*3) -> (YOUR ?*2 YOU ?*3))
((?*1 YOU ?*2 ME) -> (WHAT MAKES YOU THINK I ?*2 YOU))
```

?*1 is a variable named "1" that can match zero or more expressions in the input. Similarly, while generating a response, the value of ?* variables is spliced in.

Let the list of transformations be bound to *DB*. The default responses (when the input does not match any transformation) are stored in a list bound to *DE-FAULTS*.

The function SITA is very simple; it calls TRANSFORM to go through *DB* and tries to match the input sentence with the input patterns. When a match is found, it substitutes the values of variables in the corresponding output pattern and returns the result. When no match is found, it randomly selects a response from *DEFAULTS* and returns. The returned result is printed by SITA.

```
(DEFVAR *DB* ... )
(DEFVAR *DEFAULTS* ... )

(DEFUN SITA NIL (PRINT (TRANSFORM (READ) *DB*)))
```

```
(DEFUN TRANSFORM (SENTENCE DB)
   (DO ((REM-RULES DB (CDR REM-RULES)))
      ((NULL REM-RULES)
       (NTH (RANDOM (LENGTH *DEFAULTS*)) *DEFAULTS*))
      (LET ((CUR-MATCH (MATCH-GENERAL2
                          (CAAR REM-RULES)
                          SENTENCE NIL)))
         (COND [(NOT (FAIL-P CUR-MATCH))
                (RETURN (SUBST-VARS-GENERAL
                          (CADAR REM-RULES)
                          CUR-MATCH))]))))
```

A RANDOM of N returns a random number within the range 0 to $(N - 1)$. It depends on the particular LISP implementation. SUBST-VARS-GENERAL substitutes values of variables in a pattern as defined earlier.

Exercise 4.12 Implement and test SITA with the following transformations in *DB*:

1. (?*1 YOU ?*2 ME ?*3) ->(WHAT MAKES YOU THINK I ?*2 YOU)
2. (?*1 MY ?*2 ME ?*3) -> (YOUR ?*2 YOU ?*3)
3. (?*1 I AM NOT ?*2) -> (DO YOU THINK YOUR COMING HERE
                          WILL HELP YOU TO BE ?*2)
4. (?*1 I AM ?*2) -> (DO YOU THINK YOUR COMING HERE
                      WILL HELP YOU NOT TO BE ?*2)
5. (?*1 MOTHER ?*2) -> (TELL ME MORE ABOUT YOUR FAMILY)
6. (?*1 BROTHER ?*2) -> (TELL ME MORE ABOUT YOUR FAMILY)
7. (?*1 FATHER ?*2) -> (WHAT ELSE COMES TO YOUR MIND
                        WHEN YOU THINK ABOUT YOUR FATHER)
8. (?*2 SISTER ?*2) -> (WHAT ELSE COMES TO YOUR MIND
                        WHEN YOU THINK ABOUT YOUR SISTER)
9. (?*1 ?*2 FEEL DEPRESSED *3) -> (I AM SORRY TO HEAR
                                   ABOUT DEPRESSION)

and the following patterns in *DEFAULTS*:

1. (IN WHAT WAYS)
2. (CAN YOU THINK OF A SPECIFIC EXAMPLE)
3. (PLEASE GO ON)
4. (VERY INTERESTING)

Exercise 4.13 Combine the transformations involving MOTHER and BROTHER above into one, and do the same for FATHER and SISTER. (*Hint*: You will have to define a suitable predicate such as FAMILYP and use ?? and MATCH-MOST-GENERAL.)

Exercise 4.14 Modify SITA to store the first output generated as a result of matching any one of the first four transformations. Let it be bound to *PREV-OUTPUT*. Now add the following to *DEFAULTS*:

```
(DOES THAT HAVE ANYTHING TO DO WITH THE
         FACT THAT *PREV-OUTPUT*)
```

You will have to modify TRANSFORM to be able to substitute *PREV-OUTPUT* when necessary.

Exercise 4.15 What new transformations or features can you add to SITA to make its dialogue more impressive?

The database of SITA consists of two lists (bound respectively to *DB* and *DEFAULTS*). The matching process is quite expensive because each of the transformations in *DB* are tried sequentially. One way to speed up the process is to index the transformations by keywords. For example, transformation 1 can be indexed from YOU and ME, transformation 2 from MY and ME, and so on. Indexing can be implemented by storing references to the appropriate transformations on the property list of keywords. Before starting to perform matching we look for keywords in the input sentence, and on finding a keyword we attempt a match with appropriate patterns. The keywords can be ordered by specificity. For example, "like" is more specific than "you." A side benefit of this might be better and more specific responses.

Exercise 4.16 Implement keywords along with rules to improve the performance of SITA.

FURTHER READINGS

Pattern matching can be found in most AI books. For sample dialogues with ELIZA and information about the social impact of AI in particular and new technologies in general, see Weizenbaum (1976).

CHAPTER
5

LOGIC PROGRAMMING

Logic programming is a growing movement in computer science in which logic is used as a programming language. It gives a procedural interpretation to a subset of first-order logic. Just as LISP is based on giving a procedural interpretation to functional expressions, similarly PROLOG, a popular logic programming language, is based on giving a procedural interpretation to the horn-clause subset of first-order logic. One of the benefits of this paradigm is that in specifying the logic program one concentrates on *what* is to be computed rather than on *how* it is to be computed.

In this chapter we will first take a look at logic programming and how it can be used to solve problems and will then study how it can be implemented in LISP. The next chapter shows how it can be used in building expert systems.

5.1 RULES

In the last chapter, we looked at matching patterns with items. The patterns, in general, had variables, while the items did not have any. In Sec. 4.3 we saw how the patterns could be used for querying a database of items. The example database consisted of parental relationships. Let us extend the example to illustrate the need for rules.

Suppose we wanted to store not just parental relationships but also grandparent relationships. One way of storing the new relationship is to manually identify the grandparent relationships and enter them into the database. For example, the following

```
(GRANDPARENT RAM SAMIR)
(GRANDPARENT RAM SHEILA)
(GRANDPARENT RAM KUSUM)
```

could be entered into the database of Sec. 4.3. This is undesirable for at least two reasons: (*a*) When the database is large, manually working these out is tedious; (*b*) the new items occupy space.

An alternative to the above is to store a rule defining the new relationship in the database. The rule(s) can be used to answer a query regarding the new relationship when necessary. For example, the grandparent rule in English might look like the following:

```
X is the GRANDPARENT OF Y if:
        X is the PARENT of PARENT of Y.
```

Or equivalently

```
X is the GRANDPARENT of Y if:
    X is the PARENT of some Z, and
    Z is the PARENT of Y.
```

Since the application of rules can be automated, this avoids the need for manually computing the new relationships and for storing them. Moreover, by storing the definition of relationship we move closer to how humans do it. We will see later that there are other advantages as well in this approach.

Now all that needs to be worked out is what the nature of the rules should be and how they can be applied in answering a query! In this section, we will present an informal answer. In the subsequent sections the answer will be made more formal and presented in terms of the logic programming framework.

One way the rules may be written is that they have two parts: a head and a body. The head states the relationship being defined, while the body states the relationships that must be true for the definition to hold. The grandparent relationship, for example, could be written as

```
(GRANDPARENT ?X ?Y) <- (PARENT ?X ?Z) (PARENT ?Z ?Y)
```

The symbol <- separates the head from the body and can be read as "if." Similarly the great-grandparent relationship can also be defined:

```
(GREAT-GRANDPARENT ?X ?Y) <-
        (PARENT ?X ?Z) (GRANDPARENT ?Z ?Y)
```

Now, we can make the following observations:

1. Symbols preceded by ? are variables (much like the variables discussed in the last chapter).
2. The scope of variables is a rule. If there are multiple occurrences of a variable in the head and the body of a rule, they refer to the same entity (and hence must be bound to the same value). Variables in two different rules are different even though

they may have the same name. Thus, there are two occurrences of variable ?X in the definition of GREAT-GRANDPARENT, and they refer to the same person. However, they are not related to ?X in the definition of GRANDPARENT.

3. In the body of a rule, we are free to refer to any relationships including those for which there is a definition.

The rules can be used to answer queries by giving them a procedural interpretation. Given a query about a relationship defined by a rule, the definition can be used by reading it as "to establish the relationship given in the head, establish the relationships in the body." For example, if the query is whether RAM is the GREAT-GRAND-PARENT of ANITA (from the example in Sec. 4.3):

```
(GREAT-GRANDPARENT RAM ANITA)
```

we can use the definition to generate two new queries:

```
(PARENT RAM ?Z)
(GRANDPARENT ?Z ANITA)
```

which can again be answered, respectively, by looking up the database and applying a rule. Thus, ?Z will be bound to JAMIR in answer to the first query. The second query now becomes

```
(GRANDPARENT JAMIR ANITA)
```

and can be answered by applying the rule for GRANDPARENT. We shall study in considerable detail the procedure by which rules get applied.

When a rule gets applied as a result of queries generated by another rule, it is called chaining of rules. Thus, in the example above, GRANDPARENT is chained to GREAT-GRANDPARENT.

5.2 REVIEW OF LOGIC AND THE RESOLUTION PRINCIPLE

In standard first-order logic, two types of objects are defined: terms and well-formed formulas (or just formulas). Terms occur as arguments of predicates in the formulas and usually denote things. A formula on the other hand takes a truth value. Here we will deal with a subset of formulas called the horn clauses (just clauses here). Both terms and clauses will be written in the S-expr notation.

A *term* is one of the following:

1. A variable. A symbolic atom beginning with a ? (e.g., ?x, ?person, ?p3).
2. A constant. An atom or number (e.g., 3, 5.6, RED).
3. A function-arguments combination. A list of the form

```
(<f> <p1> ... <pn>)
```

where <f> is the function symbol and <p1> to <pn> are the arguments (which are terms). Consider for example,

```
(+ ?X 3)
```

where the function + is followed by its two arguments. (MAKE-TREE ?L VALUE ?R) is similarly another term. [Note, however, that since the variables are clearly distinguishable from constants, there is no need for the quote mark. In any case, a term is not necessarily computed. (+ ?X 3), for example, is a term, and it need not be computed; in fact, it cannot be computed if ?X does not have a value.]

A *horn clause* is of the form

$$B \text{ <- } A1 \ldots An \text{ with } n \geq 0 \tag{5.1}$$

Where B and A1 to An are atomic formulas. B is called the *head* or the *consequent*, and A1 to An the *body* or the *antecedent*.

An *atomic formula* is a predicate-arguments combination where the predicate is a symbol, and the arguments are terms. It is represented as a list. For example,

```
(PARENT RAM JAMIR)
```

is an atomic formula having PARENT as a predicate and RAM and JAMIR as its arguments. Similarly,

```
(SIZE (MAKE-TREE ?L VALUE ?R) 30)
```

is another atomic formula with SIZE as the predicate.

Let us look at examples of clauses:

```
(GRANDPARENT ?X ?Y) <- (PARENT ?X ?Z) (PARENT ?Z ?Y)
(SIZE (MAKE-TREE ?L ?VAL ?R) (+ 1 (+ ?N1 ?N2)))
        <- (SIZE ?L ?N1) (SIZE ?R ?N2)
```

If the antecedent is empty, i.e., *n* in Eq. (5.1) is equal to 0, it reduces to an atomic formula (and the symbol ← may be dropped).

An atomic formula is true provided the predicate holds for the arguments. For example, the following are true (in the example in Sec. 4.3) and might be stored in a database:

```
(PARENT   RAM   JAMIR)
(PARENT   SARAH  JAMIR)
```

A true clause of the form

$$B \leftarrow A1 \quad \ldots \quad An$$

means that atomic formula B is true whenever the formulas A1 to An are true. Thus if we wish to find whether an atomic formula B is true, one method is to check whether A1 to An are true. Of course, B is unconditionally true if it has a nil antecedent (n = 0), in which case it is the atomic formula B. True clauses (including true atomic formulas) are called *assertions*.

Take as an example the following assertion:

```
(GRANDPARENT RAM SAMIR)
  <- (PARENT RAM JAMIR) (PARENT JAMIR SAMIR)
```

RAM is a grandparent of SAMIR provided the atomic formulas in its antecedent are true.

A variable in an assertion is *universally quantified*. It means that the assertion holds for all values of the variable. For example, the following

```
(COLOR ?X RED) <- (IN ?X BOX1) (SHAPE ?X ROUND)
```

asserts that for all values of ?X if (IN ?X BOX1) and (SHAPE ?X ROUND) are true, then (COLOR ?X RED) is true, i.e., if ?X is in box1 and is round, it is red.

For variables that occur in the antecedent but not in the consequent, they may be treated as existentially quantified. For example, in

```
(GRANDPARENT ?X ?Y) <- (PARENT ?X ?Z) (PARENT ?Z ?Y)
```

it is sufficient to consider ?Z to be existentially quantified. In the example, for all ?X and ?Y if there is a ?Z such that ?X is a parent of ?Z, and ?Z is a parent of ?Y, then ?X is a grandparent of ?Y.

If an assertion has an empty antecedent it is called a *fact;* otherwise it is called a *rule*. Normally, rules have variables, while facts do not have any.

The assertions are typically stored in a database of assertions, also called a knowledge base. This is necessary because assertions look no different from clauses. They are simply clauses that are true.

Determining truth values mechanically is difficult. Therefore, we will talk in terms of *inference* or *derivation,* an analogous notion. We will define *rules of inference* by which new clauses can be derived from a given set of formulas. Of course, the rules of inference should be such that the clauses one can derive are also true.[1] We

---

[1]This is called the soundness of rules of inference. The converse, namely, that all true formulas can be derived, is called the completeness of rules of inference. Soundness is mandatory for inference to be meaningful, while completeness is desirable. The rules of inference given here are sound but not complete.

will freely talk in terms of a clause being true if it is derived by the rules of inference from the database of assertions.

There are two rules of inference which can be used to determine the truth value of a clause from a database of assertions:

1. *Universal instantiation.* Substituting a variable in an assertion yields an assertion. In other words, if we substitute for a variable in an assertion, we get another assertion.
2. *Modus ponens.* If the atomic formulas in the antecedent of an assertion are true, then the consequent is also true.

Now an atomic formula is true if it is asserted or can be inferred from the set of assertions using the rules of inference. For example, from the following assertions

```
(COLOR ?X RED) <- (IN ?X BOX1) (SHAPE ?X ROUND)
(IN SPHERE1 BOX1)
(SHAPE SPHERE1 ROUND)
```

it can be inferred by applying the two rules of inference that

```
(COLOR SPHERE1 RED)
```

is true. If we substitute SPHERE1 for ?X in the first assertion, we get the assertion (by universal instantiation)

```
(COLOR SPHERE1 RED) <- (IN SPHERE1 BOX1)
                        (SHAPE SPHERE1 ROUND).
```

Now since the formulas in its antecedent are asserted explicitly, we get the following assertion (by modus ponens):

```
(COLOR SPHERE1 RED)
```

An atomic formula whose truth value is to be determined is called a *query* or a *goal* formula. Thus, (COLOR SPHERE1 RED) above is a goal formula that turned out to be true. If the goal formula has a variable, then the binding of the variable for which the formula is true is the answer. If the formula cannot be proved true for any binding, the answer is false. For example, the following

```
(COLOR SPHERE1 ?Y)
```

is a query regarding the COLOR of SPHERE1. For the given database it will be satisfied (or be true) with

```
?Y = RED
```

Variables in a query are called *request variables,* and they are considered to be existentially quantified.

At times we will be given a set of atomic formulas in a single query or goal; all of them have to be true together for the query to be true.[2]

Exercise 5.1 Add the following assertions

```
(IN ?BLK1 ?BOX) <- (ON ?BLK1 ?BLK2) (IN ?BLK2 ?BOX)
(ON SPHERE1 OVAL1)            ;Precariously balanced.
(SHAPE OVAL1 ROUND)
```

to the assertions already present:

```
(COLOR ?X RED) <- (IN ?X BOX1) (SHAPE ?X ROUND)
(IN SPHERE1 BOX1)
(SHAPE SPHERE1 ROUND)
```

What will be the response to the following queries:

```
(IN OVAL1 BOX1)
(IN OVAL1 ?X)
```

Show the inference using the rules of universal instantiation and modus ponens.

Exercise 5.2 Take the following clauses defining ANCESTOR:

```
(ANCESTOR ?X ?Y) <- (PARENT ?X ?Y)
(ANCESTOR ?X ?Y) <- (PARENT ?X ?Z) (ANCESTOR ?Z ?Y)
```

Can you derive the following goal formulas (given the facts in Sec. 4.3)?

```
(ANCESTOR RAM KUSUM)
(ANCESTOR SARAH SAMIR)
```

5.3 RESOLUTION

The resolution rule of inference combines the two earlier rules of universal instantiation and modus ponens. It is also more efficient to implement. We will be using a particular resolution rule (called SLD resolution) for inference in horn clauses, but first let us study unification.

---

[2]Note, however, that the horn clauses are less powerful than the first-order logic. For example, they are incapable of expressing the following from first-order logic:

```
(NOT (FATHER RAM KUSUM))
```

Unification is central to resolution. It allows us to find a substitution that makes two formulas the same. Such a substitution is called a *unifying substitution* or simply a *unifier*. As we shall see, unification is a kind of pattern matching. For the following two atomic formulas

```
(PRED   ?X ?Y)
(PRED   ?Z 10)
```

the following is a unifier:

```
?Z = ?X
?Y = 10
```

Here is another:

```
?Z = CONST
?X = CONST
?Y = 10
```

Out of these two unifiers, the first one is more general than the second because it substitutes only those variables by constants that are necessary. In other words, if we substitute the first unifier in the pair of formulas, we get a formula which is more general than that obtained on substitution of the second unifier. A formula is *more general* than another if there is a substitution which makes it the same as the other. For example, on substitution the first unifier yields

```
(PRED ?X 10)
```

while the second yields

```
(PRED CONST 10)
```

The former is more general than the latter because for the substitution

```
?X = CONST
```

it becomes equal to the latter.

We can define the *most general unifier* (MGU) to be one which is more general than any other unifier. MGU is unique up to renaming of variables. Both of the following are MGUs for the earlier example:

```
?Z = ?X          ?X = ?Z
        and
?Y = 10          ?Y = 10
```

The unification algorithm given later in this chapter always finds an MGU.

We are now ready to define our *resolution* rule of inference (also called resolution principle). Given a goal formula, try to unify it with, say, a fact (atomic formula asserted to be true). If the unification is successful, the task is over and the given goal formula is true. If, on the other hand, the unification is unsuccessful, try to unify the goal with the head of a rule (a horn clause with a nonempty antecedent and which is asserted to be true). If successful, the antecedent after substitution of the unifier yields new goals. If unsuccessful, failure is reported. The same resolution rule as above has to be applied to each of the goals until either all of them are proved to be true or a goal is found which cannot be proved. The scope of variables in a set of goals is the entire set. In other words, the same variables in the set of goals must be bound, if at all, to the same value.

The following example database and goal illustrates the resolution rule

```
(COLOR ?X RED) <- (IN ?X BOX1) (SHAPE ?X ROUND).
(IN SPHERE1 BOX1)
(SHAPE SPHERE1 ROUND)
```

and a query (or goal)

```
(COLOR SPHERE1 RED)
```

In trying to answer the query, we first check whether the same fact as the query is asserted in the database. If yes, we are done and can return true. If not (as here), we try to unify the query with a consequent of a rule. Here, the unification succeeds between the consequent of the rule and the query

```
(COLOR ?X RED)
(COLOR SPHERE1 RED)
```

resulting in the unifier

```
?X = SPHERE1
```

Now, the antecedent formulas after substitution by the unifier become the new subqueries:

```
(IN SPHERE1 BOX1)
(SHAPE SPHERE1 ROUND)
```

We say that the original query is true or can be satisfied provided the subqueries can be satisfied. If the subqueries have any common variables, they must be bound, if at all, to the same value when the subqueries are satisfied. Here, the two subqueries do not have any variables and are satisfied because the same facts are asserted in the database.

Here is another example query, this time with a request variable. This query inquires about the color of SPHERE1.

```
(COLOR SPHERE1 ?Y)
```

If we follow the resolution steps for the new query, and unify with the consequent of the rule, we have the following unifier:

```
?X = SPHERE1
?Y = RED                        (request variable)
```

The subqueries here are the same as in the previous query and are true. Hence, the new query is true with the request variable bound to RED which is the answer.

Exercise 5.3 Show the unifiers for the following pairs of formulas:

(a) `(PRED1 (F1 B1 (F2 B1 B2)) RED)`
     `(PRED1 ?X ?Y)`
(b) `(PRED1 (F1 B1 (F2 B1 B2)) RED)`
     `(PRED1 (F1 ?X ?Z) ?Y)`
(c) `(PRED1 (F1 ?X (F2 ?X ?Y)) RED)`
     `(PRED1 (F1 B1 (F2 ?Z B2)) ?W)`

5.4 AN EXAMPLE—KINSHIP

We have seen the parent-child relationship earlier. Using it, grandparent and ancestor relations are defined. (See Sec. 5.2.) In this section, we extend it to other relationships, collectively called kinship.

The fundamental relationship is still parenthood. If, in addition, male or female property is known, we can define some other relationships.

First we define FATHER and MOTHER relationships:

```
(FATHER ?X ?Y) <- (PARENT ?X ?Y) (MALE ?X)              (5.2)
(MOTHER ?X ?Y) <- (PARENT ?X ?Y) (FEMALE ?Y)            (5.3)
```

The first rule above states that ?X is the father of ?Y, provided ?X is the parent of ?Y and ?X is male, and similarly for the second rule.

Now we can define (real) brother and sister as those who have the same father and mother:

```
(SIBLING ?X ?Y)        ;?X is sibling of ?Y
   <- (FATHER ?F ?X) (FATHER ?F ?Y)
      (MOTHER ?M ?X) (MOTHER ?M ?Y)                     (5.4)
```

```
(BROTHER ?X ?Y) <- (MALE ?X) (SIBLING ?X ?Y)              (5.5)
(SISTER ?X ?Y) <- (FEMALE ?X) (SIBLING ?X ?Y)             (5.6)
```

Two individuals are first cousins if a parent of one is a sibling of a parent of the other.

```
(FIRST-COUSIN ?X ?Y)
    <- (PARENT ?A ?X) (PARENT ?B ?Y)
        (SIBLING ?A ?B)                                   (5.7)
```

Similarly, second cousins are defined by

```
(SECOND-COUSIN ?X ?Y)
    <- (PARENT ?A ?X) (PARENT ?B ?Y)
        (FIRST-COUSIN ?A ?B)                              (5.8)
```

Defining cousins is also not difficult:

```
(COUSIN ?X ?Y) <- (FIRST-COUSIN ?X ?Y)                    (5.9)
(COUSIN ?X ?Y) <- (PARENT ?A ?X) (PARENT ?B ?Y)
                    (COUSIN ?A ?B)                        (5.10)
```

Let us take the family tree shown in Fig. 5-1, where sex is specified in parentheses. To represent the family tree we could have the following assertions besides those in Sec. 4.3:

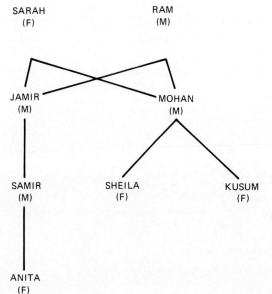

FIGURE 5-1

```
(FEMALE SARAH)
(MALE RAM)
(MALE JAMIR)
(MALE MOHAN)
(MALE SAMIR)
(FEMALE SHEILA)
(FEMALE KUSUM)
(FEMALE ANITA)
```

Now, if the following query

```
(FIRST-COUSIN SAMIR SHEILA)
```

is issued, the inference tree that gets generated (or traversed by INFER-AND) is shown in Fig. 5-2. A dotted line between two atomic formulas indicates that they unify. The one above is a goal, while the lower one is the consequent of an assertion. The consequent of an assertion is connected to the antecedent of the assertion. The connector shows that there is an AND node, namely, each of the antecedent formulas must be true for the consequent to be true.

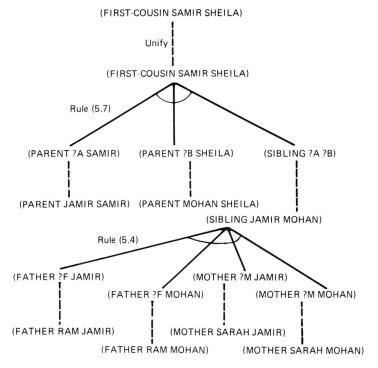

FIGURE 5-2
Inference tree.

There are many advantages in solving problems using logic programming. In it one defines rules and facts independent of how they would be used. It is declarative rather than procedural. In many situations, including the example above, it is easier to specify the "knowledge" descriptively rather than procedurally. Also, as mentioned earlier, a rule does not have predefined inputs and outputs unlike programs. For example, if we unify the following goal

```
(FIRST-COUSIN SAMIR ?Z)
```

with the consequent of rule (5.7), the first argument of FIRST-COUSIN is provided as input and the second argument is desired as output. On the other hand, in the tree in Fig. 5-2 both arguments are inputs and the output is true or false.

Exercise 5.4 Define rules for maternal grandparents.

Exercise 5.5 Define paternal uncle.

Exercise 5.6 Define mother-in-law. (*Hint*: You will first need to define the basic spouse relationship.)

Exercise 5.7 Define stepbrother and stepmother. Assume NEQ is a predicate that is true if its arguments are not equal. (*Hint*: Again, definition of spouse is needed.)

Exercise 5.8 Test run your rules in the last four exercises on a family-marital graph. Examine the inference tree.

Rules specify only one-way relationships from antecedent to consequent. For example, if we want to infer parenthood and sex based on father relationship, we will have to incorporate the following rules:

```
;; If ?X is father of ?Y, then ?X is parent of ?Y
(PARENT ?X ?Y) <- (FATHER ?X ?Y)                    (5.11)

;;Similar
(PARENT ?X ?Y) <- (MOTHER ?X ?Y)                    (5.12)

;;If ?X is the father of somebody, ?X is male
(MALE ?X) <- (FATHER ?X ?Y)                         (5.13)

;;Similar
(FEMALE ?X) <- (MOTHER ?X ?Y)                       (5.14)
```

Exercise 5.9 If you include rules (5.11) to (5.14) in your database, what happens when you issue the following query?

```
(PARENT RAM MOHAN)
```

5.5 IMPLEMENTING RESOLUTION

There are several key components that are part of a resolution-based inference system. There must typically be components for finding the most general unifier, generating unique variables, and substituting values of variables, and finally, there must be an algorithm that puts all these together. These are discussed below.

5.5.1 Unification

The function for finding the unifier (called UNIFY) is described below. It finds the most general unifier.

UNIFY has many similarities to the pattern-matching algorithm MATCH2 (Sec. 4.2). It also takes as its arguments the two things that are being matched (PAT1 and PAT2) and a substitution (ALIST) found so far. It returns an atom $FAIL if PAT1 and PAT2 cannot be unified, and an association list representing the unifying substitution if PAT1 and PAT2 can be unified. UNIFY is more general than MATCH2 because both PAT1 and PAT2 might contain variables.

UNIFY differs from MATCII2 in only the following way: It checks both PAT1 and PAT2 to see whether they are variables. If any of them is a variable, it calls VAR-UNIFY with three arguments: the variable, the other pattern, and an association list. VAR-UNIFY behaves like CHECK-ADD-BINDING when the variable does not have a value on the ALIST. If on the other hand the variable has a value, it tries to unify the value of the variable with the other parameter (PAT1 or PAT2). This additional complexity is the consequence of allowing variables in both PAT1 and PAT2. (This is illustrated later by an example.)

Variable names in PAT1 and PAT2 must be disjoint for the algorithm to work correctly. A variable, say ?X, is represented as ($VAR X) as before. (See Sec. 4.2 for definitions of IS-VAR, NAME-OF, and the read macro '?'.)

```
(DEFUN UNIFY (PAT1 PAT2 ALIST)
;;; Tries to unify PAT1 and PAT2 under the given
;;; association list ALIST. If successful, returns
;;; the new association list containing the unifier.
;;; Otherwise returns $FAIL.
    (COND [(FAIL-P ALIST) ALIST]
          [(IS-VAR PAT1) (VAR-UNIFY PAT1 PAT2 ALIST)]
          [(IS-VAR PAT2) (VAR-UNIFY PAT2 PAT1 ALIST)]
          [(AND (ATOM PAT1) (ATOM PAT2))
           (COND [(EQL PAT1 PAT2) ALIST] [T '$FAIL])]
          [(OR (ATOM PAT1) (ATOM PAT2)) '$FAIL]
          [T (UNIFY (CDR PAT1)
                    (CDR PAT2)
                    (UNIFY (CAR PAT1)
                           (CAR PAT2)
                           ALIST))]))
```

```
(DEFUN VAR-UNIFY (VAR PAT ALIST)
;;; If VAR is bound, its value is unified with PAT
;;; and the new association list is returned if successful,
;;; else returns $FAIL. If VAR is unbound, create a
;;; binding and return the new association list.
   (LET ((BINDING (ASSOC (NAME-OF VAR) ALIST)))
      (COND [(NULL BINDING)
             (CONS (LIST (NAME-OF VAR) PAT)
                   ALIST)]
            [T (UNIFY (CADR BINDING) PAT ALIST)])))
```

The following illustrates why VAR-UNIFY rather than CHECK-ADD-BINDING is necessary. If we have the following input to UNIFY

```
PAT1 = (PROP1 ?X ?X)
PAT2 = (PROP1 20 ?Z)
ALIST = ()
```

then during unification (after unifying the second elements of lists PAT1 and PAT2) we get the substitution

```
?X = 20
```

When the third elements ?X and ?Z are unified, we find that ?X already has a value. With VAR-UNIFY we do not stop here but try to unify the value of ?X with ?Z. (CHECK-ADD-BINDING would have rejected the match because the value of ?X is different from ?Z.) It results in the following unifier:

```
?X = 20
?Z = 20
```

The above UNIFY algorithm works correctly except for one problem. It does not check for circularity of bindings of variables. For example, on unifying the two atomic formulas,

```
(PRED (F ?X) ?X)
(PRED ?Y ?Y)
```

our algorithm will yield the unifier

```
?Y = (F ?X)
?X = ?Y
```

which is meaningless unless we can give a meaning to an infinite term such as (F (F

... F(X)..)). Also, our algorithm can go in an infinite recursion if a variable is bound to itself.

One way to eliminate these is to check for circularity before creating a new variable binding. Thus, VAR-UNIFY below, before creating a binding between a variable VAR and a value PAT, calls OCCURS-IN to check that in creating the binding no circularity would be introduced. This is accomplished by OCCURS-IN by making sure that VAR does not occur in PAT and also that no variable in PAT has a value in which VAR occurs, and so on.

```
(DEFUN VAR-UNIFY (VAR PAT ALIST)
;;; Same as earlier VAR-UNIFY except check for
;;; circularities
    (LET ((BINDING (ASSOC (NAME-OF VAR) ALIST)))
        (COND [BINDING (UNIFY (CADR BINDING) PAT ALIST)]
            [(EQUAL VAR PAT)
             ;; Do not bind VAR to itself.
             ALIST]
            [(NOT (OCCURS-IN VAR PAT ALIST))
             ;; Do not bind VAR to anything
             ;; containing VAR.
             (CONS (LIST (NAME-OF VAR) PAT) ALIST)]
            [T '$FAIL])))

(DEFUN OCCURS-IN (VAR PAT ALIST)
;;; Returns true if VAR occurs in PAT where variables
;;; in PAT are substituted from ALIST.
    (COND
        [(ATOM PAT) NIL]
        [(IS-VAR PAT)
         (OR (EQUAL VAR PAT)
             (LET ((BINDING (ASSOC (NAME-OF PAT) ALIST)))
                 (COND [BINDING (OCCURS-IN VAR (CADR BINDING)
                                           ALIST)]
                       [T NIL])))]
        [T (OR (OCCURS-IN VAR (CAR PAT) ALIST)
               (OCCURS-IN VAR (CDR PAT) ALIST))]))
```

As this check is very expensive (exponential in the size of the pattern), most systems do not perform it. (See Further Readings at the end of the chapter for pointers to more efficient algorithms.)

Exercise 5.10 Show that if OCCURS-IN check is not put in VAR-UNIFY, it goes into infinite recursion with the following two patterns:

```
(PRED (F ?X) ?X (F ?X))
(PRED ?Y ?Y (F ?Y))
```

5.5.2 Generating Unique Variables

We have already seen that variables in two atomic formulas that are to be unified must be disjoint. (This is because of the scopes of the variables.) To make sure that this is so we can always rename variables in one formula so that each variable is replaced by a unique name distinct from all others.

One way to generate unique variables is to generate a new symbol for every variable name and replace the variable names by the respective symbols. Thus, for example, we could generate a symbol G0032 (using GENSYM) for a variable name X, and replace X in all occurrences of ($VAR X) by ($VAR G0032). The problem with this approach is twofold. First, the user-defined variable names are changed to something else, affecting the readability of atomic formulas. This will be particularly serious when the debugging or tracing aids show the formula during inference. Second, this approach causes a large number of symbols to be generated.

We present a novel approach here which does not suffer from the above defects and which has advantages if we need to substitute values of variables. The basic idea in our approach is that the structure representing a variable is made unique rather than its name. Thus, for example, all occurrences of variable X in an assertion are represented by the same cons cell for ($VAR X). Variable X in other assertions is also represented by the list structure ($VAR X) but consists of a different cons cell. (With this change, we shall have to store in the association list not just the name but the list structure for the variable.) Thus, in this method, the variable names given by the user are retained and unnecessary atoms are not generated.

To make non-EQ representations print differently, we will put a unique integer in the representation of a variable. This will be useful in debugging, say. For example, all occurrences of a variable ?X in a clause might become

```
($VAR X . 25)
```

while in another all the occurrences might become

```
($VAR X . 73)
```

The point to be noted, however, is that while testing for equality of variables, we never need to compare the integers in them. A simple and fast EQ test is sufficient.

Function RENAME-VARS takes a pattern and produces its copy in which all occurrences of every variable are substituted by their respective unique list structures as explained above. The actual task of substitution is performed by CHECK-GEN-NEW-VAR. It takes a representation of the variable and makes it unique. It maintains an association list between the variable name and its unique representation in *VAR-NAMES*. Given a variable name, it first checks whether it is on *VAR-NAMES*. If yes, it returns its value; otherwise it generates a list structure for it and creates and places the association on *VAR-NAMES* before returning.

```
(DEFVAR *NUM* 0)
(DEFVAR *VAR-NAMES* ())
```

```
(DEFUN RENAME-VARS (S)
;;; Initialize *VAR-NAMES* to () (for every call).
;;; Increment *NUM* by 1. Call
;;; RENAME-VARS-AUX to do the actual work
;;; of making variable names unique.
   (SETQ *VAR-NAMES* ())
   (SETQ *NUM* (+ 1 *NUM*))
   (RENAME-VARS-AUX S))


(DEFUN RENAME-VARS-AUX (S)
;;; Returns a pattern corresponding to S so that all
;;; the variables have been made unique.
   (COND [(IS-VAR S) (CHECK-GEN-NEW-VAR S)]
         [(ATOM S) S]
         [T (CONS (RENAME-VARS-AUX (CAR S))
                  (RENAME-VARS-AUX (CDR S)))]))


(DEFUN CHECK-GEN-NEW-VAR (V)
;;; Check whether the variable V has already been
;;; encountered, by looking up *VAR-NAMES*.
;;; If yes, return its unique entry.
;;; If not, put a unique entry for V in *VAR-NAMES*
;;; and return it.
   (LET ((X (ASSOC (NAME-OF V) *VAR-NAMES*)))
     (COND
      [(NULL X)
       ;; Create a unique variable entry
       (LET ((UNIQUE (LIST (NAME-OF V)
                           (CONS '$VAR
                                 (CONS (NAME-OF V)
                                       *NUM*)))))
          (SETQ *VAR-NAMES* (CONS UNIQUE *VAR-NAMES*))
          (CADR UNIQUE))]
      [T (CADR X)])))
```

The above implementation generates a new copy of the pattern in which variables with the same name are represented by the same unique cons cell.

A new copy is generated by RENAME-VARS-AUX for the entire pattern without sharing any substructure. In the worst case, even if a pattern contains no variables, it is copied. To avoid this waste we redefine RENAME-VARS-AUX which calls on COMBINE to make a copy only when necessary.

```
(DEFUN RENAME-VARS-AUX (S)
   (COND [(IS-VAR S) (CHECK-GEN-NEW-VAR S)]
         [(ATOM S) S]
```

```
      [T (COMBINE S (RENAME-VARS-AUX (CAR S))
                    (RENAME-VARS-AUX (CDR S)))]))

(DEFUN COMBINE (S HEAD TAIL)
;;; HEAD = Possibly transformed head of S
;;; TAIL = Possibly transformed tail of S
;;; If no transformation has taken place, return S.
;;; Otherwise combine the HEAD and TAIL to yield a new S
    (COND [(AND (EQL HEAD (CAR S)) (EQL TAIL (CDR S)))
           S]
          [T (CONS HEAD TAIL)]))
```

For the new representation of the variables, VAR-UNIFY needs to be redefined. UNIFY remains unchanged.

```
(DEFUN VAR-UNIFY (VAR PAT ALIST)
;;; If VAR is bound, its value is unified with PAT.
;;; (In case of failure returns $FAIL as usual.)
;;; Else VAR is bound to PAT and adds the
;;; new unifier to ALIST and returns it.
    (LET ((BINDING (ASSOC VAR ALIST))) ;Uses VAR instead of
                                       ;(NAME-OF VAR) earlier
       (COND [(NULL BINDING)
              (CONS (LIST VAR PAT) ALIST)]
             [T (UNIFY (CADR BINDING) PAT ALIST)])))
```

Exercise 5.11 Instead of keeping the associations between variable names and their respective unique representations using a special variable *VAR-NAMES*, pass them as a parameter. Compare the complexity of your function with the ones given here.

Exercise 5.12 If no special variables were used, how would you implement RENAME-VARS?

5.5.3   Representation of Assertions

We have already seen how atomic formulas are represented—a list consisting of the predicate name followed by its arguments.

Before proceeding further we must select a representation for the assertions. An assertion of the form

```
B ← A1 A2 ... An
```

will be represented by an S-expr of the form

```
(B (A1 ... An) <name>)
```

where <name> is an optional atom naming the assertion, and B and A1 to An are atomic formulas.

We will represent the database of assertions as a list of assertions *DBASRTS*. As a result, the search will be linear and quite inefficient, but it will do for now. We will be able to concentrate on the inference algorithm.

5.5.4 Resolution

We are now ready to define INFER-AND, a function that puts it all together and implements resolution. It takes QLIST, a list of query formulas ANDed together, and ALIST, an association list that keeps the bindings of variables (initially ()). It returns $FAIL if the query formulas cannot be derived from the database of facts and rules, and an association list otherwise.

This is how INFER-AND works: It takes the first query Q from QLIST and tries to unify it under the given association list with the consequent of an assertion. If none unifies, it means Q cannot be unified under the given ALIST and failure is returned.

On the other hand, if Q unifies with the consequent of an assertion, say *b* (yielding a new association list RES), then there are two cases:

1. *b* has a nil antecedent. In this case Q has succeeded and remaining goals in QLIST are tried under RES by a recursive call.
2. *b* has a nonnil antecedent. In this case Q has succeeded provided the atomic formulas in the antecedent of *b* are satisfied. To test this, a recursive call is made with the antecedent of *b* added to the tail of QLIST under the RES association list. (A tag, $AND, is also put on the new QLIST. This will be explained later.)

Now, if the recursive call returns failure, Q is matched with the consequent of another assertion, if possible, and the above is repeated. If, on the other hand, the recursive call succeeds, it means that the ANDed query has succeeded, and the new association list is returned.

```
(DEFSTRUCT (ASRT (:CONSTRUCTOR MAKE-ASRT
                              (CONSEQ ANTEC NAME))
              (:TYPE LIST))
          CONSEQ ANTEC NAME)
(DEFVAR *DBASRTS*    ... )

(DEFUN INFER-AND (QLIST ALIST)
;;; QLIST is a list of goals or queries.
;;; ALIST is the current association list (initially ()).
;;; Returns an association list if successful in
;;; satisfying the queries, $FAIL if not.
  (COND
    [(NULL QLIST) ALIST]
    [(EQL '$AND (CAAR QLIST))
```

```
;; Needed later in Sec. 6.1.4. Ignore for now.
(INFER-AND (CDR QLIST) ALIST)]
[T ;; Carry out the inference. Search the database.
(LET ((Q (CAR QLIST)) (RES NIL))
  (DO*
        ([ASRTS *DBASRTS* (CDR ASRTS)]
         [DBASRT (RENAME-VARS (CAR ASRTS))
                 (RENAME-VARS (CAR ASRTS))])
        (NULL ASRTS) '$FAIL)
    (SETQ RES (UNIFY Q (ASRT-CONSEQ DBASRT) ALIST))
    (COND
      [(EQL '$FAIL RES)
       ;; Fail to match with conseq of DBASRT.
       ;; Do nothing. Will loop.
       ]
      [T ;; Q succcessfully matched. Try antec of Q
         ;; and the rest of QLIST.
         (SETQ RES
          (COND
            [(NULL (ASRT-ANTEC DBASRT))
             (INFER-AND (CDR QLIST) RES)]
            [T (INFER-AND (APPEND (ASRT-ANTEC DBASRT)
                                  (CONS (LIST '$AND)
                                        (CDR QLIST)))
                          RES)]))
         (COND [(EQL '$FAIL RES)] ;Do nothing. Will loop.
               [T ;; Success. Return the new ALIST.
                  (RETURN RES)])])))]))
```

Exercise 5.13 Take the family relationships and goals given in Exercise 5.2 and show how INFER-AND will prove the goals to be true.

Exercise 5.14 Define the iterative version of INFER-AND, that is, it should not make a recursive call.

Exercise 5.15 Test your iterative implementation in the previous exercise with the kinship example.

Exercise 5.16 When the database includes rules (5.11) to (5.14) and those given in the kinship example, INFER-AND goes into an infinite loop when given the following goal:

```
(FATHER RAM MOHAN)
```

Verify that it indeed does so. (*Note*: This is not due to the resolution principle but rather to the depth-first search strategy used in INFER-AND. If the breadth-first strategy were used, this would have yielded an answer. Verify using paper and pencil.)

Exercise 5.17 Implement either the breadth-first or best-first strategy in INFER-AND. Repeat Exercise 5.16 to check whether the INFER-AND goes into infinite recursion.

5.5.5 Ultimate Substitution of Variables

Frequently, we need to substitute values of variables from the association list. For example, once we have succeeded in resolving a goal clause we might like to display the goal with values of variables substituted.

Let us define a function called SUBST-VARS-ULT that takes a formula and an association list and substitutes for variables that have a value. If the value of a variable contains another variable, that other variable is also substituted if possible, and so on. It is called ultimate substitution.

```
(DEFUN SUBST-VARS-ULT (S ALIST)
    (COND [(IS-VAR S)
            ;; Get the value of variable S.
            (LET ([BIND (ASSOC S ALIST)])
                (COND [(NULL BIND)
                        ;; S does not have a value.
                        ;; Unable to substitute.
                        S]
                      [T (SUBST-VARS-ULT (CADR BIND)
                                            ALIST)])))]
          [(ATOM S) S]
          [T (COMBINE S (SUBST-VARS-ULT (CAR S) ALIST)
                        (SUBST-VARS-ULT (CDR S) ALIST))]))
```

A more efficient version of SUBST-VARS-ULT does not copy; instead it makes changes in-place in the pattern using SETF. If the value of a variable is a list, the representation of the variable is changed destructively to the value.

```
(DEFUN DSUBST-VARS-ULT (S ALIST)
    (COND [(ATOM S) S]
          [(IS-VAR S) ;Degenerate case. Initial S a var.
            (LET ((BIND (ASSOC S ALIST)))
                (COND [(NULL BIND)
                        ;; Variable S does not have
                        ;; a value. Return it
                        ;; without substitution.
                        S]
                      [T (DSUBST-VARS-ULT (CADR BIND)
                                            ALIST)]))]
          [(IS-VAR (CAR S))
            ;;Normal termination case. Head of S a var.
            (LET ((BIND (ASSOC (CAR S) ALIST)))
```

```
(COND [(NULL BIND)
       ;; Variable in the head of S
       ;; does not have a value.
       ;; Continue substitution on
       ;; the tail of S.
       (DSUBST-VARS-ULT (CDR S) ALIST)
       S]
      [T ;; Var in head of S has a value.
       ;; Find the ultimate value and
       ;; substitute.
       ;; Then continue with the tail of S.
       (LET ((VAL (DSUBST-VARS-ULT
                    (CADR BIND) ALIST)))
            (SETF (CAR S) VAL)
            (DSUBST-VARS-ULT (CDR S)
                (CONS (LIST (CAR BIND) VAL)
                    ALIST))
            S)])]
      [T (DSUBST-VARS-ULT (CAR S) ALIST)
         (DSUBST-VARS-ULT (CDR S) ALIST)
         S]))
```

Exercise 5.18 The tail of a formula cannot be a symbol in the representation selected in this chapter. However, if it were permitted, DSUBST-VARS-ULT would not be able to handle it. How would you change it if you were asked to handle this?

Exercise 5.19 If variables are represented by a unique list structure, and if the value of a variable is a list, then the value can be substituted destructively in the unique list structure. It results in substitution of all occurrences of the variable. (Values that are atoms have to be substituted separately for each occurrence.) Define a function that takes a pattern and an association list and substitutes as described. (*Note*: For variables that are substituted in the above manner, their bindings can be removed from the association list. Why?)

Exercise 5.20 Change INFER-AND such that on successful unification of a query with the consequent of an assertion, the unifier is substituted in the antecedent of the assertion, yielding new goals, and the same old association list is passed. How does it affect the efficiency of inference?

5.6 NEGATION AS FAILURE

So far we have not allowed negation of atomic formulas. There is an interesting idea that can be applied to deal with negation: Failure to derive a formula is considered equal to deriving its negation. This is based on the so-called *closed world assumption,* in which it is assumed that what cannot be derived is false.

Whenever we have to derive a goal formula that is the negation of an atomic formula, we try to derive the atomic formula. If we are successful, the goal formula cannot be derived and is false. If we are unsuccessful, the goal formula is considered derived.

Exercise 5.21 Modify INFER-AND to incorporate negation as failure.

Exercise 5.22 Just as programs have to be debugged, similarly in logic programming a set of assertions has to be debugged for mistakes, discrepancies, or inefficiency. In the INFER-AND defined here, no special aids are provided for debugging. The user would have to rely on the LISP debugger. What aids can you think of providing to the user? Incorporate some of them in INFER-AND.

FURTHER READING

For an introduction to logic programming using PROLOG and how it can be used in diverse applications see Clocksin and Mellish (1984). Logic programming using horn clauses is described in Kowalski (1979). To read about implementation of logic programming see Robinson (1979) and Boyer (1972). A linear algorithm for unification with an OCCURS-IN check is described in Martelli and Montaneri (1982) and Kapur, Krishnamoorthy, and Narendran (1986).

To read about efficient implementations of logic programming consult Warren (1977), Malhotra (1987), and Kumar (1987). The literature is fast exploding in this area and is generally reported in Conferences in Logic Programming, Foundations of Software Technology, and Theoretical Computer Science (proceedings published by Springer Verlag), and in the journals of *Logic Programming* and *New Generation Computing,* among many others.

For an introduction to logic, read any one of Gallier (1987), Enderton (1972), or Smullyan (1968). For mechanical theorem proving see Chang and Lee (1973). Foundations of logic programming are discussed in Lloyd (1984).

CHAPTER

6

AN EXPERT SYSTEMS SHELL

In the last chapter we developed algorithms and functions that are at the heart of logic programming. Before they can be used in an application, however, they must be incorporated in a system that has provision for efficient storage and retrieval of assertions, an appropriate user interface, ability to pose questions to the user when facts and rules fail, etc. Such a system is called an expert systems shell, named after its most dominant application.

We have already seen that in logic programming we match the goal with assertions in the database, which in general yields a new set of goals, and so on. This is called *backward chaining* because one begins with the goal and goes "backward" toward facts. Naturally, the expert systems shell described in this chapter will use backward chaining since it is based on logic programming.

In contrast to the above, the next chapter discusses production systems. There *forward chaining* is used where one begins with the assertions and moves toward goals.

In the first section, we select a data structure and design a simple shell. Also incorporated in it are facilities for user interaction. Next we augment the shell with computational predicates and functions. In the third section, functional dependencies are discussed. Examples from auto repair, heat-exchanger design, and blocks world illustrate the use of the shell.

6.1 A SIMPLE SHELL

The first issue that needs to be addressed while building a shell is the organization of the database of assertions.

119

In the last chapter, we saw how an individual assertion may be represented: as a triple containing the consequent, antecedent, and name. We will continue to use the same representation. The database of assertions was organized as a linear list in the last chapter. This, however, is too inefficient and was assumed for illustration purposes only. A straightforward method to speed up the access is to store the assertions on the property list of the predicate in its consequent. Thus, for example, the assertions

```
(ANCESTOR RAM KUSUM)
(ANCESTOR ?X ?Y) <- (PARENT ?X ?Y)
```

would be stored on the property list of ANCESTOR. We store them under the attribute ASRTS.

This permits efficient access to relevant assertions. Given a goal, we no longer need to search the entire database. We merely search the assertions associated with the goal predicate. The resulting subgoals, if any, again require a search of only the assertions associated with their respective predicates, and so on. This brings about a major improvement in speed.

> **Exercise 6.1** Redefine INFER-AND given in the last chapter where facts and rules are not in a global list but attached to predicates as described here. (*Hint*: See later in this chapter if you have difficulty.)

6.1.1   Posing Questions

Frequently, in expert systems not all the information is available in the database of assertions. At times, the information has to be elicited from the user. In the naive approach, before the inference begins, all the questions can be asked of the user and the answers stored as facts. This, however, does not work satisfactorily. First, usually not all questions need to be asked. Based on the goal and the user's responses only some of the questions need to be posed to the user. Second, questions are asked in some order keeping focus and user's responses in mind. In fact, what questions to ask and in what order to ask them should be tied to the inference or reasoning processes.

This is accomplished in our shell by introducing rules that cause questions to be issued. Such rules make use of a built-in predicate called ASK-USER. The rules are not treated in any special manner, but we call them question rules to emphasize that they are used for asking questions.

ASK-USER is a special predicate that behaves differently from other predicates. The database is not searched to test the truth value of a formula involving ASK-USER. Instead, a function with the same name is called that interacts with the user. If the user is unable to provide the answer, the formula is not true and it is recorded that the user does not know the answer. Otherwise the formula is satisfied and an appropriate fact is asserted.

Before defining ASK-USER let us look at some examples. They are from the domain of automobile repair.

```
(ENGINE-HOT) <- (TEMPR COOLANT HIGH)                        (6.1)
(TEMPR ?X ?Y )
 <- (ASK-USER (SOURCE ?X)
              (TARGET ?Y)
              (QUESTION IS THE TEMPERATURE
                 OF ?X HIGH NORMAL OR LOW))             (6.2)
(TEMPR ?X ?Y)
 <- (ASK-USER (SOURCE ?X ?Y)
              (TARGET)
              (QUESTION IS IT TRUE THAT THE
                 TEMPERATURE OF ?X IS ?Y))              (6.3)
```

The first rule above asserts that the engine is hot if the temperature of the coolant is high. The second and the third are question rules. Their antecedents contain ASK-USER. When the second rule is invoked, the truth value of the antecedent is to be determined. If ?X (the source variable) is known and ?Y (the target variable) is not, the question is issued asking for the temperature of ?X. The user response, other than DONTKNOW, supplies the value of ?Y. Similarly, to determine the truth value of the antecedent in the third rule, a question is issued when ?X and ?Y are known, to confirm whether the temperature of ?X is equal to ?Y. As the second and the third rules show, ASK-USER allows different questions to be issued depending on what is known (the source variables) and what needs to be known (the target variables).

More formally, ASK-USER takes three parameters of type: SOURCE, TARGET, and QUESTION. The SOURCE and TARGET parameters contain lists of variables called source and target variables, respectively. The question in the QUESTION parameter is issued to the user only if all the source variables have variable-free values (i.e., on ultimate substitution of a source variable, the result does not contain any variable) and none of the target variables have a value (i.e., on ultimate substitution of a target variable we get a variable). The response of the user normally provides values of the target variables, and the formula containing ASK-USER becomes true. If there are no target variables, the answer must be YES, NO, TRUE, or FALSE. If the answer is YES or TRUE, the formula is true; otherwise it is false. The user is free to say DONTKNOW in response to any question. It causes the formula containing ASK-USER to fail.

What does the above imply for the question rules in our examples? To determine whether the antecedent of the second rule (6.2) is true, first, a check is made that ?X, the source variable, has a variable-free value and that ?Y, the target variable, does not have a value. If the check regarding source and target variables fails, then the question is not issued and the rule fails. If the check yields true, the question is issued after substituting values of variables in it. The response of the user other than DONT-KNOW provides the value for ?Y, and the antecedent formula containing ASK-USER is satisfied. If the user answers DONTKNOW, the antecedent is not satisfied and the rule fails. On a failure, another rule must be tried as usual.

The third rule (6.3) is similar to the second except the question is issued when

both variables ?X and ?Y have a variable-free value. There are no target variables; hence, the answer yes or no, true or false simply determines the truth value of the formula. It does not provide a value to any variable.

6.1.2   An Example—Auto Repair

To illustrate the above ideas we take an extended example pertaining to automobile repair. An automobile repair expert system takes the user through steps leading to repair of the automobile. The knowledge needed for the expert system is shown in a tree like the structure in Fig. 6-1. The nodes represent symptoms, faults, etc. The tree shows the relationship between the nodes and is useful primarily in thinking about the knowledge. Informally, a node representing a symptom or a fault is true, provided its successor nodes are true. We shall call such a tree the knowledge tree.

Here the root node is labeled auto-repair. It has three successors each corresponding to a different fault. The first fault is engine-does-not-turn. It has three successors which together stand for the following: If the ignition switch is on and the engine is not turning, then it should be investigated whether the starter motor is getting power. The first two of the successors are marked by a # which indicates that the truth value of the node is determined by asking a question. In other words, question rule is present, and invoking the rule causes the question to be issued.

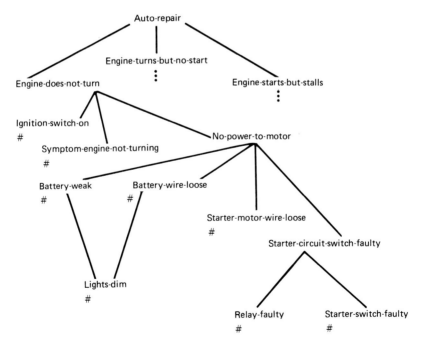

FIGURE 6-1
Knowledge structure for auto repair.

arguments COOLANT and HIGH, no question will be issued. Similarly, if the user had answered DONTKNOW in response to the question in rule (6.2), where ?X was bound to COOLANT, then

```
(COOLANT ?Y)
```

would be stored in a list under the attribute DONTKNOW. Next time we have a goal of the form

```
(TEMPR COOLANT ?Z)
```

rule (6.2) will fail because the above has the same arguments (up to renaming of variables) as the ones on the property list under DONTKNOW. No question will be issued.

GET-DONTKNOW and STORE-DONTKNOW retrieve and store information for the predicate in a goal Q for which the user has answered DONTKNOW. This will be called DONTKNOW LIST. USER-DONTKNOW-P takes a goal Q and returns true if for the same arguments as in Q, the user has answered DONTKNOW or FALSE or NO.

```
(DEFMACRO GET-DONTKNOW (Q)
   `(GET (CAR ,Q) 'DONTKNOW))

(DEFUN STORE-DONTKNOW (Q ALIST)
;;; On the attribute DONTKNOW of the predicate in Q
;;; add the arguments of Q to the existing DONTKNOW LIST.
   (SETF (GET-DONTKNOW Q)
         (CONS (SUBST-VARS-ULT (CDR Q) ALIST)
               (GET-DONTKNOW Q))))

(DEFUN USER-DONTKNOW-P (Q)
   (DO ((DONTKNOW-LIST (GET-DONTKNOW Q) (CDR DONTKNOW-LIST))
        (RES NIL))
       ((NULL DONTKNOW-LIST) NIL)
     ;; Check for equality between the first
     ;; element of DONTKNOW LIST and tail of Q.
     (SETQ RES
           (DO ((D (CAR DONTKNOW-LIST) (CDR D))
                (REM-Q (CDR Q) (CDR REM-Q)))
               ((OR (NULL D) (NULL REM-Q))
                (AND (NULL D) (NULL REM-Q)))
             (COND [(AND (IS-VAR (CAR D))
                         (IS-VAR (CAR REM-Q)))
                    T]
                   [(EQUAL (CAR D) (CAR REM-Q)) T]
```

```
               [T ;; Match fails between Q and the
                  ;; present head of DONTKNOW-LIST.
                  (RETURN NIL)])))
      (COND [RES (RETURN T)])))
```

Having outlined the strategy and defined the support functions, let us look at the overall implementation of INFER-AND. First, since there might be a need to store intermediate results and the DONTKNOW response, some extra information about the rule whose antecedent is being tested must be carried around. It consists of the consequent, a flag indicating whether the results are to be stored, and the name of the rule. These three are passed in the first three arguments, respectively. The other two arguments are QLIST and ALIST as before.

Now, when a list beginning with $AND is the first element of QLIST, it indicates that all the clauses in the antecedent of the current rule have been satisfied. FLAG is tested, and if it is true, the consequent after the ultimate substitution of variables is stored. Following that, the $AND entry is popped and information about the previous rule that was being tried is retrieved, and, as usual, a recursive call is made.

If the first clause on QLIST has ASK-USER, DONTKNOW information is searched first. If nonempty, it means that the question has been answered earlier by the user as DONTKNOW. No question is issued and failure is returned. Similarly, if the above turns out to be false and a question gets issued (on call on the function ASK-USER), then the user response is stored in a variable *ANS*. This is examined later to see whether the user has answered NO or DONTKNOW. If so, appropriate information is stored under the DONTKNOW LIST for the predicate.

Second, while searching the database of rules, if there is a match between the goal and the consequent, the $AND entry containing the consequent, etc., is pushed on QLIST.

```
(DEFUN INFER-AND (CONSEQ FLAG NAME QLIST ALIST)
;;; See the description above for the function.
   (DECLARE (SPECIAL *ANS*)) ;Set by ASK-USER
                             ; to user response.

   (COND
      [(NULL QLIST) ALIST]
      [(EQL '$AND (CAAR QLIST))
       ;; For the current rule all antecedent formulas
       ;; have been successful. Store consequent if necessary.
       (COND [FLAG (STORE-ASRT
                      (MAKE-ASRT (SUBST-VARS-ULT
                                    CONSEQ ALIST)
                                 NIL
                                 (LIST NAME (GENSYM))))])
       ;; Continue with the inference on tail of QLIST.
```

```
          ;; Restore consequent, etc. saved earlier in $AND entry.
        (INFER-AND (CADAR QLIST)
                   (CADDAR QLIST)
                   (CADDDR (CAR QLIST))
                   (CDR QLIST)
                   ALIST)]
   [T ;; Carry out the inference.
    (LET ((Q (CAR QLIST)) (RES NIL))
       (COND
         [(EQL 'ASK-USER (CAR Q))
          ;; Non-database predicate encountered.
          (COND [(USER-DONTKNOW-P
                  (SUBST-VARS-ULT CONSEQ ALIST))
                 ;; Question already asked and answered
                 ;; as FALSE or DONTKNOW.
                 (SETQ RES '$FAIL)]
                [T ;; Issue question to user.
                 (SETQ RES (ASK-USER ALIST (CDR Q)))
                 ;; User response available in *ANS*.
                 (COND [(MEMBER (CAR *ANS*)
                                '(N NO FALSE DONTKNOW))
                        (STORE-DONTKNOW
                          (SUBST-VARS-ULT CONSEQ ALIST)
                          ALIST)])
                 (SETQ *ANS* NIL)])
          (COND [(EQL '$FAIL RES) RES]
                [T ;;Continue inference with new ALIST RES
                 (INFER-AND CONSEQ FLAG NAME (CDR QLIST)
                            RES)])]
         [T ;; Search the database of assertions to infer Q.
          (DO*
            ((ASRTS ... ) ;Same as in the last section.
             (DBASRT ... );Same as in the last section.
            ((NULL ASRTS) '$FAIL)
            (SETQ RES
                  (UNIFY Q (ASRT-CONSEQ DBASRT) ALIST))
            (COND
              [(EQL '$FAIL RES) '$FAIL]
              [T ;; Q successfully matched.Try antecedent of Q
               ;; and the rest of QLIST. Use RES as the
               ;; new association list.
               (SETQ RES
                 (COND
              [(NULL (ASRT-ANTEC DBASRT))
               ;; DBASRT has nil antecedent.
```

```
                    ;; Continue with the tail of QLIST.
                    (INFER-AND CONSEQ FLAG NAME
                               (CDR QLIST) RES)]
               [T
                ;; Continue inference with antecedent
                ;; of DBASRT and tail of QLIST.
                (INFER-AND Q
                    (OR (IS-INTERMEDIATE
                            (ASRT-CONSEQ DBASRT)
                            CONSEQ FLAG NAME DBASRT)
                        (HAS-QUESTION
                            (ASRT-ANTEC DBASRT)))
                    (ASRT-NAME DBASRT)
                    (APPEND (ASRT-ANTEC DBASRT)
                            (CONS (LIST '$AND
                                        CONSEQ FLAG
                                        NAME)
                                  (CDR QLIST)))
                    RES)]))
               (COND [(EQL '$FAIL RES) RES]
                     [T ;; Success. Return new ALIST.
                      (RETURN RES)])])))])))])))

(DEFUN IS-INTERMEDIATE (PRED CONSEQ FLAG NAME ASRT)
   (AND (EQL (CAR PRED) (CAR CONSEQ))
        FLAG
        (EQL NAME (ASRT-NAME ASRT))))

(DEFUN HAS-QUESTION (ANTEC)
   (LET ((ASK (ASSOC 'ASK-USER ANTEC)))
      (NOT (NULL (ASSOC 'QUESTION (CDR ASK))))))

(DEFUN STORE-ASRT (ASRT)
   (LET ((CONSEQ (ASRT-CONSEQ ASRT)))
      (SETF (GET (CAR CONSEQ) 'ASRTS)
            (CONS ASRT (GET (CAR CONSEQ) 'ASRTS)))))
```

ASK-USER is the same as before, and the user response stored in the variable *ANS*
is available.

Exercise 6.8 We wish to provide an elaboration facility by which the user can see more
details regarding the question that has been asked. When the user says WHAT or ELAB-
ORATE, text regarding the predicate in the CONSEQ is presented after substituting
variables in it.

Select an appropriate representation for the same, and modify ASK-USER to handle it.

Exercise 6.9 Test your elaboration facility in the previous exercise by providing elaboration text for the predicates in Fig. 6-1.

Exercise 6.10 We wish to provide an explanation facility in the system. When the user says WHY or EXPLAIN in response to a question, the system displays the rule which has caused the question to be issued. The rule can be presented using an elaboration facility (see Exercise 6.8) for each of the formulas in the rules. When the user says WHY, the rule before the one displayed is shown.

Implement the above in a system in which you are manipulating the stack yourself. (See Exercise 6.4.)

6.2   COMPUTATIONAL PREDICATES AND FUNCTIONS

So far we have seen that to determine truth values of formulas we have to search in the database of assertions. In this section, we examine *computational* predicates that are "computed" (i.e., applied to their arguments like functions) to determine the truth value of the formula in which they occur.

As an example, consider the predicate $<$. The following are true:

```
(< 0 1)
(< 0 2)
(< 0 3)
     .
     .
     .
(< 1 2)
(< 1 3)
     .
     .
     .
```

But clearly, it is not possible to store all such facts. The solution is to compute and determine whether a formula involving $<$ is true.

A similar thing holds for the terms. The following two terms would be considered different by our system:

```
7
(+ 3 4)
```

This is because their structure is different and UNIFY does not recognize $+$ as a computational function. If we want the above two to be unified, we must recognize that $+$ is a function and apply it to its arguments before trying to unify them.

Predicates or functions which are applied to their arguments are said to be of computational type (as opposed to database type). Atomic formulas and terms involving them are called computational formulas and computational terms, respectively.

Exercise 6.11 The rules below allow the temperature to be input in Fahrenheit or centigrade scale depending on the user's choice. The value of ?T in the predicate TEMP-VALUE is in centigrade irrespective of what scale was used by the user.

```
(TEMPR-VALUE ?X ?T)
  <- (ASK-USER (SOURCE ?X)
               (TARGET ?U)
               (QUESTION DO YOU WANT TO ENTER
                  THE TEMPERATURE OF ?X IN CENTIGRADE OR
                  FAHRENHEIT))
     (ASK-USER (SOURCE ?X ?U)
               (TARGET ?VAL)
               (QUESTION WHAT IS THE
                  TEMPERATURE OF ?X IN ?U))
     (CONVERT-TO-CENTIGRADE ?VAL ?U ?T)
  (CONVERT-TO-CENTIGRADE ?VAL CENTIGRADE ?C)
     <- (= ?VAL ?C)
  (CONVERT-TO-CENTIGRADE ?VAL FAHRENHEIT ?C)
        <- (F-TO-C ?VAL ?C).
  (F-TO-C ?F ?C) <- (= ?C (* (/ 5 9) (- ?F 32))).
```

Extend the above so that the Reaumur scale is also included.

6.2.1   Computational Terms in Unification

First, let us look at a unification algorithm that handles *computational* functions occurring in terms. A function is considered computational if there is a lambda expression defined for it. FBOUNDP tests whether the symbol given to it has a function definition. A computational function can be applied to its arguments provided they have variable-free values (as defined for SOURCE variables in ASK-USER). The ultimate substitution and application of the computational function is accomplished by EVAL-TERM. (EVAL-TERM must evaluate the arguments of the term recursively, because they may be computational terms themselves.) It returns $FAIL-EVAL if it is unable to evaluate the term.

```
(DEFUN EVAL-TERM (EXPR ALIST)
;;; EXPR is possibly a computational term and ALIST the
;;; association list.
;;;  Apply the function in EXPR to the arguments in EXPR
;;; after substituting for variables, evaluating
;;; computational subterms if any, and checking that no
;;; variables remain in the arguments.
;;; Otherwise return $FAIL.
```

```
    (LET ((ARGS (EVAL-TERMS-LIST (CDR EXPR) ALIST)))
      (COND [(EQL '$FAIL-EVAL ARGS) '$FAIL-EVAL]
            [(FUNCP (CAR EXPR))
             (APPLY (CAR EXPR) ARGS)]
            [T (CONS (CAR EXPR) ARGS)])))

(DEFUN EVAL-TERMS-LIST (L ALIST)
;;; L is a list of terms and ALIST the association list.
;;; Each of the terms in L is evaluated and a list of the
;;; results is returned.
    (DO ((REM-L L (CDR REM-L))
         (VAL-LIST NIL (CONS VAL VAL-LIST))
         (VAL NIL))
        ((NULL REM-L) (NREVERSE VAL-LIST))
      (SETQ VAL
            (COND [(IS-VAR (CAR REM-L))
                   (SUBST-VARS-ULT (CAR REM-L) ALIST)]
                  [(ATOM (CAR REM-L)) (CAR REM-L)]
                  [T (EVAL-TERM (CAR REM-L) ALIST)]))
      (COND [(OR (EQL '$FAIL-EVAL VAL) (HAS-VAR VAL))
             (RETURN '$FAIL-EVAL)])))

(DEFUN FUNCP (S)
;;; Returns true if S is a function name.
  (AND (SYMBOLP S) (FBOUNDP S)))
```

UNIFY given below carries out the actual unification. Whenever any of the patterns PAT1 or PAT2 is a list, it is tested for a computational term. If yes, it is evaluated using EVAL-TERM, before proceeding with the unification. If EVAL-TERM returns failure (i.e., $FAIL-EVAL) or unification of the evaluated term fails, then unification is attempted without evaluating the computational term.

```
(DEFUN UNIFY (PAT1 PAT2 ALIST)
    (COND [(IS-VAR PAT1) (VAR-UNIFY PAT1 PAT2 ALIST)]
          [(IS-VAR PAT2) (VAR-UNIFY PAT2 PAT1 ALIST)]
          [(ATOM PAT1)
           (COND [(ATOM PAT2)
                  (COND [(EQL PAT1 PAT2) ALIST]
                        [T '$FAIL])]
                 [(FUNCP (CAR PAT2))
                  (COND [(EQL PAT1 (EVAL-TERM PAT2 ALIST))
                         ALIST]
                        [T '$FAIL])]
          [T ;; PAT2 is not an atom, nor does it
             ;; evaluate to an atom. Match not possible.
```

```lisp
                  '$FAIL])]
      [(ATOM PAT2) (UNIFY PAT2 PAT1 ALIST)]
      [T (UNIFY-EXPR PAT1 PAT2 ALIST)]))


(DEFUN UNIFY-EXPR (PAT1 PAT2 ALIST)
;;; PAT1 or PAT2 might be computational terms.
;;; Unify them after evaluating them using EVAL-TERM.
  (LET
      ((VAL1 (COND [(FUNCP (CAR PAT1))
                    (EVAL-TERM PAT1 ALIST)]
                   [T '$FAIL-EVAL]))
       (VAL2 (COND [(FUNCP (CAR PAT2))
                    (EVAL-TERM PAT2 ALIST)]
                   [T '$FAIL-EVAL])))
    (COND
      [(EQL '$FAIL-EVAL VAL1)
       ;; Unable to obtain value of PAT1.
       ;; Unify them as they are.
       (COND [(EQL '$FAIL-EVAL VAL2)
       ;;Unable to obtain value of PAT2
       (LET ((MLIST (UNIFY (CAR PAT1)
                           (CAR PAT2)
                           ALIST)))
          (COND [(EQL '$FAIL MLIST) '$FAIL]
                [T (UNIFY-LISTS (CDR PAT1)
                                (CDR PAT2)
                                MLIST)]))]
             [T (UNIFY PAT1 VAL2 ALIST)])]
      [(EQL '$FAIL-EVAL VAL2)
       (UNIFY VAL1 PAT2 ALIST)]
      [T (UNIFY VAL1 VAL2 ALIST)])))


(DEFUN UNIFY-LISTS (PAT1 PAT2 ALIST)
;;; PAT1 or PAT2 are lists of terms of arguments in a
;;;   computational term.
;;; Unify the respective terms in the lists.
    (COND [(IS-VAR PAT1) (VAR-UNIFY PAT1 PAT2 ALIST)]
          [(IS-VAR PAT2) (VAR-UNIFY PAT2 PAT1 ALIST)]
          [(AND (ATOM PAT1) (ATOM PAT2))
           (COND [(EQL PAT1 PAT2) ALIST] [T '$FAIL])]
          [(OR (ATOM PAT1) (ATOM PAT2)) '$FAIL]
          [T (LET ((NEWMLIST (UNIFY (CAR PAT1)
                                    (CAR PAT2)
                                    ALIST)))
               (COND [(EQL '$FAIL NEWMLIST) '$FAIL]
```

```
                    [T (UNIFY-LISTS (CDR PAT1)
                                    (CDR PAT2)
                                    NEWMLIST)])))]))


(DEFUN VAR-UNIFY (VAR PAT ALIST)
;;; If VAR is bound, its value is unified with PAT,
;;; else VAR is bound to PAT and the new ALIST returned.
  (LET ((BIND (ASSOC VAR ALIST)))
        (COND
           [(NULL BIND)
            (CONS
                (LIST VAR
                      (COND [(ATOM PAT) PAT]
                            [(FUNCP (CAR PAT))
                             (LET ([VAL (EVAL-TERM PAT ALIST)])
                                 (COND [(EQ '$FAIL VAL) PAT]
                                       [T VAL]))]
                            [T PAT]))
                ALIST)]
           [T (UNIFY (CADR BIND) PAT ALIST)])))
```

6.2.2   Computational Predicates in Inference

Now let us see how INFER-AND can be modified to deal with formulas involving
computational predicates. We assume that computational predicates will have the
function stored under the attribute COMPUTEPRED. Thus, for the predicate < we
will have

```
(SETF (GET '< 'COMPUTEPRED) #'<)
```

Whenever INFER-AND is called with a clause involving a computational predicate,
it should apply the function, rather than looking it up in the database. However, before
applying the function, it should first check that all the arguments have variable-free
values.[1] If any of the arguments does not have variable-free value, the formula cannot
be satisfied and INFER-AND should return $FAIL.

An equality predicate must be handled in a special way, however. When both
its arguments have variable-free values, they can be tested for equality as before. If,
on the other hand, the values contain variables, one need not give up. For example,
if

```
(= ?X 30)
```

---

[1] This restriction has been placed to keep the semantics simple. More work is needed to investigate the
relaxation on this condition. One area where such a relaxation should be permitted, for example, is when
the function is a constructor function.

is given to INFER-AND, it should return true with essentially ?X bound to 30 (if it is not already bound to something incompatible). This is accomplished by simply calling UNIFY. The new definition of INFER-AND is given below. (For the sake of uniformity, it assumes that ASK-USER and = are marked as computational predicates, since for them we need to perform some computations rather than looking them up in the database.)

```
(DEFUN INFER-AND (CONSEQ FLAG NAME QLIST ALIST)
  (DECLARE (SPECIAL *ANS*))
  (COND
      [(NULL QLIST) ... ]
      [(EQ '$AND (CAAR QLIST)) ... ]
      [T ;; Carry out the inference.
       (LET ((Q (CAR QLIST)) (RES NIL))
         (COND
            [(GET-COMPUTEPRED Q)
             ;; Nondatabase predicate encountered.
             (COND
             [(EQ 'ASK-USER (CAR Q)) ...] ;Same as in last section
             [(EQ '= (CAR Q))
              (SETQ RES (UNIFY (CADR Q) (CADDR Q) ALIST))]
             [T
              ;; Prepare to apply computational predicate.
              ;; Requires that computational terms be
              ;; evaluated first.
              (LET ((ARGS (EVAL-TERMS-LIST (CDR Q) ALIST)))
                (COND
                  [(HAS-VAR ARGS)
                   ;; A variable without a value in ARGS.
                   (SETQ RES '$FAIL)]
                  [T
                   ;; Apply the function.
                   (SETQ RES
                     (COND
                        [(NOT (FAIL-P (APPLY (GET-COMPUTEPRED
                                                        Q)
                                            ARGS)))
                         ALIST]
                        [T '$FAIL])))])))])
             ;; Continue inference with tail of QLIST.
             (COND [(OR (EQ '$FAIL RES)
                        (EQ '$FAIL-EVAL RES))
                    '$FAIL]
                   [T (INFER-AND CONSEQ FLAG NAME (CDR QLIST)
                                 RES)])])
```

```
[T ;; Search database of assertions to infer Q.
   ;; Same as earlier.
   ...]))
```

```
(DEFMACRO GET-COMPUTEPRED (Q)
 `(GET (CAR ,Q) 'COMPUTEPRED))
```

As an illustration of computational predicates, consider an example first introduced in Sec. 6.1. To determine whether the engine is running hot, it was left to the
judgment of the user whether the temperature of the coolant was high. With the avail-
ability of computational predicates, the user can be asked for the value of the temperature, and it can be computed whether it is high.

```
(ENGINE-HOT) <- (TEMPR COOLANT HIGH).                        (6.4)
(TEMPR COOLANT HIGH) <- (TEMPR-VALUE COOLANT ?Y)
                          (> ?Y 90).                          (6.5)
(TEMPR GEARBOX-OIL HIGH) <- (TEMPR-VALUE GEARBOX-OIL ?Y)
                              (> ?Y 70).                      (6.6)
(TEMPR-VALUE ?X ?Y)
   <- (ASK-USER (SOURCE ?X)
               (TARGET ?Y)
               (QUESTION WHAT IS THE
                         TEMPERATURE OF ?X IN
                         DEGREES CENTIGRADE)).                (6.7)
(TEMPR ?X ?Y)
   <- (ASK-USER (SOURCE ?X)
               (TARGET ?Y)
               (QUESTION IS THE TEMPERATURE OF ?X
                         HIGH NORMAL OR LOW)).                (6.8)
```

A few observations are in order about the above rules. Rule (6.5), when matched with
the goal, sets up two subgoals. The first subgoal causes rule (6.7) to fire which issues
a direct question to the user. If the user answers DONTKNOW (e.g., no temperature
gauge is available), rules (6.5) and (6.7) fail and the next rule which fires is (6.8).
Rule (6.8) is the same as the earlier rule (6.2) that asks the user whether the engine
is running hot and relies on the judgment of the user. Secondly, rules (6.5) and (6.6)
show that the temperature that is considered high depends upon the type of fluid
(coolant or gear-box oil) being considered.

> **Exercise 6.12** The use of computational terms or predicates is not without a price. Their
> use places restrictions on which arguments of a predicate or a function can be used as
> input and which as output. For example, the first rule below converts from Fahrenheit
> to centigrade, and the second one in the reverse direction.

```
(F-AND-C ?F ?C)
     <- (= ?X (- ?F 32)) (= ?C (* .555 ?X)).

(F-AND-C ?F ?C)
     <- (= ?X (* 1.8 ?C)) (= ?F (+ ?X 32)).
```

Moreover the antecedents are procedural. If the order of atomic formulas in the antecedent of any of the rules above is changed, it fails to work. What can be done to remove some of the above problems?

6.3 FUNCTIONAL DEPENDENCIES

Frequently, in the real world, values of some of the properties of objects are unique. For example, temperature of a fluid is unique, i.e., it has only one temperature at a given time (assuming uniform temperature). Logic programming introduced thus far does not allow us to express the above. For example, the assertion

```
(TEMPR-VALUE COOLANT 80)
```

states that a temperature of the coolant is 80°. By itself, it does not make any statement whether the coolant can have other temperatures at the same time. If the two assertions

```
(TEMPR-VALUE COOLANT 80)
(TEMPR-VALUE COOLANT 70)
```

are present in the database, the logic programming system does not complain.

The above notion can be captured by *functional dependencies* (FDs) on the arguments of predicates as follows: If we could assert, for example, that the first argument of TEMPR-VALUE functionally determines the second argument, then we would be assured that there cannot be two or more facts with the predicate TEMPR-VALUE having the same first argument but different second argument. Thus, the following would not be allowed to be present simultaneously.

```
(TEMPR-VALUE COOLANT 80)
(TEMPR-VALUE COOLANT 70)
```

(If the above were to be present in a set of assertions, it would be called an inconsistent set.)

If the arguments i_1 to i_k functionally determine the ith argument for a predicate P, it is written as

$$i_1, \ldots i_k \rightarrow i \text{ on } P$$

Now, if the following is in the database

$$(P\ y_1\ \ldots\ y_n)$$

where

$$(y_{i_1} = c_{i_1}, \dots y_{i_k} = c_{i_k}, y_i = c_i)$$

and the C_i's are constants, then the following holds:

```
not (P z₁ ... zₙ )
```

where

$$(z_{i_1} = c_{i_1}, \dots z_{i_k} = c_{i_k}, z_i \neq c_i)$$

As another example, suppose we have bottles containing chemical samples. Shelf number and bottle number uniquely identify a bottle. Chemicals in every bottle have a unique mass (obviously) and pH factor. Thus, the shelf number and bottle number functionally determine the mass and the pH factor. The predicate CHEMICAL is as follows:

```
(CHEMICAL <shelf-no> <bottle-no> <mass> <pH>)
```

Therefore, we have the following two dependencies:

```
1,2 -> 3      on CHEMICAL
1,2 -> 4      on CHEMICAL
```

In a short form, we will write them as

```
1,2 -> 3,4   on CHEMICAL
```

> **Exercise 6.13** In a zoo, elephants are uniquely identified by their name. Identify the FDs for the predicate ELEPHANT having weight, height, and foods liked.
>
> ```
> (ELEPHANT <name> <wt> <ht> <food>)
> ```

There are two advantages in declaring FDs on predicates in a database.

1. It allows inconsistencies to be detected as described earlier.
2. It can speed up inference. When we try to infer a goal and find an assertion that matches on the arguments that functionally determine some of the other arguments, and there is a disagreement on the dependent arguments, we say that a counter-example has been found. The goal fails and no further search is done in trying to infer it. FDs can also be used for intelligent backtracking.

> **Exercise 6.14** Write a program that when given a set of FDs and a database, finds if there are any inconsistencies.

Exercise 6.15 (Difficult) Implement FDs in INFER-AND. Choose an appropriate representation for storing the FDs and using them in inference.

Exercise 6.16 What is the effect of FDs on question rules? Suppose there is a predicate for which specified FDs match the SOURCE and TARGET variables in the ASK-USER in its question rule. What will be its effect? Discuss.

Exercise 6.17 Can you draw a similarity between "dontknow" information stored for a predicate and FDs for the predicate? Discuss.

6.4   AN EXAMPLE—EXPERT SYSTEM FOR HEAT EXCHANGERS

In this section, a fragment of rules from an expert system for the design of heat exchangers is described [Bhaskare (1986)]. The purpose is to show the user interaction, computational predicates and functions, and FDs all together. The particular expert system described here is used for the design of shell-and-tube–type heat exchangers. Such a heat exchanger has a shell in which is placed a tube bundle. (See Fig. 6-2.)

The two fluids between which the heat transfer has to take place flow in the shell and the tube, respectively. The system designs the heat exchanger depending on the inlet and outlet temperatures, mass-flow rates, specific heats, and other properties such as corrosiveness and fouling nature.

The rules given below select between the hot and the cold fluid to be on the tube side. Rule ST5 states that if the hot fluid is corrosive, make it tube-side fluid. Rule ST7 states a similar rule for a fouling hot fluid. If ST5 or ST7 are not able to select the tube-side fluid, ST9 selects based on the mass-flow rates.

```
;;;If the hot fluid named ?NAME-H is corrosive,
;;; make it the tube-side fluid.
ST5: (TUBE-SIDE-FLUID ?NAME-H)
        <- (FLUID-NAME HOT ?NAME-H) (CORROSIVE ?NAME-H).
```

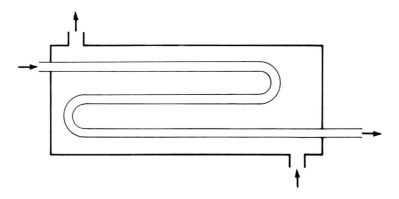

FIGURE 6-2

```
;;;If the hot fluid is fouling, make it the tube-side fluid.
ST7: (TUBE-SIDE-FLUID ?NAME-H)
       <- (FLUID-NAME HOT ?NAME-H) (FOULING ?NAME-H)

;;;If the hot fluid has a higher mass-flow rate than
;;; the cold fluid, make it the tube-side fluid.
ST9: (TUBE-SIDE-FLUID ?NAME-H)
       <- (FLUID-NAME HOT ?NAME-H)
          (FLUID-NAME COLD ?NAME-C)
          (MASS-FLOW-RATE-COLD ?NAME-C ?VAL1)
          (MASS-FLOW-RATE-HOT ?NAME-H ?VAL2)
          (> ?VAL2 ?VAL1).
;;; Opposite case of rule ST9.
ST10 (TUBE-SIDE-FLUID ?NAME-C)
       <- (FLUID-NAME HOT ?NAME-H)
          (FLUID-NAME COLD ?NAME-C)
          (MASS-FLOW-RATE-COLD ?NAME-C ?VAL1)
          (MASS-FLOW-RATE-HOT ?NAME-H ?VAL2)
          (>= ?VAL1 ?VAL2).
```

In trying to infer the antecedent formulas a number of questions are put to the user. They get issued when the following rules are invoked. STQ1 asks the user the name of the hot or the cold fluid, as the case may be. The other rules, similarly, are self-explanatory.

```
STQ1: (FLUID-NAME ?H-C ?FLUID)
       <- (ASK-USER (SOURCE ?H-C)
                    (TARGET ?FLUID)
                    (QUESTION WHAT IS THE NAME OF THE
                    ?H-C FLUID)).

STQ2: (FOULING ?FLUID)
       <- (ASK-USER (SOURCE ?FLUID)
                    (TARGET)
                    (QUESTION IS IT TRUE THAT ?FLUID
                              IS FOULING)).

STQ3: (CORROSIVE ?FLUID)
       <- (ASK-USER (SOURCE ?FLUID)
                    (TARGET)
                    (QUESTION IS IT TRUE THAT
                    ?FLUID IS CORROSIVE)).

;;;In the following rules, TYPES allows type checking
;;; to be performed.
```

```
STQ4: (MASS-FLOW-RATE-COLD ?FLUID ?VAL)
         <- (ASK-USER (SOURCE ?FLUID)
                      (TARGET ?VAL)
                      (QUESTION WHAT IS THE MASS FLOW
                              RATE OF ?FLUID IN KG/SEC)
                      (TYPES NUMBER)).

STQ5: (MASS-FLOW-RATE-HOT ?FLUID ?VAL)
         <- (ASK-USER (SOURCE ?FLUID)
                      (TARGET ?VAL)
                      (QUESTION WHAT IS THE MASS FLOW
                              RATE OF ?FLUID IN KG/SEC)
                      (TYPES NUMBER)).

STQ6: (INLET-TEMP ?FLUID ?T)
         <- (ASK-USER (SOURCE ?FLUID)
                      (TARGET ?T)
                      (QUESTION WHAT IS THE INLET TEMPERATURE
                              OF ?FLUID IN DEGREES CENTIGRADE)
                      (TYPES NUMBER)).

STQ7: (OUTLET-TEMP ?FLUID ?T)
         <- (ASK-USER (SOURCE ?FLUID)
                      (TARGET ?T)
                      (QUESTION WHAT IS THE OUTLET TEMPERATURE
                              OF ?FLUID IN DEGREES CENTIGRADE)
                      (TYPES NUMBER)).
```

Note that if the user answers DONTKNOW to corrosivity question STQ3, rule ST5 fails. However, there are still rules ST7, ST9, and ST10 that can help decide the tube-side fluid. On the other hand if the user does not know the names of the fluids, inference will not be able to continue.

The tree given in Fig. 6-3 shows how the rate of heat transfer (heat-rate) and log-mean-tempr-diff can be computed. A node with AND successors indicates that all of its successor nodes must be successful (i.e., have a value) for it to be successful. (# as before indicates that the user is asked for the value.) They are represented by the following rules:

```
ST22: (HEAT-RATE ?Q)
         <- (FLUID-NAME COLD-FLUID ?NAME-C)
            (MASS-FLOW-RATE-COLD ?NAME-C ?M-C)
            (SPECIFIC-HEAT ?NAME-C ?CP-C)
            (INLET-TEMP ?NAME-C ?TCI)
            (OUTLET-TEMP ?NAME-C ?TCO)
            (= ?Q (* ?M-C ?CP-C (- ?TCI ?TCO))).
```

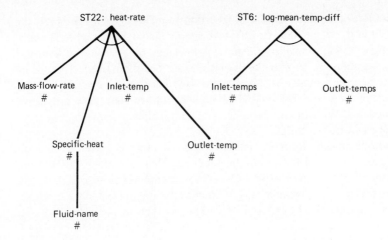

FIGURE 6-3

```
ST6: (LOG-MEAN-TEMP-DIFF ?X)
     <- (FLUID-NAME HOT-FLUID ?NAME-H)
        (FLUID-NAME COLD-FLUID ?NAME-C)
        (INLET-TEMP ?NAME-H ?THI)
        (INLET-TEMP ?NAME-C ?TCI)
        (OUTLET-TEMP ?NAME-H ?THO)
        (OUTLET-TEMP ?NAME-C ?TCO)
        (= ?X (* (- (- ?THI ?TCO)
                    (- ?THO ?TCI))
                 (LN (* (- ?THI ?CO)
                        (- ?THO ?TCI)))))).
```

Exercise 6.18 Develop a front end for the expert systems shell described in this chapter. Define a macro DEFASRT by which a user can define assertions. (They should be typed in a form similar to that shown in this section.) Similarly, the user should be able to assert that a predicate is of computational type, intermediate type, etc., and specify elaboration text. All this information should be readable from and writable to a file as well.

6.5   MODELING DYNAMIC SITUATIONS— BLOCKS WORLD

All the examples considered so far in this chapter have steady-state models. Whether we have dealt with automobile repair or heat-exchanger design, we have modeled them statically. The database of assertions does not model changes that take place as the engine starts or fluids flow. In fact, a static model involving steady-state temperatures (when the engine is running) and mass-flow rate of fluids, etc. is sufficient in the analysis and design. Thus, even though the real-world situations have been dynamic, we have used static models.

This is not to say that the database of assertions remains unchanged. Surely the database changes (e.g., when ASK-USER or an intermediate-type predicate is used), but it only changes to add previously unknown knowledge, not because of a change in the modeled situation. As a corollary, assertions are never removed. There is no need to, because in a static model what has been asserted continues to be true forever.

In this section, we take an example—blocks world—to show how a dynamic world can be modeled. We will only be concerned with maintaining the current state, however. History will not be stored.

Before introducing the example, let us look at two special predicates that are used for adding and removing facts from the database. They are called ASSERT and RETRACT, respectively. Each of them takes an atomic formula as its argument. The former adds it to the database, while the latter removes it if it is present in the database.

The blocks world consists of a set of labeled blocks lying on a table and possibly one over the other. The position and configuration of the blocks is known. There is a robot arm that can move the blocks.

The robot arm can perform three operations. It can open or close its gripper to grasp or ungrasp a block. It can also move to a desired position.

There are three special predicates called action predicates that relate to the actions of the robot arm:

```
(DO-GRIP)                Close the gripper.
(DO-UNGRIP)              Open the gripper.
(DO-MOVEHANDTO ?P)       Move the hand to position ?P.
```

Determining the truth value of these predicates causes the robot arm to be actuated.

Appropriate predicates have to be found to model the state as well as actions in the blocks world. Let us model the state by the following predicates:

```
(POS ?X ?P)     True if block ?X is at position ?P.
(ON ?X ?Y)      True if block ?X is on block ?Y.
(CLEAR ?X)      True if there is nothing on top of block ?X.
(HANDEMPTY)     True if the hand is empty.
```

Let the actions be modeled by the predicates given below. These actions not only cause operation of the arm but also manipulate the database.

```
(DO-PLACE ?X ?P)     Place block ?X at position ?P.
(DO-GRASP ?X)        Grasp block ?X.
(DO-UNSTACK ?X)      Remove block ?X from over some
                     block and place it on the table.
```

There is a computational predicate NEQ and a computational function FIND-EMPTYPOS. The former is true if its two arguments are different; the latter returns the position of an empty space when called.

Our knowledge base consists of seven rules followed by nine facts.

```
S1: (POS ?X ?P) <- (NEQ ?X HAND) (DO-PLACE ?X ?P)
     ;; Position of the block ?X is ?P, if it
     ;; is placed at ?P.

S2: (DO-PLACE ?X ?P) <- (POS ?X ?OLD) (DO-GRASP ?X)
                        (POS HAND ?P) (DO-UNGRIP)
                        (RETRACT (POS ?X ?OLD))
                        (ASSERT (POS ?X ?P)).
     ;; A block ?X is placed at position ?P
     ;; if it is grasped by hand. The
     ;; position of the hand is changed to ?P, and
     ;; it is released.

S3: (DO-GRASP ?X) <- (CLEAR ?X) (HANDEMPTY) (POS ?X ?P)
                     (POS HAND ?P) (DO-GRIP)
                     (RETRACT (HANDEMPTY)).
     ;; A block ?X is grasped if there is
     ;; nothing over ?X. The position of hand and
     ;; the block is the same, and it is
     ;; gripped.

S4: (POS HAND ?P) <- (POS HAND ?OLD) (DO-MOVEHANDTO ?P)
                     (RETRACT (POS HAND ?OLD)).
     ;; Hand is at position ?P if it is
     ;; moved to it from somewhere.

S5: (CLEAR ?X) <- (ON ?Y ?X) (DO-UNSTACK ?Y)
                  (RETRACT (ON ?Y ?X)).
     ;; Block ?X is clear if block ?Y on
     ;; ?X is removed.

S6: (DO-UNSTACK ?Y) <- (POS ?Y ?P) (= ?Q (FINDEMPTYPOS))
                       (DO-PLACE ?Y ?Q).
     ;; A block ?Y is unstacked if it is
     ;; placed somewhere else on the table.

S7: (HANDEMPTY) <- (= ?Q (FINDEMPTYPOS)) (POS HAND ?Q)
                   (DO-UNGRIP).
     ;; To make the hand empty, find a vacant spot and
     ;; place whatever hand is holding there.
```

The retract predicate used in rules S3 and S7 removes the specified fact from the database. The assert predicate is not used because the state predicates (POS, ON, CLEAR, and HANDEMPTY) are of intermediate type. Whenever a goal or a subgoal containing them is satisfied, it is automatically asserted.

```
G1: (POS A J).    ; Block A is at position J.
G2: (POS B K).
G3: (POS C L).
G4: (ON A B).     ; Block A is on block B.
G5: (ON B C).
G6: (ON C D).
G7: (CLEAR A).    ; Block A does not have anything over it.
G8: (POS HAND M).; HAND is positioned at M.
G9: (HANDEMPTY). ; HAND is empty.
(DEFUN FINDEMPTYPOS () (GENSYM))
```

Exercise 6.19 Introduce an actual coordinate system in the above example. So far only atoms P, Q, etc. have been used. (*Note*: Two blocks one of which is over the other have the same x and y coordinates.)

Exercise 6.20 Introduce shapes and refer to blocks by their shapes. Also introduce rules about balancing (e.g., a spherical or conical block cannot be below another block.)

Exercise 6.21 Assume there are two robot arms. Introduce rules for them.

There is a major disadvantage with ASSERT and RETRACT: Backtracking is lost. When backtracking occurs over a rule containing ASSERT or RETRACT, the changes made to the database by them are not undone.

If history has to be maintained, ASSERT and RETRACT are not used. Instead, an additional argument representing the state must be introduced in each of the predicates. Thus, for example, POS will now be a three-place predicate:

```
(POS <block> <position> <state>)
```

An action causes a change in the state. Thus, if a block B at position P1 in state S1 is moved to position P2, a new state results. It could be written as follows:

```
(POS B P2 (DO (MOVE B P1 P2) S1))
```

In fact, we could write a general rule:

This approach turns out to be extremely expensive in terms of time as well as in terms of space. The major cause of the inefficiency is the frame axioms which assert that when we get a new state as a result of an action on an object, the other objects are not affected. A frame axiom corresponding to the above action is as follows:

```
(POS ?C ?R (DO (MOVE ?B ?Q ?P) ?S))
        <- (NEQ ?C ?B) (POS ?C ?R ?S)
```

It asserts that if a block ?B is moved resulting in a new position for it in a new state, then block ?C maintains its old position in the new state (provided ?C is not ?B).

Exercise 6.22 How will you implement ASSERT and RETRACT in the shell? (*Hint*: Any variable in their argument formula must be substituted if possible before performing the operation.)

Exercise 6.23 PROLOG has ASSERTA and ASSERTZ that add at the beginning and the end of the database, respectively. Similarly there are RETRACTA and RETRACTZ. Implement them here.

Exercise 6.24 (Difficult) Change the implementation so that on backtracking, changes made by ASSERTA, ASSERTZ, RETRACTA, and RETRACTZ are undone. (*Hint*: Note that RETRACT removes an assertion only if it is present.)

Exercise 6.25 Maintain a history for the blocks world described here. (*Hint*: Incorporate the actions in a state by including them as part of the state terms. They will no longer be predicates.)

FURTHER READINGS

Read about the details of some specific expert systems. For example, for an expert system based on logic programming that designs heat exchangers see Srinivas (1987), Bhaskare (1986), and Kumar (1986). MYCIN, an expert system regarding diagnosis and therapy of bacterial infections, is described in Shortliff (1976). For a short, readable introduction on expert systems see Sell (1985).

The shell described here together with various extensions in the exercises is a system called VIDHI [Sangal (1986)].

Functional dependencies in the context of relational databases are described in most books on databases. See for example Date (1986) and Ullman (1983). To incorporate functional dependencies in INFER-AND see Dashora (1988) and Dashora et al. (1988).

The blocks world example with state and frame axioms is described in Mukherjee (1988). It also contains the design of a temporal logic programming system in which frame axioms do not cause any extra computation.

CHAPTER
7

PRODUCTION SYSTEMS

There is another rule-based scheme that is quite popular. It is called a production system. A rule or a *production* consists of an antecedent and a consequent, similar to before. The rules are also said to be of *situation-action* (or if-then) type because the antecedent represents situations or conditions and the consequent represents actions. Usually, the productions are applied in the forward direction in which the conditions in the antecedent of a rule are matched against a global database (similar to facts), and on success, actions in the consequent are executed which alter the database. This process goes on until either the desired goal facts are obtained or no rule is applicable.

There are many variations on the basic scheme above. Here, we will study the basic scheme in detail. Some of the variations will be discussed at the end of the chapter.

While discussing the implementation, two general ideas will be described. The first one pertains to a state-restoring mechanism that undoes changes made to the database. It can be generalized to other situations where changes have to be undone. The second one pertains to discrimination nets, a data structure that is efficient for partial matches. Such a net could also have been used in VIDHI for a faster matcher.

7.1   PRODUCTION SYSTEMS

A production system consists of three components:

1. A global database
2. A set of production rules
3. A control system

150

The *global database* is a central data structure used to store the relevant information (facts) regarding the problem being solved. The complexity of the data structure is dependent on the problem. It could be an array (e.g., if the four-queens problem is being solved), or it could be a larger, complex structure (e.g., if a heat exchanger is being designed). Making a correct choice is extremely important for efficiency.

A *production rule* has an antecedent and a consequent. The antecedent contains conditions, and the consequent contains actions. A rule is *satisfied* (or is *applicable*) if all the antecedent's conditions match structures in the global database. When a rule is *applied* (or *fired*), actions in its consequent are carried out. These change the database. Rules are independent of each other, and the only method by which they communicate is the global database.

The *control system* manages the firing of rules. It has to decide which of the rules are applicable. It selects one of them (called *conflict resolution*) and fires it. Finally, it has to check whether the goal has been reached, in which case it returns the sequence of rule applications that led to it. Also if no rule is applicable and the goal is not reached, that is, a *dead end* has been reached, it must recognize this and take appropriate action. Resolving conflict among applicable rules and dealing with dead ends constitute the major part of what is called the control strategy.

Conflict resolution is done by means of heuristics that are special to the problem at hand. There are two major kinds of control strategies: irrevocable and tentative. In the *irrevocable* strategy once a conflict is resolved and the selected rule fired, the other choices are not available. If the fired rule leads us to a dead end, we fail. In the *tentative* strategy, even if a rule is selected out of the conflict set and fired, it is possible to try other rules in the conflict set on the same global database. Thus, if a dead end is reached, the system tries to select some other rule at the earlier state and apply it. The tentative strategy can be implemented by backtracking wherein the global database is restored to its original state for trying out the other rules, or by means of a best-first search wherein multiple states of the global database are maintained and the most promising state explored further. (See Chap. 3 for details on different kinds of search.)

Normally, the irrevocable strategy can be used in three situations only:

1. When our conflict resolution strategy is perfect and is guaranteed to select the best rule (e.g., eight-puzzle)
2. When the firing of the selected rule leaves the applicability of the remaining rules untouched (e.g., rules carrying out type inheritance for a set of types)
3. When the task at hand is so hopelessly complex that the resources at hand simply do not permit a revocable strategy (e.g., opening move in a chess game)

Needless to say, when any of the above occurs, irrevocable strategy should be adopted for efficiency.

Whether an irrevocable or tentative strategy is used, there is, at times, a need to detect cycles in rule application. A *cycle* occurs when firing a rule makes the global database what it was at an earlier stage. On detection of a cycle in the tentative strategy, it should be treated just like a dead end. Therefore, an alternative rule must be fired in an appropriate state. Cycle detection can be expensive.

Consider the blocks world as an example of production systems. Some labeled blocks are lying on the table in some configuration. We have a set of rules that cause the blocks to be moved around. The global database consists of a set of items expressing relationships among the blocks (much like the atomic formulas in the last chapter). For example, if A is on B, B is on C, etc. we have the situation shown in Fig. 7-1.

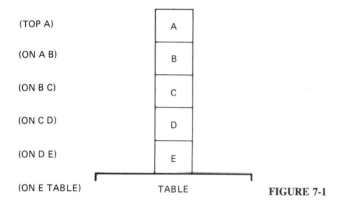

(TOP A)	A
(ON A B)	B
(ON B C)	C
(ON C D)	D
(ON D E)	E
(ON E TABLE)	TABLE

FIGURE 7-1

A rule which causes a set of stacked blocks to be unstacked looks as follows:

```
(UNSTACK ?X ?Y) (TOP ?X) (ON ?X ?Z)
    -> (ON ?X TABLE) (TOP ?X) (TOP ?Z) (UNSTACK ?Z ?Y)
```

It says that if blocks starting from ?X to ?Y have to be unstacked, ?X is on top, and ?X is on ?Z, then on moving ?X to the table, ?Z becomes the top and now ?Z to ?Y have to be unstacked. Whenever the antecedent (or left-hand side) of a rule matches the global database, the matched items are deleted from the database, and the consequent (or right-hand side) is added to the global database.

Now if we want to unstack blocks A to C, we include

```
(UNSTACK    A    C)
```

in the global database and provide the goal

```
(TOP    C)
```

to the production system. As we can see, the above rule will be applied twice resulting in A and B being placed on the table and the goal being reached. The following shows the state of the database while the rules are being applied (where the items that match the antecedent and the ones produced by the consequent are underlined):

```
(TOP A) (ON A B) (ON B C)..(ON E TABLE) (UNSTACK A C)
        ↓  rule application
(ON A TABLE) (TOP A) (TOP B) (ON B C)..(ON E TABLE) (UNSTACK B C)

(ON A TABLE) (TOP A) (TOP B) (ON B C)..(ON E TABLE) (UNSTACK B C)
                     ↓  rule application
(ON A TABLE) (TOP A) (ON B TABLE) (TOP B) (TOP C) (ON C D)..
(ON E TABLE) (UNSTACK B C)
```

As another example, let us consider a production system that follows a tentative control strategy using backtracking. Cycles are not detected because the nature of rules is such that we are guaranteed to be free of cycles.

The task at hand is to accept sentences belonging to a (trivial) subset of English given its grammar. The *terminal* symbols of the grammar are

```
RAM   SCHOOL   LAUGHED   WENT THE   A   TO AT
```

The *nonterminals* are

```
S   NP   VP   N   V   DET   PREP
```

(standing for, respectively, sentence, noun phrase, verb phrase, noun, verb, determiner, and preposition). The last four of the nonterminals are special in that they match a single terminal symbol each. They are also called *lexical categories* or preterminals. They must match exactly one terminal. Each of the first three nonterminals may match zero or more terminal symbols.

Suppose we have the following context-free grammar for our subset of English (with arrows reversed compared to the usual notation):

```
NP VP       -> S                                            (7.1a)
DET N       -> NP                                           (7.2a)
N           -> NP                                           (7.3a)
V PREP NP   -> VP                                           (7.4a)
V           -> VP                                           (7.5a)
```

The left-hand side is a list of nonterminals indicating the order in which they should be present in the sentence. The right-hand side, or the consequent, is a single nonterminal which should replace the matched nonterminals. The first rule says that if NP is followed by VP, then they can be combined yielding S, and so on.

Since our production system operates on sets of items where there is no implied order, the position of nonterminals with respect to the sentence must be suitably encoded. Here are our production rules with the encoding.

```
(?I NP ?J) (?J VP ?K) (FULLSTOP ?K) -> (?I S ?K)      (7.1b)
(?I DET ?J) (?J N ?K)              -> (?I NP ?K)        (7.2b)
(?I N ?J)                          -> (?I NP ?J)        (7.3b)
(?I V ?J) (?J PREP ?K) (?K NP ?L)  -> (?I VP ?K)        (7.4b)
(?I V ?J)                          -> (?I VP ?J)        (7.5b)
```

The first rule says that if ?I to (?J - 1) words in the sentence constitute NP, and ?J to (?K − 1) constitute VP, and the sentence has (?K − 1) words, then replace these items with S covering from ?I to (?K − 1) words.

For the lexical categories we have

```
(?I RAM ?J)     -> (?I N ?J)
(?I SCHOOL ?J)  -> (?I N ?J)
(?I LAUGHED ?J) -> (?I V ?J)
(?I WENT ?J)    -> (?I V ?J)
(?I THE ?J)     -> (?I DET ?J)
(?I A ?J)       -> (?I DET ?J)
(?I TO ?J)      -> (?I PREP ?J)
(?I AT ?J)      -> (?I PREP ?J)
```

These could also have been made part of a dictionary rather than part of rules.

The initial global database is a set of items representing the sentence to be recognized (i.e., a list of words or terminal symbols enclosed by their positions). Our system follows the heuristic which says: Choose a rule for lexical category, if one is applicable; otherwise choose an applicable rule out of the remaining. Let us now examine an example sentence: Ram went to school. A trace of changing global database is shown as the rules are applied.

```
(1 RAM 2) (2 WENT 3)(3 TO 4) (4 SCHOOL 5) (FULLSTOP 5)
      .
      .
      .
      ↓
(1 N 2) (2 V 3) (3 PREP 4) (4 N 5) (FULLSTOP 5)
   ↓   rule (7.3)
(1 NP 2) (2 V 3) (3 PREP 4) (4 N 5) (FULLSTOP 5)
   ↓   rule (7.3)
(1 NP 2) (2 V 3) (3 PREP 4) (4 NP 5) (FULLSTOP 5)
   ↓   rule (7.4)
(1 NP 2) (2 VP 5) (FULLSTOP 5)
   ↓   rule (7.1)
(1 S 5)
```

Note in the above that if instead of rule (7.4), rule (7.5) was applied, we would have reached a dead end and would have been forced to backtrack.

Exercise 7.1 In the blocks world described earlier, suppose we want to reverse a stack as shown in Fig. 7-2. Define a set of rules which cause the reversal shown in the figure to take place. [*Hint*: An item of the form (REVERSE A E) in the database should start the reversal.]

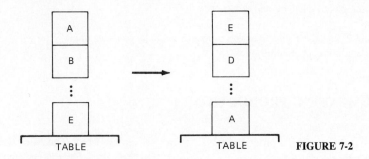

FIGURE 7-2

Exercise 7.2 Again in the blocks world we want to unstack a set of blocks but not necessarily beginning from the top. The stack should be changed such that the specified blocks are removed from the stack leaving others unchanged. (See Fig. 7-3.) Define an appropriate set of rules.

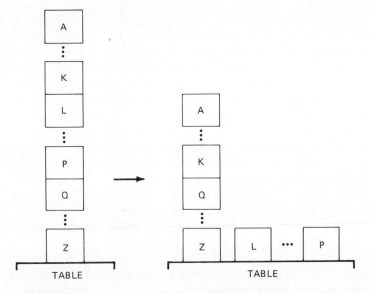

FIGURE 7-3

Exercise 7.3 Take the blocks world example in Sec. 6.5 and solve it using production systems.

Exercise 7.4 For the eight-puzzle, select a representation for the global database and write the production rules. What control strategy will you follow for solving it?

Exercise 7.5 Solve the four-queens problem using production systems. (For details of the four-queens problem see Sec. 3.1.2.)

Exercise 7.6 In the language example discussed here, suppose we were interested in the parse structure and not just recognition of a sentence. What changes would need to be made to the global database and the rules?

Exercise 7.7 Introduce adjectives and pronouns in the language example. You will have to define additional production rules.

7.2 IMPLEMENTING PRODUCTION SYSTEMS

Let us now discuss how such a production system can be implemented. The rules will be matched in the order in which they are specified. The first rule that matches will be applied, which is a simple method of conflict resolution. The system will, however, follow a tentative regime which will be implemented by backtracking.

7.2.1 Representation for the Database and Rules

As usual, the first task is to select a data structure. Let an item be represented by the corresponding list object, and the global database by a list of items. Thus, the following will be the representation for the global database of the blocks world discussed in the last section:

```
((ON A B) (ON B C) (ON C D) (ON D E) (UNSTACK A C))
```

In the next section, we will consider a more efficient representation.

We will represent a rule by the same structure as the one used for representing assertions in logic programming:

```
(DEFSTRUCT   (ASRT   (:CONSTRUCTOR   MAKE-ASRT
                        (CONSEQ   ANTEC   NAME)))
          CONSEQ   ANTEC   NAME)
```

The set of rules will simply be a list of such structures. Thus, the following will generate a list of one rule for the blocks world:

```
(LIST   (MAKE-ASRT
          '((ON ?X TABLE) (TOP ?X) (TOP ?Z)
            (UNSTACK ?Z ?Y))
          '((UNSTACK ?X ?Y) (TOP ?X)
            (ON ?X ?Z))
          'BW1))
```

7.2.2 State-Restoring Mechanism—Transition-Saving Approach

We have to implement the tentative control strategy using backtracking. In other words, when a rule that is selected and applied fails to lead to the goal, the global database must be restored and a new rule tried, if possible. All this needs a mechanism by which the state of the global database can be restored. This is the subject matter of this section.

There are two basic methods for restoring the state. One is based on the state-saving approach and the other on the transition-saving approach. In the state-saving approach, a copy is made of the state and saved on a history stack. In case backtracking occurs, the state is restored from the stack. This can be expensive if the state contains a large amount of information.

In the transition-saving approach, just the information needed to undo the change is saved, which means the following:

1. In case of destructive changes to the list structure, the position in the list structure and the old value in that position is saved.
2. In case of assignment to a variable, the name and the old value of the variable is saved.

The implementation in this section is based on the transition-saving approach.

In our implementation, we have to take care of only the destructive changes to the list structure, because no assignment is made to any LISP variable. A nonnull list of items represents the global database. When a rule is applied, some of the items are deleted and new ones are added. How should these be undone if necessary? The answer is actually not very difficult. We will record the cons cells that undergo a change together with the old information in them. Later the information can be restored if necessary.

To delete a set of items from the global database, we will replace the items by NIL. The length of the list will remain the same except some of the items would have been replaced by NILs. The replaced items along with their positions in the list will be saved on a stack.

Let us do the above as a two-step process. In the first step, a list (called a mark list) of positions and items to be deleted is made. Next, the NILs are put instead of the items (that are to be deleted). The mark list can then be put on the stack. For example, if (ON A B) and (UNSTACK A C) have to be deleted from

```
((ON   A   B)   (ON   B   C)   (UNSTACK   A   C))
```

which is represented as shown in Fig. 7-4, then we will form a mark list of the form

```
((p   (ON   A   B))   (r   (UNSTACK   A   C)))
```

Next, NILs will be put in the CARs of *p* and *r*, resulting in

```
(NIL   (ON   B   C)   NIL)
```

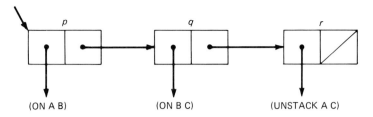

FIGURE 7-4

The implementation below uses a free variable called *MARKED-ITEMS* to store the mark list. It is a special variable in LISP. Every time a cons cell is to be placed in the mark list, MARK-DB is called which places it on *MARKED-ITEMS*. DEL-MARKED-ITEMS is called with the mark list to actually replace the items by NILs.

```
(DEFUN MARK-DB (DBPOS)
;;; Put the cons cell DBPOS and its CAR
;;; in the list *MARKED-ITEMS*.
    (DECLARE (SPECIAL *MARKED-ITEMS*))
    (PUSH (LIST DBPOS (CAR DBPOS)) *MARKED-ITEMS*))

(DEFUN DEL-MARKED-ITEMS (L)
;;; L is a list of pairs: (<DB position> <item>).
;;; For each pair in L delete the database item
;;; by changing its head to NIL.
    (COND [(NULL L) T]
          [T (SETF (CAAAR L) NIL)
             (DEL-MARKED-ITEMS (CDR L))]))
```

Undoing the deletion is easy, given the mark list. Simply take the items from the pairs and put them in the CARs of the cons cells (in the pairs) as shown below.

```
(DEFUN UNDEL-MARKED-ITEMS (L)
;;; L is a list of pairs: (<DB position> <item>).
;;; For each pair, make <item> the head of <DB position>.
    (COND [(NULL L) T]
          [T (SETF (CAAAR L) (CADAR L))
             (UNDEL-MARKED-ITEMS (CDR L))]))
```

To add new items at the front of a list a similar strategy is followed. It is best illustrated by an example. Suppose we have to add

```
((TOP  B)  (ON  A  TABLE)  (TOP  A))
```

which is represented as shown in Fig. 7-5, to the database

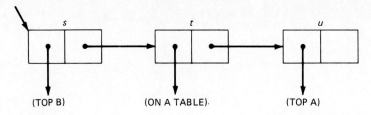

(TOP B)　　　　　(ON A TABLE).　　　　(TOP A)

FIGURE 7-5

```
(NIL  (ON  B  C)  NIL)
```

which is represented as shown in Fig. 7-6. We will make suitable changes resulting in the list

```
((TOP  B)  (ON  A  TABLE)  (TOP  A)  NIL  (ON  B  C)  NIL)
```

which is represented as shown in Fig. 7-7. An important point to note is that p continues to be the first cons cell of the list. g, h, and i are the new cons cells. The old item in p is copied into i, and the new items are stored in p, g, and h resulting in a database that contains new items at the beginning. All this is accomplished by ADD-ITEMS. UNADD-ITEMS undoes the above and restores the earlier database.

```
(DEFUN ADD-ITEMS (DB L)
;;; See description in text above.
  (LET ((TEMP (CONS (CAR DB) (CDR DB))))
    (SETF (CDR DB) (APPEND (CDR L) TEMP))
    (SETF (CAR DB) (CAR L))
    DB))
(DEFUN UNADD-ITEMS (DB L)
  (LET ((TEMP (NTHCDR (LENGTH L) DB)))
    (SETF (CAR DB) (CAR TEMP))
    (SETF (CDR DB) (CDR TEMP))
    DB))
```

Exercise 7.8 Define ADD-ITEMS and UNADD-ITEMS that add or remove new items at the end of the database list.

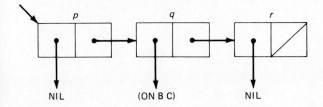

NIL　　　　　(ON B C)　　　　NIL

FIGURE 7-6

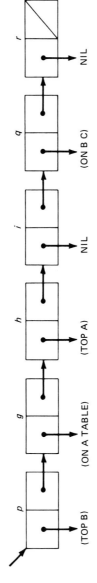

FIGURE 7-7

Exercise 7.9 Suppose we were permitted to destructively change the argument list (containing items to be added to the database). Redefine ADD-ITEMS and UNADD-ITEMS so that a more efficient version results.

Exercise 7.10 In deletion of items in the database, lots of NILs might lie around slowing down the search. Can you think of a more efficient implementation?

Exercise 7.11 Implement deletion of items without using free variables.

7.2.3   Application of Rules

Now that we have the machinery for restoring states, we can move over to the rule applier. The rule applier is implemented by APPLYRULE. It takes as its arguments the global database and the rule to be applied. It tries to apply the rule; it returns NIL if unsuccessful and T if successful. In the latter case, the database is changed and the transition is pushed on the history stack (bound to *HISTORY*).

APPLYRULE calls MATCH-ANTEC to match the antecedent of the rule with the global database. It returns the association list if successful and $FAIL if not (consistent with earlier matchers). In the former case, *MARKED-ITEMS* is bound to the mark list as a side effect. Now, if the match succeeds, APPLYRULE deletes marked items from the database, substitutes the associations into the consequent of the rule, and adds them to the database. The mark list, the add list, and the rule are pushed onto *HISTORY*.

```
(DEFUN APPLYRULE (DB RULE)
;;; See the description in text above.
  (DECLARE (SPECIAL *MARKED-ITEMS* *HISTORY*))
  (LET ((NEW-ALIST (MATCH-ANTEC DB (ASRT-ANTEC RULE)
                                   NIL)))
     (COND [(FAIL-P NEW-ALIST) NIL]
           [T (LET ((ITEMS (SUBST-VARS (ASRT-CONSEQ RULE)
                                          NEW-ALIST)))
                 (PUSH (LIST *MARKED-ITEMS* ITEMS RULE)
                       *HISTORY*)
                 (DEL-MARKED-ITEMS *MARKED-ITEMS*)
                 (ADD-ITEMS DB ITEMS)
                 T)])))


(DEFUN MATCH-ANTEC (DB ANTEC ALIST)
  (COND
        [(NULL DB) '$FAIL]
        [(NULL ANTEC) ALIST]
        [T ;; Match (CAR ANTEC) then continue.
          (DO ((DBREM DB (CDR DBREM)))
              ((NULL DBREM) '$FAIL)
```

```
(LET ((NEW-ALIST (MATCH2 (CAR ANTEC)
                         (CAR DBREM)
                         ALIST)))
  (COND [(FAIL-P NEW-ALIST)
         ;; Do nothing. Will loop.
         ]
        [T (LET ((FINAL-ALIST (MATCH-ANTEC DB
                                (CDR ANTEC)
                                NEW-ALIST)))
             (COND [(FAIL-P FINAL-ALIST)
                    ;; Do nothing. Will loop.
                    ]
                   [T ;; All antecedents matched.
                    (MARK-DB DBREM)
                    (RETURN FINAL-ALIST)]))]))
)]))
```

7.2.4 The Control

PRODSYS given below implements our control strategy. It takes the global database,
a list of rules, and the goal item, and tries the rules one by one until a rule succeeds.
It repeats the above process until a goal or a dead end is reached. In the former case,
the *HISTORY* stack contains the list of rules that got applied in reverse order (i.e.,
first rule at the bottom of the stack). In the latter case, it undoes the changes to the
database by calling UNDO to restore the state (using the mechanism described in the
last section) and continues to try the remaining rules in that state.

```
(DEFVAR *DBRULES* ...) ;Global database of rules

(DEFUN PRODSYS (DB RULES GOAL)
;;; Returns T if successful in reaching goal. Also the
;;; database DB gets modified.
;;; Otherwise returns NIL, and DB remains unchanged.
  (DECLARE (SPECIAL *MARKED-ITEMS*))
  (COND
    [(MEMBER GOAL DB :TEST #'EQUAL) T]
    [(NULL RULES) NIL]
    [T (LET ((RES (LET ((*MARKED-ITEMS* NIL))
                    (APPLYRULE DB (CAR RULES)))))
         (COND [(FAIL-P RES)
                ;; First rule in RULES fails to apply,
                ;; try remaining.
                (PRODSYS DB (CDR RULES) GOAL)]
               [T ;; Continue from new DB.
                (LET ((X (PRODSYS DB *DBRULES* GOAL)))
```

```
(COND [X ;; Reached goal.
       T]
      [T ;; Failed to reach goal.
       (UNDO DB)
       (PRODSYS
          DB (CDR RULES) GOAL)
      ])])])

(DEFUN UNDO (DB)
  (DECLARE (SPECIAL *HISTORY*))
  (COND [(NULL *HISTORY*) NIL]
        [T (LET* ((X (POP *HISTORY*))
                  (DELETED (CAR X))
                  (ADDED (CADR X)))
             (UNADD-ITEMS DB ADDED)
             (UNDEL-MARKED-ITEMS DELETED))]))
```

Exercise 7.12 Design an interface that allows the user to control the application of rules interactively. In particular the interface should allow single stepping (application of a single rule) and undoing of the last rule.

Exercise 7.13 Implement another control strategy, say best-first search, in PRODSYS. How will you tackle multiple states (i.e., one for each node in OPEN list as discussed in Chap. 3)?

7.3 DISCRIMINATION NETS OR TRIES

In the implementation just described, there is a source of great inefficiency. To match each of the items in the antecedent of a rule, we have to traverse a list of items matching each item with the database as we go. This is inefficient for two reasons. First, a list has to be traversed linearly. Second, matching each item is an independent process, and a partial match with one item does not help the matching of another item.

In Chap. 6 on expert systems shells, we saw how the search could be reduced by the use of property lists. But the second problem was not addressed there either. In this section we will introduce a data structure that will address both issues at the same time. This data structure is called the *discrimination net*.

To understand the basic idea behind discrimination nets, let us take the example of trees first. In a tree, the data is stored in the nodes in such a way that if data being searched (call it search key or search item) is not present in the node, it is possible to decide in what child subtree it might be present, and, therefore, the search is reduced to that subtree only. A *discrimination trie* (or just *trie*) is similar, but with one difference: In a tree, the keys or items are wholly contained in a node, while in a trie only parts of the item are stored in a node. The whole item is implicit in the path that is traversed in the trie. The consequence of this is that to decide what child subtrie to follow while searching for an item, only a part of the search item needs to be considered.

Let us take an example to illustrate the difference between the two. Let there be a database of the following items:

```
(OVER A B)
(OVER A C)
(OVER A D)
(OVER B C)
(OVER A)          ; to indicate A is at the top
(UNSTACK A C)
```

Figure 7-8 shows a tree representation (where the items are ordered lexicographically over lists). The trie representation for the same database is shown in Fig. 7-9 (where * indicates the existence of the item). Note that * could be at a nonleaf node as well. In general, instead of just a * we could associate useful information with the item.

Now, given a search item, say (OVER A C), and the tree data structure, the comparison test is expensive because the item at the node has to be compared (or matched) with the search item every time. In contrast to this, in a trie structure at each node we will only be comparing part of the item. Thus, the search (or match) will be faster. Trie might also take less memory if many items share prefixes.

The discrimination net is a generalization of a discrimination trie when it is a network instead of just a tree. In a net, two nodes might have a common child node.

Let us now turn our attention to the implementation. The following is a representation of the trie node:

```
(DEFSTRUCT (TRIE (:CONSTRUCTOR MAKE-TRIE
                                 (SUBKEY ENTRY SONS)))
           SUBKEY ENTRY SONS)
```

It has three parts, a subkey (which leads to the current trie node from its parent), an entry (which is NIL if this is not a database item, and * or the item itself otherwise), and a list of sons (each of which is a trie node). The following would be the rep-

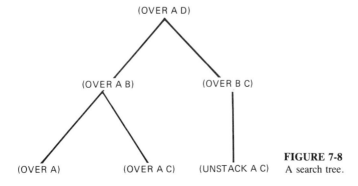

FIGURE 7-8
A search tree.

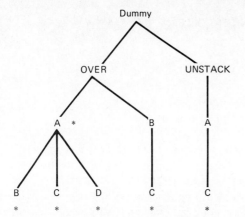

FIGURE 7-9
A discrimination trie.

resentation of the example database [square brackets have been shown instead of #S(...) for the trie nodes for readability].

```
[DUMMY ()
    ([OVER       ()   ([A    *    ([B    *    ()]
                                   [C    *    ()]
                                   [D    *    ()])]
                 [B    ()  ([C    *    ()])])]
     [UNSTACK ()  (  [A    ()  ([C    *    ()])])])]
```

Let us now define two basic functions: SEARCH-TRIE-NODE and INSERT-TRIE. The former takes an item and a trie and searches for it in the trie. If the item is not found, the function returns NIL; otherwise it returns the last trie node corresponding to the item. The latter takes an item, a nonnull value, and a nonnull trie. It enters the item in the trie and puts the value with the item as its ENTRY. (As mentioned earlier, the value will normally be the item itself or some associated information rather than just *.) The first time INSERT-TRIE is called, it is given the trie node

```
(MAKE-TRIE 'DUMMY () ())
```

Both functions given below are self-explanatory.

```
(DEFUN SEARCH-TRIE-NODE (REM-ITEM TRIE)
    (COND [(NULL REM-ITEM) TRIE]
          [T (LET ((MATCH (ASSOC (CAR REM-ITEM)
                                  (TRIE-SONS TRIE)
                                  :KEY #'TRIE-SUBKEY)))
               (COND [MATCH (SEARCH-TRIE-NODE
                              (CDR REM-ITEM)
                              MATCH)]
                     [T NIL]))]))
```

```
(DEFUN INSERT-TRIE (REM-ITEM ITEM TRIE)
  (COND
    [(NULL REM-ITEM)
     (SETF (TRIE-ENTRY TRIE) ITEM)]
    [T (LET ((SON (ASSOC (CAR REM-ITEM)
                         (TRIE-SONS TRIE)
                         :KEY #'TRIE-SUBKEY)))
         (COND [(NULL SON)
                (LET ((NEW-TRIE (MAKE-TRIE (CAR REM-ITEM)
                                           NIL NIL)))
                  (SETF (TRIE-SONS TRIE)
                        (APPEND (TRIE-SONS TRIE)
                                (LIST NEW-TRIE)))
                  (INSERT-TRIE (CDR REM-ITEM)
                               ITEM NEW-TRIE)
                  TRIE)]
               [T (INSERT-TRIE (CDR REM-ITEM) ITEM SON)
                  TRIE]))]))
```

Using SEARCH-TRIE-NODE we can define SEARCH-TRIE that is like the former except returns the entry only. DEL-TRIE deletes the item from the trie.

```
(DEFUN SEARCH-TRIE (ITEM TRIE)
  (LET ((X (SEARCH-TRIE-NODE ITEM TRIE)))
    (COND [X (TRIE-ENTRY X)])))

(DEFUN DEL-TRIE (ITEM TRIE)
  (SETF (TRIE-ENTRY (SEARCH-TRIE-NODE ITEM TRIE)) NIL))
```

We are now ready to define a matcher for the trie data structure. It is given a pattern (that is, a condition from the antecedent of a rule), and it returns a list of all those trie nodes that match. Variable bindings are not created however. (That can be done by matching the condition with the entries in the retrieved nodes.) MATCH-TRIE-NODES is very similar to SEARCH-TRIE-NODE except that when the search item contains a variable, it tries to follow each of the son tries and returns all those that match in a list.

```
(DEFUN MATCH-TRIE-NODES (REM-ITEM TRIE)
  (COND
    [(NULL REM-ITEM) (LIST TRIE)]
    [(IS-VAR (CAR REM-ITEM))
     (MAPCAN #'(LAMBDA (TR)
                 (MATCH-TRIE-NODES (CDR REM-ITEM) TR))
             (TRIE-SONS TRIE))]
    [T (LET ((MATCH (ASSOC (CAR REM-ITEM)
                           (TRIE-SONS TRIE)
```

```
                    :KEY #'TRIE-SUBKEY)))
    (COND [MATCH (MATCH-TRIE-NODES (CDR REM-ITEM)
                                    MATCH)]
          [T NIL])))])))
```

Exercise 7.14 Write a function called TRAVERSE-TRIE that prints all the entries in a trie.

Exercise 7.15 Build tries for the conditions in the rules in the production system. Whenever a variable appears, treat it as if the atom $VAR has been encountered. (*Note*: The name of the variable is ignored while building the trie.)

Exercise 7.16 Using the trie representation for rules in the production system, try matching a condition with the database.

Exercise 7.17 So far we have permitted only lists of atoms to be stored in the trie structure. To deal with arbitrary lists we have to make just one observation: A list can be written as a special symbol, say $CONS, followed by its CAR and CDR written in a similar fashion. This yields a list of atoms that is unique for the list structure.

Following are some example lists written in the above fashion:

```
(EQU RED (COLOR A))
(EQU RED $CONS COLOR $CONS A NIL)

(EQU (COLOR A) (COLOR B))
(EQU $CONS COLOR $CONS A NIL
     $CONS COLOR $CONS B NIL)

(EQU (COLOR (RIGHT-OF C)) RED)
(EQU $CONS COLOR $CONS $CONS RIGHT-OF
     $CONS C NIL NIL RED)
```

Write SEARCH-TRIE-NODE and INSERT-TRIE functions that work on arbitrary lists.

Exercise 7.18 There is another way of representing a list as a sequence of atoms provided no CDR of its sublists is a symbol. Although it is less general than that suggested in the previous exercise, it is more compact. In this notation,

```
(EQU (COLOR A) (COLOR B))
```

is written as

```
(EQU $OPEN COLOR A $CLOSE
     $OPEN COLOR B $CLOSE)
```

It can be generalized, however, to take care af all possibilities by including another special symbol, say $DOT. For example,

```
(EQU (COLOR . A) (COLOR . B))
```

is written as

```
(EQU $OPEN COLOR $DOT A $CLOSE
     $OPEN COLOR $DOT B $CLOSE)
```

Implement SEARCH-TRIE-NODE and INSERT-TRIE for this scheme.

Exercise 7.19 The trie data structure can be used to make the list expression unique. Define a function called INTERN-LIST that takes a list and enters it in the trie data structure bound to, say, *LIST-OBJECTS*. Use it to implement a property list mechanism for lists.

Exercise 7.20 Reimplement INTERN-LIST to make every sublist in a given list unique.

Exercise 7.21 Redefine MATCH-TRIE-NODES to return a list of association lists containing the bindings of variables in the search pattern. The one defined here returns only the items, which must be further matched to obtain the bindings. (*Note*: This generally results in a less efficient matcher for usual kinds of databases.)

Exercise 7.22 The trie structures described here are designed for a left-to-right match. Suppose we wanted to carry out a right-to-left match. How will you build the trie structure?

Exercise 7.23 Can you combine two trie structures to provide both left-to-right and right-to-left access to items? (*Hint*: You will end up with a discrimination net rather than a trie.)

7.4 PRODUCTION SYSTEM USING DISCRIMINATION TRIES

Let us now incorporate the discrimination nets in the implementation of production systems. In particular, let us represent the global database using discrimination tries. The items in the database are lists of atoms without any variables. The rules will continue to be represented as a list of ASRT structures as before.

Also as before, we must first develop a mechanism for restoring the state. The mark list is a list of pairs of positions and entries, as before, except now the position is a trie node. Each of the functions MARK-DB, DEL-MARKED-ITEMS, and UN-DEL-MARKED-ITEMS given below are similar to before (in Sec. 7.2.2). The only difference is that now the trie node is passed as the database position. ADD-ITEMS and UNADD-ITEMS actually become simpler; all they have to do is call on INSERT-TRIE.

```
(DEFUN MARK-DB (NODE)
;;; Node is a trie node. Make a pair of the node and its
;;; entry and put it on *MARKED-ITEMS*.
```

```
(DECLARE (SPECIAL *MARKED-ITEMS*))
(PUSH (LIST NODE (TRIE-ENTRY NODE))
      *MARKED-ITEMS*))


(DEFUN DEL-MARKED-ITEMS (L)
;;; L is a list of pairs: (<trie node> <its entry>).
;;; In the <trie node>s in the pairs make the entry NIL.
   (COND [(NULL L) T]
         [T (SETF (TRIE-ENTRY (CAAR L)) NIL)
            (DEL-MARKED-ITEMS (CDR L))]))


(DEFUN UNDEL-MARKED-ITEMS (L)
;;; L is a list of pairs as before. Put the
;;; entries in <trie node>s.
   (COND [(NULL L) T]
         [T (SETF (TRIE-ENTRY (CAAR L)) (CADAR L))
            (UNDEL-MARKED-ITEMS (CDR L))]))


(DEFUN ADD-ITEMS (DB L)
;;; Add the list of items in L into the database DB.
(COND [(NULL L) T]
      [T (INSERT-TRIE (CAR L) (CAR L) DB)
         (ADD-ITEMS DB (CDR L))]))


(DEFUN UNADD-ITEMS (DB L)
;;; Do the opposite of ADD-ITEMS.
(COND [(NULL L) T]
      [T (DEL-TRIE (CAR L) DB)
         (UNADD-ITEMS DB (CDR L))]))
```

Exercise 7.24 In the function DEL-MARKED-ITEMS, we simply make the ENTRYs of the concerned trie nodes NIL. This may result in "dead branches" in the trie that do not contain any entries. The dead branches slow down the matching. Redefine MARK-DB and DEL-MARKED-ITEMS so that the dead branches are removed and saved.

Now let us examine the application of rules. APPLYRULE remains unchanged, and in PRODSYS there is just one change: Instead of MEMBER we must use SEARCH-TRIE to test whether a goal is in the database. They are not shown here. MATCH-ANTEC is also similar to its earlier definition except that now instead of going through the list of rules, we first retrieve the matching nodes using MATCH-TRIE-NODES and then go through them. The definition of MATCH-ANTEC is given below.

```
(DEFUN MATCH-ANTEC (DB ANTEC ALIST)
  (COND
     [(NULL ANTEC) ALIST]
     [T ;; Match (CAR ANTEC) then continue with the rest.
```

```
(DO ((NODES (MATCH-TRIE-NODES (CAR ANTEC) DB)
             (CDR NODES)))
    ((NULL NODES) '$FAIL)
  (LET((NEW-ALIST (MATCH2 (CAR ANTEC)
                          (TRIE-ENTRY (CAR NODES))
                          ALIST)))
    (COND [(FAIL-P NEW-ALIST)
           ;; Do nothing. Will loop.
           ]
          [T (LET ((FINAL-ALIST (MATCH-ANTEC DB
                                  (CDR ANTEC)
                                  NEW-ALIST)))
               (COND [(FAIL-P FINAL-ALIST)
                      ;; Do nothing. Will loop.
                      ]
                     [T ;; All antecedents matched.
                      (MARK-DB (CAR NODES))
                      (RETURN FINAL-ALIST)])))])
    )]))
```

Exercise 7.25 Reimplement INFER-AND in VIDHI using a trie structure to store assertions.

Exercise 7.26 In production systems, keep the conditions of rules in the same trie structure as the database. Whenever a new item is added to the database, the matching process goes on simultaneously. Thus we can immediately know which of the rules might become applicable. The reverse information about what rules become inapplicable can similarly be identified when an item is deleted.

Use the above idea to implement an extremely efficient production system. (*Note*: It is also quite suitable for a demon facility.)

7.5 DISCUSSION

Throughout the chapter we have assumed a forward-driven system in which the antecedent is matched with the database. The reverse is also possible, however. We can match the given goal state with the consequent of rules and generate a new set of goals. This process can continue until all the generated goals are present in the database. This is called a backward-driven or backward-chained system.

In some production systems, the rules are partitioned into classes or sets. At any given time, only a single set is active, that is, available for matching. There are rules, however, for switching between the rule sets. This approach is useful when the solution to the problem can be naturally partitioned into such rule sets.

Sometimes the rules and items are not known with definiteness but only with some probability. In such a situation probabilities are associated with both items and

rules. When a rule is applied, instead of deleting items we only change the probabilities. (An item having a lower probability than a threshold can be deleted.) Such systems are said to possess fuzzy reasoning.

FURTHER READINGS

For a thorough discussion on the relative advantages and disadvantages of production systems see Davis and King (1977). Waterman and Hayes-Roth (1978) describe a number of variations on production systems. OPS5, a well-known production system, is described in Brownston et al. (1985). Theoretical aspects are discussed in Nilsson (1980). For a discussion on implementation of rule sets see Diwan (1986). MYCIN is a well-known system employing fuzzy reasoning [Shortliffe (1976)].

Tries are described in Knuth (1973). Discrimination nets are discussed in detail in Charniak (1980).

For a theory of context-free grammars and formal languages see Hopcroft and Ullman (1979). Natural language parsing is discussed in Winograd (1983).

FUNCTIONAL PROGRAMMING

CHAPTER
8

HIGHER-ORDER FUNCTIONS

Functions that take a function as their argument or return a function as their result are called *higher-order functions*. These provide a powerful mechanism for solving problems and for avoiding the use of recursion as well as explicit iteration. Mapping functions like MAPCAR with which the reader is already familiar are an example. They take a function and apply it to every member of one or more given lists. In this chapter, we introduce a set of additional higher-order functions. Most of the higher-order functions discussed in this chapter take a function as one of their arguments and operate on the data. They do not return a function as their value.

In Chap. 10, all the higher-order functions return functions, which can be applied on the data. It provides a structure to the higher-order functions. The intervening chapter discusses streams. In case of streams, one operates on data which get generated on demand. The data actually contain functions which get applied when necessary.

8.1 WHY HIGHER-ORDER FUNCTIONS

Higher-order functions can be used to capture a whole pattern of computation. The pattern holds across many applications—what might be different is the specific function in the pattern. For example, if we square every element or take the cube of every element of a list, the pattern of computation (namely, performing an operation on every element of a list) is the same. The only difference is in the specific function which is part of the pattern (namely, square in one case and cube in the other).

The following two functions could be defined for the above two cases as

```
(DEFUN SQUARE-EACH (L)
    (COND [(NULL L) ()]
          [T (CONS (SQR (CAR L))
                   (SQUARE-EACH (CDR L)))]))

(DEFUN CUBE-EACH (L)
    (COND [(NULL L) ()]
          [T (CONS (CUBE (CAR L))
                   (CUBE-EACH (CDR L)))]))
```

On identifying the pattern we can define a higher-order function called EACH that takes a function as its argument.

```
(DEFUN EACH (F L)
    (COND [(NULL L) ()]
          [T (CONS (FUNCALL F (CAR L))
                   (EACH F (CDR L)))]))
```

Once EACH, or any pattern of computation for that matter, has been identified and defined, it provides us with a very powerful method.[1] For example, if we have to take the square root of every number in a list L, we only have to write

```
(EACH #'SQRT L)
```

Exercise 8.1 Define a higher-order function called SIGMA that parallels the summation operator in mathematics:

$$\sum_{i=a}^{b} f(i) = f(a) + \cdots + f(b)$$

Exercise 8.2 Define SIGMA-RECURRENCE, a higher-order function similar to SIGMA except that it uses a recurrence relation and the value of the previous term to compute the next term in the series. For example,

$$S = \sum_{i=1}^{b} g^i(a_0) = g(a_0) + g^2(a_0) + \cdots + g^b(a_0)$$

or

$$t_i = g^i(a_0)$$

---

[1]EACH here is nothing but a special case of MAPCAR which takes a monadic function as its first argument.

$$S^i \sum_{i=0}^{b-1} g(t_i)$$

(*Note*: This would frequently be a much more efficient method of computing the sum of a series. A variation of this method covers many commonly occurring series. Can you find it?)

Exercise 8.3 There is a list of lists of numbers representing the marks obtained by students in different sections. Using MAPCAR compute the averages of each of the sections.

Exercise 8.4 Repeat Exercise 8.3, but compute the overall average. (*Hint*: The overall average is the weighted average of the individual averages of the sections.)

Exercise 8.5 Define a function called MATCH-LIST using MAPCAR that takes a pattern and a list of items and returns a list containing trues and falses depending on whether the corresponding item matched the pattern or not.

```
(MATCH-LIST '(A ? B)
            '((A 1 B) (C D) (A 2 B) (A B)))
     =>     (T NIL T NIL)
```

(*Hint*: See Sec. 4.1 for matching.)

In the rest of the chapter we will define some higher-order functions which are particularly important in symbol processing.

8.2 REDUCTION FUNCTIONS

Reduction functions apply a function of two arguments repeatedly to elements of a list. For example, consider a function reduce-right defined as follows:

$$\text{reduce-right } (g, x, a) = g(x_1, g(x_2, \cdots, g(x_k, a)))$$

where x is a list $(x_1 x_2 \cdots x_k)$ of k elements. It applies a diadic function (function of two arguments) g to the first element of x and to the result of applying g to the rest of the list repeatedly. Thus, it reduces a list from the right or the end. If we have the diadic addition function +, we can use it in LISP to sum the numbers in a list as follows:

```
(REDUCE-RIGHT #'+ '(3 8 2 1) 0) => 14
```

Similarly, with *, the diadic multiply (that takes two arguments),

```
(REDUCE-RIGHT #'* '(3 3 2) 1) => 18
```

REDUCE-RIGHT can be defined as follows:

178 FUNCTIONAL PROGRAMMING

```
(DEFUN REDUCE-RIGHT (G X A)
   (COND [(NULL X) A]
         [T (FUNCALL
                G (CAR X) (REDUCE-RIGHT G (CDR X) A) )]))
```

We can define APPEND using CONS and REDUCE.

```
(DEFUN OUR-APPEND (L1 L2)
   (REDUCE-RIGHT #'CONS L1 L2) )
```

Binary functions MAX2 and MIN2 can be used to find the maximum and the minimum, respectively, of a list of numbers.

```
(DEFUN MAX2 (N1 N2)
   (COND [(> N1 N2) N1] [T N2] ))

(REDUCE-RIGHT #'MAX2 '(5 8 3) -999999)
   => 8

(DEFUN MIN2 (N1 N2)
   (COND [(< N1 N2) N1] [T N2] ))

(REDUCE-RIGHT #'MIN2 '(5 8 3) +999999)
   => 3
```

where -999999 and $+999999$ are used as the smallest and largest integers (i.e., negative infinity and positive infinity), respectively.

In another example, consider an arithmetic function SUMPROD-AUX that takes a number n and a list of two numbers (which hopefully consists of the sum and the product of numbers in some list) and produces a list of two numbers by adding n to the first number in the list (sum) and multiplying n by the second number in the list (product).

```
(DEFUN SUMPROD-AUX (N X)
   (LIST (+ N (CAR X)) (* N (CADR X))) )
```

By reducing a list of numbers by SUMPROD-AUX we get the same effect as SUM-PROD that returns the sum and product of numbers in a list. For example,

```
(REDUCE-RIGHT #'SUMPROD-AUX '(2 4 3) '(0 1)) => (9 24)
```

As we have seen, the mapping functions allow us to apply a given function to every element of a list (or lists); the result is a list of length equal to the argument list(s). The reduction functions, on the other hand, apply a given function to elements of a

list yielding a single element or a shorter list. In the two examples below, REDUCE-RIGHT and MAPCAR are combined to get additional power.

Given a list of lists of numbers, we get a list of numbers by reducing each list of numbers in the top-level list. Let S be bound to ((3 2 5) (2 1 0) (9 2 8 7)), then

```
(MAPCAR #'(LAMBDA (L) (REDUCE-RIGHT #'+ L 0)) S)
    => (10 3 26)
```

To add all the numbers in S we write the following:

```
(REDUCE-RIGHT #'+
        (MAPCAR #'(LAMBDA (L) (REDUCE-RIGHT #'+ L 0)) S)
        0)
    =>    39
```

Exercise 8.6 Let ADD-SUMCOUNT be a function that takes two arguments: a number n and a list consisting of sum and count (for a list of numbers). It returns a list of new sum and new count.

```
(ADD-SUMCOUNT 5 '(38 3))
        => (43 4)
```

Using ADD-SUMCOUNT and REDUCE-RIGHT compute the average of a list of numbers.

Exercise 8.7 There is a list of lists of numbers representing the marks obtained by students in different sections (same as in Exercise 8.3). Compute the averages of each of the sections using MAPCAR and REDUCE-RIGHT.

Exercise 8.8 Repeat Exercise 8.7 but compute the overall average.

Exercise 8.9 Define a function that takes a pattern and a list of items and returns a number equal to the number of items that match the pattern.

Exercise 8.10 Define REDUCE-LEFT which is like REDUCE-RIGHT except it associates from the left. For example,

```
(REDUCE-LEFT #'- '(8 4 3 5) 0)
    ;equals (((0 - 8) - 4) - 3) - 5 in infix notation
        => - 20
(REDUCE-RIGHT #'- '(8 4 3 5) 0)
    ;equals 8 - (4 - (3 - (5 - 0))) in infix notation
        => 2
```

COMMON LISP has a built-in function called REDUCE that combines the power of REDUCE-LEFT and REDUCE-RIGHT. For details see Steele (1984).

8.3 PARTIAL APPLICATION

In *partial application* we take an *n*-adic function and *k* number of arguments ($0 < k < n$) and produce a function of $(n - k)$ number of arguments; the resultant function can be applied to $(n - k)$ arguments yielding a result that would be produced if the original function was applied to *n* arguments of which the first *k* are the same as those used in partial application, and the remaining $(n - k)$ are the same as those supplied later. We assume for simplicity that there are no free variables in the body of the definition of function. We define a function PART-APPLY-2 that takes a dyadic function and an argument and partially applies the function.

```
(PART-APPLY-2 #'+ '5) => <lambda-expr1>
```

Thus, if F is bound to <lambda-expr1> then when F is applied to a number, it adds 5 to it.

```
(FUNCALL F 3) => 8
(FUNCALL F 4) => 9
```

For a given function <lambda-expr> that takes two arguments the result of its partial application to <S-expr> is the following:

```
(LAMBDA (X) (FUNCALL #'<lambda-expr> '<S-expr> X))
```

The following definition of PART-APPLY-2 produces a lambda expression of the above form:

```
(DEFUN PART-APPLY-2 (F S)
   #'(LAMBDA (X) (FUNCALL F S X)) )

(PART-APPLY-2 #'(LAMBDA (X Y) (+ X Y)) '5)
   =equivalent to=>
      (LAMBDA (X) (FUNCALL #'(LAMBDA (X Y) (+ X Y))
                            '5 X))
```

In the solution just outlined, the given function is applied in the body of a new lambda expression which has one argument less than the given function.

Partial application can be useful in a variety of ways. Suppose we wanted to add a number, say 4, to each of the numbers in a list. We could write it as

```
(MAPCAR (PART-APPLY-2 #'+ 4) '(3 8 9))
   => (7 12 13)
```

While defining CART-PROD in Sec. 1.5.2, we had defined a function called ELEM-PROD that takes an object and a list and produces a list of pairs of the given object and elements of the given list.

```
(ELEM-PROD '3 '(2 4 6)) => ((3 2) (3 4) (3 6))
```

ELEM-PROD can be defined using MAPCAR and PART-APPLY-2:

```
(DEFUN ELEM-PROD (E L)
   (MAPCAR (PART-APPLY-2 #'LIST E) L))
```

> **Exercise 8.11** Define MATCH-LIST defined in Exercise 8.5 using partial application and mapping functions.

> **Exercise 8.12** The SUCCESSORS function takes a node N and generates its successors. (See Sec. 3.3.) Using partial application and mapping functions, generate a list of edges (or pairs) from N to its successors.
> How would you generate the list of reverse edges in which N is the second element of the pair?

8.4 FILTERING

Filtering is a process by which some or all of the elements of a list are selected, resulting in a list containing, usually, only some of the elements of the input list. The selection is done by means of a monadic predicate, called a *sieve* (through which passes the input list). The unary predicate is applied to each element of the input list; if the result is nonnull, the element "passes through the sieve" and is included in the resultant list, otherwise it fails and is not included in the resultant list. For example, the following selects zeros from a list of numbers:

```
(FILTER #'ZEROP '(1 23 0 0 84 0))
   => (0 0 0)
```

If we wish to select all nonzero elements from a list of numbers, we would define an appropriate sieve and apply the FILTER function:

```
(FILTER #'(LAMBDA (X) (NOT (ZEROP X)))
      '(1 23 0 0 84 0))
   => (1 23 84)
```

FILTER can be defined as follows:

```
(DEFUN FILTER (F L)
   (COND [(NULL L) ()]
         [(FUNCALL F (CAR L))
           (CONS (CAR L) (FILTER F (CDR L)))]
         [T (FILTER F (CDR L))] ))
```

There is a built-in function called REMOVE-IF-NOT that is like FILTER.
Predicates of two arguments can be partially applied to generate appropriate

sieves. For example, to select all the elements not less than 3 in a list of numbers, we apply $<$ or LESSP partially:

```
(FILTER (PART-APPLY-2 #'< 3)
        '(1 23 0 0 84 0) )
  => (23 84)
```

Similar to FILTER we can define a function called PASS-MULTI-SIEVES-P that takes a list of sieves and an element and returns true if the element passes through each of the sieves. Here is the definition:

```
(DEFUN PASS-MULTI-SIEVES-P (SIEVES ELEM)
   (COND [(NULL SIEVES) T]
         [(FUNCALL (CAR SIEVES) ELEM)
          (PASS-MULTI-SIEVES-P (CDR SIEVES) ELEM)]
         [T NIL]))
```

Using the above it is a simple matter to define FILTER-MULTI-SIEVES that takes a list of sieves and a list, and returns a list of those elements that pass through every sieve.

```
(DEFUN FILTER-MULTI-SIEVES (SIEVES L)
   (COND [(NULL L) ()]
         [(PASS-MULTI-SIEVES-P SIEVES (CAR L))
          (CONS (CAR L)
                (FILTER-MULTI-SIEVES SIEVES (CDR L)))]
         [T (FILTER-MULTI-SIEVES SIEVES (CDR L))]))
```

Exercise 8.13 Define a function that takes a list of triangles and filters the right-angle triangles. (*Hint*: Represent a triangle by a list of three pairs of cartesian coordinates of its vertices.)

Exercise 8.14 Given a list of lists of numbers, compute the averages of each of the sublists. Include those sublists whose average is greater than AMIN to compute the overall average. Use FILTER besides MAPCAR, REDUCE-LEFT, and ADD-SUMCOUNT.

Exercise 8.15 Define a function that takes a list of sets L and a set S and returns a list of those sets in L which are subsets of S. (Assume a suitable representation for sets.)

Exercise 8.16 Define a function called FILTER-UNTIL that takes a sieve and a list like FILTER and passes the elements in the list until there is one which does not pass. For example,

```
(FILTER-UNTIL #'(LAMBDA (X) (NOT (ZEROP X)))
              '(1 23 0 0 84 0))
    => (1 23)
```

Exercise 8.17 Identify the computation pattern in the following functions:

```
(DEFUN APPEND (L1 L2)
   (COND [(NULL L1) L2]
         [T (CONS (CAR L1)
                  (APPEND (CDR L1) L2))]))

(DEFUN CART-PROD (S1 S2)
   (COND [(NULL S1) ()]
         [T (APPEND (ELEM-PROD (CAR S1) S2)
                    (CART-PROD (CDR S1) S2))]))
```

Define a higher-order function, say RECURSE1, that captures the pattern. Now redefine APPEND and CART-PROD in terms of RECURSE1.

Can you use RECURSE1 to define other similar functions, say LENGTH?

Exercise 8.18 Identify the computation pattern in tail recursive functions like REVERSE.

8.5   AN EXAMPLE—COMPUTING PRIMES

We now show how sieves of Eratosthenes can be used to find prime numbers and can be implemented using higher-order functions. To find the $(n + 1)$th prime number given the first n prime numbers $p_1, p_2, \ldots, p_n$, we form a sieve for each of the n prime numbers (see Fig. 8.1); the sieve s_i for p_i allows only those numbers to pass

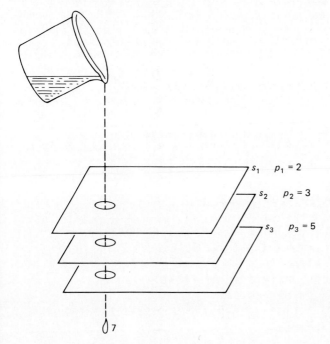

FIGURE 8.1
Sieves of Eratosthenes.

through it that are not divisible by p_i. Now we begin with the number $(p_n + 1)$ and see whether it passes through all the sieves s_1 to s_n; if it does, it is the $(n + 1)$th prime number; otherwise the same thing is repeated with $(p_n + 2)$, and so on. We are given that 2 is the first prime number. After 2, since no even number is prime, only odd numbers need to be considered. In other words, given n ($n > 1$) primes we need to consider numbers $(p_n + 2)$, $(p_n + 4)$, and so on.

We first define a function called NEXT-PRIME that is given a list of sieves (corresponding to the prime numbers found so far starting from 2), and a number NUM. It returns the next prime number greater than or equal to NUM. A typical sieve for prime number 5 is

```
(LAMBDA (N) (NOT (ZEROP (REM N 5))))
```

If it is applied to a number, it evaluates to true only if it is not divisible by 5. NEXT-PRIME is now straightforward.

```
(DEFUN NEXI-PRIME (SIEVES NUM)
    (COND [(PASS-MULTI-SIEVES-P SIEVES NUM) NUM]
          [T (NEXT-PRIME SIEVES (+ NUM 2))]))
```

Now using the above, we can define a function N-PRIMES that takes an argument n and generates a list of the first n primes. It calls N-PRIMES-AUX that takes four arguments: N (the number of primes yet to be generated), PRIMES (a list of primes generated so far), SIEVES (a list of sieves corresponding to the primes), and NUM (the next number to be tested for primeness). It is initially called with the prime number 2 and corresponding other arguments. Subsequently, it keeps adding to the list of PRIMES.

```
(DEFUN N-PRIMES (N)
;;; Returns list of first N primes.
    (N-PRIMES-AUX (- N 1)
                  (LIST 2)
                  (LIST (GEN-NOT-DIVISIBLEP 2))
                  3))

(DEFUN N-PRIMES-AUX (N PRIMES SIEVES NUM)
;;; See description in text above.
    (COND [(EQL N 0) PRIMES]
          [T (LET ((PRIME (NEXT-PRIME SIEVES NUM))))
              (N-PRIMES-AUX
                (- N 1)
                (NCONC PRIMES (LIST PRIME))
                (NCONC SIEVES
                       (LIST (GEN-NOT-DIVISIBLEP PRIME)))
```

```
                (+ PRIME 2)))]))

(DEFUN GEN-NOT-DIVISIBLEP (P)
  #'(LAMBDA (N) (NOT (ZEROP (REM N P)))))
```

Exercise 8.19 Define NEXT-PRIME and N-PRIMES without using filtering. Compare the definitions with those given here.

8.6   AN EXAMPLE—QUERY PROCESSOR

Let us take the query processor discussed in Sec. 4.3 and implement it using higher-order functions. To facilitate the task, we first define a higher-order function called FILTER-XFORM that transforms the elements after filtering them. The sieve function is used not only for filtering but for transformation as well.

```
(DEFUN FILTER-XFORM (SIEVE L)
;;; Filters elements of L and then transforms them.
;;; FAIL-P determines which elements fail to pass filter.
   (COND [(NULL L) ()]
         [T (LET ((RES (FUNCALL SIEVE (CAR L))))
              (COND [(FAIL-P RES)
                      (FILTER-XFORM SIEVE (CDR L))]
                    [T (CONS RES
                             (FILTER-XFORM SIEVE (CDR L)))])])]))
```

Now SIMP-QUERY-PROCESSOR can be defined using FILTER-XFORM and a sieve formed by incorporating the input query and association list. When the sieve is applied to the items of the database, it returns association lists for items with which the query matches.

```
(DEFUN SIMP-QUERY-PROCESSOR (SIMP-QUERY DB ALIST)
;;; See description in text above.
   (FILTER-XFORM
       #'(LAMBDA (DBITEM) (MATCH2 SIMP-QUERY DBITEM ALIST))
       DB))
```

Exercise 8.20 (Difficult) Implement the QUERY-PROCESSOR of Section 4.3 using suitable higher-order functions.

Exercise 8.21 Implement the operators you thought of in Exercise 4.2 using higher-order functions.

Exercise 8.22 Implement the enriched set of operators as described in Exercise 4.3 using higher-order functions.

8.7 FREE VARIABLES AND HIGHER-ORDER FUNCTIONS

One must be careful of free variables when dealing with higher-order functions. Free variables in functions that are arguments of higher-order functions sometimes cause unexpected results. The question that arises is whether the free variables should take their value from the environment when the function was created or when it is applied. Usually, the answer is the former. See, for example, the free variable P in the lambda that is generated by GEN-NOT-DIVISIBLEP. Since COMMON LISP has lexical closures, free variables are resolved correctly in the lambda expression generated by GEN-NOT-DIVISIBLEP. The closure is taken by #' or FUNCTION. The free variable P in the lambda gets bound to the environment inside GEN-NOT-DIVISIBLEP in this call. If closures were not available, we would have to ensure there were no free variables. This means that free variables, if any, must be substituted by their value. In the example of GEN-NOT-DIVISIBLEP, we would have to write

```
(DEFUN GEN-NOT-DIVISIBLEP (P)
   `(LAMBDA (N) (NOT (ZEROP (REM N ,P)))) )
```

such that the value of P is substituted when the lambda is formed.

FURTHER READINGS

For an interesting introduction to higher-order functions see Abelson and Sussman (1985).

CHAPTER
9

STREAMS AND DELAYED EVALUATION

In this chapter we study the explicit delaying of evaluation as realized by streams.[1]

In the last chapter we looked at higher-order functions—functions that take a function as an argument or return it as a value. The programmer and the user of the higher-order function must be consciously aware of this fact. In contrast, *streams* are data structures which contain unevaluated expressions (or function applications). They are passed as data structures to a function that operates on them, and get evaluated when needed. The function that operates on the stream data structure is like a higher-order function by our definition, but the abstraction provided is that of a function manipulating a data structure.

9.1 STREAMS

When we are dealing with very large (even infinite) amounts of data, it may not be desirable (or even possible) to store the data in memory. Streams are an elegant method of dealing with the situation. A stream is a data structure that contains unevaluated parts. As the unevaluated parts of a stream are accessed, they are evaluated yielding data and perhaps some other unevaluated parts.

---

[1] No relationship to input and output streams.

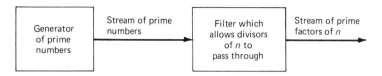

FIGURE 9-1

The elegance of streams lies in the fact that the program accessing the stream data structure need not be aware of the fact that the data is being generated on demand. It accesses it like any other data structure. This allows us to separate the task of building the data structure from the programs that access it. This separation makes programming easier.

Consider for example the problem of finding the prime number divisors (also called prime factors) of a given number n. It can be solved by considering prime numbers and testing whether they are divisors of n. The number of prime numbers needed, though finite, is not known a priori. On the other hand if we have an ordered "list" of prime numbers, it is a simple matter to find the divisors. Such a problem is an ideal candidate for the use of streams. It can be broken up into two parts: (a) generating an ordered stream of prime numbers, and (b) selecting ones that are divisors of n. Solving each of the two parts separately is a lot easier than solving the original problem in one shot.

Analogy with signal processing in electrical engineering helps in thinking about streams. There is a "signal generator" that generates a stream. The stream passes through various "filters" and signal processing components until the desired result is obtained. For the above example, we can view it as a system in which there is a "signal" generator of prime numbers and a "filter" of divisors of n (see Fig. 9-1). It can be further simplified as shown in Fig. 9-2.

The use of streams leads to more modular solutions as well. The solutions are cleaner and easier to understand, and the components of the solutions are likely to be more general and hence usable by other programs as well. For example, once we have a generator of prime numbers, it can be used in situations other than finding divisors. Similarly, it is easier to take a solution that utilizes streams and use it to construct a solution to a related problem. For example, if we want to find common prime factors of n_1 and n_2, we need to cascade another filter for factors of n_2 to the original solution. All the earlier components can be used as they are.

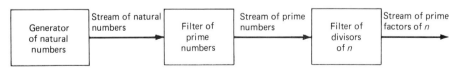

FIGURE 9-2

9.2   IMPLEMENTING STREAMS—
A SIMPLE SOLUTION

As described earlier, streams are data structures that are not fully formed (i.e., contain unevaluated parts). We will call the unevaluated parts *recipes* or *promises*. For example, a stream of natural numbers can be represented as

```
(1 . <recipe for generating natural numbers starting from 2>)
```

The head of the stream is 1, while the tail is a recipe. If we try to access the second element, the recipe gets evaluated yielding

```
(2 . <recipe for generating natural numbers starting from 3>)
```

and so on.

Recipes can be implemented by storing the name of an appropriate function followed by its arguments. Evaluating or *forcing* the recipe means applying the function in the recipe to its arguments and returning the result. A tag, say RECIPE, is also necessary to distinguish a recipe from ordinary data. Thus, the representation of a recipe is

```
(DEFSTRUCT (RECIPE (:CONSTRUCTOR MAKE-RECIPE (FUNC ARGS)))
           FUNC ARGS)

#S(RECIPE  FUNC <fn>  ARGS (<arg1> ... <argN>))
```

where <fn> is the name of a function, and <arg1> to <argN> are its arguments. A stream of natural numbers is given below, where GINT is a function that takes an integer as its argument and produces a stream of integers starting from its argument.

```
(1 . #S(RECIPE FUNC GINT ARGS (2)))
```

The following are equivalent ways of representing the same stream differing in the extent of unevaluated parts:

```
(1  2  3  . #S(RECIPE FUNC GINT ARGS (4)))
(1  2  3  4  . #S(RECIPE FUNC GINT ARGS (5)))
#S(RECIPE FUNC GINT ARGS (1))
```

GINT is called a *generator* or a *stream function*, since (GINT <n>) produces a list whose first element is <n> and the rest of the list is a recipe containing GINT and <n> + 1. It is defined as

```
(DEFUN GINT (N)
    (CONS N (MAKE-RECIPE 'GINT (+ 1 N))))
```

Therefore,

```
(GINT  3)  =>  (3 . #S(RECIPE FUNC GINT ARGS  (4)))
(GINT  4)  =>  (4 . #S(RECIPE FUNC GINT ARGS  (5)))
```

More formally then, a *stream* is either (*a*) a recipe, or (*b*) a list containing zero or more recipes. A recipe on being forced yields a stream.[2]

For traversing a stream, we use SCAR and SCDR instead of CAR and CDR. These functions force the recipes, if necessary, while traversing a stream.

A stream is said to be in a *normal form* if it is not a recipe. For a normalized stream no recipe needs to be forced to get the first or the rest of the elements of the stream. Thus,

```
(1 . #S(RECIPE FUNC GINT ARGS (2)))
(1  2  3 . #S(RECIPE  FUNC GINT ARGS (4)))
```

are in normal form, while

```
#S(RECIPE FUNC GINT ARGS (1))
```

is not. Clearly, a stream must be in a normal form before its first element or the rest of its elements can be obtained. Definitions of SCAR, SCDR, and NORMALIZE are given below. SCAR and SCDR assume that their argument stream is normalized and return a normalized stream (for efficiency reasons, to be discussed later).

```
(DEFUN SCAR (S)  (NORMALIZE (CAR S)))

(DEFUN SCDR (S)  (NORMALIZE (CDR S)))

(DEFUN NORMALIZE (S)
    (COND [(IS-RECIPE S)
             (NORMALIZE (APPLY (RECIPE-FUNC S)
                               (RECIPE-ARGS S)))]
          [T S]))

(DEFUN IS-RECIPE (R)  (EQL 'RECIPE  (TYPE-OF R)))
```

---

[2]Streams can be generalized to include atoms. A recipe, in that case, may evaluate to an atom as well.

NORMALIZE forces the stream passed to it until it is in a normal form. The repeated forcing is necessary because a recipe on being forced might yield another recipe.

An advantage of always dealing with a normalized stream is that testing for null streams becomes simpler, and the first element of the stream can be accessed without forcing the stream.

To take a closer look at the definitions, let us study some examples. GAPPEND is a generator that appends two streams to yield a new stream:

```
(DEFUN GAPPEND (S1  S2)
    (COND [(NULL S1) S2]
          [T (CONS  (SCAR  S1)
                    (MAKE-RECIPE
                      #'GAPPEND (LIST (SCDR S1) S2)))]))
```

The resulting stream is normalized. The first element is available directly; the rest of the elements, however, are represented by a recipe. Thus,

```
(GAPPEND '(10 11 12)  '(7  8))
        => (10 . #S(RECIPE  FUNC GAPPEND
                           ARGS ((11 12)  (7  8))))
```

To see how a finite stream would result in a list as it is forced, we define a function called FORCE-N that forces up to a specified number of elements of a given stream (counting from 0). Like SCAR and SCDR it assumes normalized streams.

```
(DEFUN FORCE-N  (N  S)
;;; Forces first N elements of stream S
;;; counting from 0.
    (COND  [(NULL  S)  ()]
           [(=  0  N)  S]
           [T (CONS  (SCAR S)
                     (FORCE-N (- N 1) (SCDR S)))]))
```

Thus, if

```
RES = (10 . #S(RECIPE  FUNC GAPPEND
                      ARGS ((11 12)  (7 8 9))))
```

then

```
(FORCE-N  0  RES)
   => (10 . #S(RECIPE FUNC GAPPEND ARGS ((11 12) (7 8 9))))
```

```
(FORCE-N  1  RES)
   => (10 11 . #S(RECIPE FUNC GAPPEND ARGS ((12) (7 8 9))))
(FORCE-N  2  RES)
   => (10 11 12 . #S(RECIPE FUNC GAPPEND ARGS (() (7 8 9))))
(FORCE-N  3  RES)
   => (10  11  12  7  8  9)
(FORCE-N  7  RES)
   => (10  11  12  7  8  9)
```

GAPPEND can also take streams as its arguments. Let us first introduce a generator GINT-RANGE that generates a finite stream of integers in a specified range:

```
(DEFUN GINT-RANGE (LO  HI)
   (COND  [(>  LO  HI)  ()]
          [T (CONS  LO
                      (MAKE-RECIPE #'GINT-RANGE
                                   (LIST (+ 1 LO) HI)))]))
```

Let T1 and T2 be set to a finite stream of integers as follows:

```
(SETQ  T1  (GINT-RANGE  21  23))
(SETQ  T2  (GINT-RANGE  35  36))
```

Therefore,

```
T1  =  (21 . #S(RECIPE  FUNC GINT-RANGE  ARGS (22 23)))
T2  =  (35 . #S(RECIPE  FUNC GINT-RANGE  ARGS (36 36)))
```

and

```
(GAPPEND  T1  T2)
   => (21 . #S(RECIPE
                FUNC GAPPEND
                ARGS
                ((22 . #S(RECIPE  FUNC GINT-RANGE
                                   ARGS (23 23)))
                 (35 . #S(RECIPE  FUNC GINT-RANGE
                                   ARGS (36 36))))))
```

Let the above result be bound to RES. On forcing the elements of RES (using FORCE-N) we get

```
(FORCE-N 1 RES)
   => (21 22
```

```
       . #S(RECIPE
             FUNC GAPPEND
             ARGS
                ((23 . #S(RECIPE   FUNC GINT-RANGE
                                   ARGS (24 23)))
                 (35 . #S(RECIPE   FUNC GINT-RANGE
                                   ARGS (36 36)))))))

(FORCE-N  2 RES)
   =>   (21 22 23
          . #S(RECIPE
                FUNC GAPPEND
                ARGS
                  (()
                   (35 . #S(RECIPE  FUNC GINT-RANGE
                                    ARGS (36 36)))))))

FORCE-N  3 RES)
    =>   (21 22 23 35 . #S(RECIPE FUNC GINT-RANGE
                          ARGS (36 36)))

(FORCE-N  6 RES)
    => (21 22 23 35 36)
```

Exercise 9.1 Define FORCE-N without using SCAR or SCDR. (Use IS-RECIPE and NORMALIZE directly.) Also modify it to accept both normalized and unnormalized streams.

We can build a stream of streams where each of the streams is infinite. To construct a stream of the following form

```
((1 2 ...) (11 12 ...) (21 22 ...) ...)
```

in which the first element of the stream is a stream of natural numbers starting from 1, the second element is a stream of natural numbers starting from 11, and so on, we have the following generator:

```
(DEFUN GINF (N)
   (CONS (GINT N)
         (MAKE-RECIPE #'GINF (LIST (+ 10 N))) ))
```

Now,

```
(GINF 1) => ( (1 . #S(RECIPE FUNC GINT ARGS (2)))
             . #S(RECIPE FUNC GINF ARGS (11)))
```

```
(FORCE-N 1 (GINF 1))
   => ( (1 . #S(RECIPE FUNC GINT ARGS (2)))
        (11 . #S(RECIPE FUNC GINT ARGS (12)))
      . #S(RECIPE FUNC GINF ARGS (21)))
(SCAR (SCDR (GINF 1)))
   => (11 . #S(RECIPE FUNC GINT ARGS (12)))
```

Let two infinite streams be interleaved by GTHREAD2:

```
(GTHREAD2 (GINT 1) (GINT 11))
```

producing

```
(1 11 2 12 3 13 ... )
```

The following is its definition:

```
(DEFUN GTHREAD2 (S1 S2)
   (CONS (SCAR S1)
         (MAKE-RECIPE #'GTHREAD2 (LIST S2 (SCDR S1)))))
```

Exercise 9.2 Define GWEAVE that takes a stream S of streams and interleaves the elements of the streams in S. For example,

```
(GWEAVE (GINF 1))
```

produces a stream of the form (1 11 21 ...). What does the following evaluate to when forced:

```
(FORCE-N N (GWEAVE
              (LIST (GINT 0) (GINT 10) (GINT 20))))
```

for three different values of N: 0, 1, and 2?

Exercise 9.3 Generate a stream in which elements of a list repeat ad infinitum.

```
(GREPEAT '(1 2 3))
      => (1 2 3 1 2 3 1 2 ...)
```

Exercise 9.4 Repeat Exercise 9.3 but specify the number of repetitions. For example,

```
(GREPEAT-N 0 '(1 2 3)) => ()
(GREPEAT-N 1 '(1 2 3)) => stream equivalent to (1 2 3)
(GREPEAT-N 2 '(1 2 3)) => stream equivalent to
                          (1 2 3 1 2 3)
```

A characteristic of recipes is that they consist of a function followed by its arguments that are the result of evaluating parameters at the time recipe is formed. This ensures that the parameters are evaluated in the environment in which the function would have been applied had it not been delayed.

All the functions that have been delayed are pure; that is, they have no side effects and do not depend on any free (global) variables that might change during the time a function is delayed. Handling side effects, in full generality, is quite an impossible task and goes against the very idea of streams. Delay of a function having side effects delays the side effect it would have produced; and if the user is forced to consider the effects of delay, the advantages of streams are lost.

9.3   IMPLEMENTING STREAMS USING CLOSURE

Once we understand the basic idea, we can improve upon the implementation. We can construct recipes using lexical closure.[3] The idea is as follows: If the evaluation of an expression <e> is to be delayed, the lambda expression

```
#'(LAMBDA () <e>) => <closure-of-lambda-containing-<e>>
```

is constructed and placed in a recipe:

```
#S(RECIPE <closure-of-lambda-containing-<e>> ())
```

When the recipe is forced, the closure of the lambda expression is applied to nil arguments. The closure ensures that the evaluation, whenever it takes place, is carried out in the desired original environment.

As an example, consider the new definition of GAPPEND:

```
(DEFUN GAPPEND (S1 S2)
   (COND [(NULL S1) S2]
         [T (CONS (SCAR S1)
                  (MAKE-RECIPE
                     #'(LAMBDA ()
                          (GAPPEND (SCDR S1) S2))
                     ()))]))
```

If as before,

```
T1 = (21 . #S(RECIPE  FUNC GINT-RANGE ARGS (22 23)))
T2 = (35 . #S(RECIPE  FUNC GINT-RANGE ARGS (36 36)))
```

[3]Some earlier implementations of LISP did not support taking closure. Most of the ones that did, did not allow full closures, e.g., the closures could not be returned. Hence, the technique described in this section would be inapplicable there.

and GAPPEND is called, we get

```
(GAPPEND T1 T2)
   => (21 . #S(RECIPE FUNC <closure1> ARGS ()))
```

where <closure1> is the closure of

```
(LAMBDA () (GAPPEND (SCDR S1) S2))
```

When the recipe is forced, the body of the lambda expression is evaluated in the environment in which closure was taken (i.e., in which S1 was bound to the value of T1, and S2 to that of T2).

This new scheme of taking closure has the advantage over the previous one that parameters of function calls that are delayed are not evaluated before the recipe is formed. In case a recipe is never evaluated, this can be very important. First, such evaluation is not needed and hence is inefficient. More importantly, however, such an evaluation might be nonterminating in which case the stream implemented with the former method will be an undefined object. (For an example, see the next section.)

There is another important advantage in using closures. In case a function has local or free variables, their values are preserved in the closure and are available when the recipe is forced. In the earlier implementation without using closures, values of local or free variables were not available. Hence, care had to be taken that values of such variables are appropriately included as arguments (by introducing additional arguments). Definition of NORMALIZE remains the same because the structure of the recipe is unchanged. It contains a niladic function (actually a closure) followed by zero arguments.

9.4 MAKING GENERATORS OF STREAMS MORE NATURAL

If we compare the definitions of APPEND and GAPPEND, we find that the definition of GAPPEND does not naturally follow from that of APPEND. Details of how a recipe is represented must be learned before GAPPEND can be written or understood.

```
(DEFUN APPEND (L1 L2)
   (COND [(NULL L1) L2]
         [T (CONS (CAR L1)
                  (APPEND (CDR L1) L2) )]))

(DEFUN GAPPEND (S1 S2)
   (COND [(NULL S1) S2]
         [T (CONS  (SCAR S1)
                   (MAKE-RECIPE #'GAPPEND
                                (LIST (SCDR S1) S2)))]))
```

or

```
(DEFUN GAPPEND (S1 S2)
   (COND [(NULL S1) S2]
         [T (CONS (SCAR S1)
                  (MAKE-RECIPE
                       #'(LAMBDA ()(GAPPEND
                                    (SCDR S1) S2))
                       ()))]))
```

A better syntax using DELAY is given below. To define GAPPEND, we just have to put an explicit delay in the body of APPEND. With this, GAPPEND is just like APPEND except that instead of the recursive call a recipe is formed.

```
(DEFUN GAPPEND (S1 S2)
   (COND [(NULL S1) S2]
         [T (CONS (SCAR S1)
                  (DELAY (GAPPEND (SCDR S1) S2)))]))
```

The definition of DELAY that makes the above possible is easy to arrange. Two definitions are given below. The first definition constructs a recipe by evaluating the parameters but without taking closure. The second one takes closure.

```
(DEFMACRO DELAY (E)
;;; Value of E is of the form
;;;    (<fn> <parm1> ...<parmn>)
;;; Each of the parameters is evaluated and a
;;; recipe is formed
;;;    (RECIPE  FUNC <fn>  ARGS <arg1> ... <argN>)
;;; To generate the recipe, the macro must expand into
;;;    (MAKE-RECIPE '<fn>
;;;                 (LIST <parm1> ... <parmN>))
   `(MAKE-RECIPE  ',(CAR E)  (LIST ,@(CDR E))))
```

After macro expansion, the following is produced

```
(MAKE-RECIPE
    '<fn>
    (LIST <parm1> ... <parmN>))
```

which on evaluation produces the desired recipe. Parameters of the function to be delayed are evaluated after the macro expansion and then put in the recipe. NOR-MALIZE and FORCE-N are the same as before.

The second definition of DELAY constructs a recipe based on taking closures.

```
(DEFMACRO DELAY (E)
  `(MAKE-RECIPE  #'(LAMBDA () ,E)  ()))
```

Thus,

```
(DELAY <e>)
```

expands into

```
(MAKE-RECIPE
     (FUNCTION (LAMBDA () <e>))
     ())
```

which on evaluation takes the closure of the lambda expression and puts it in the recipe. In the rest of this chapter, we will use and assume the second definition of DELAY.

The generators introduced in Sec. 9.1 are redefined below using DELAY. Any one of the above two definitions of DELAY may be used here.

```
(DEFUN GINT (N)
   (CONS N (DELAY (GINT (+ 1 N)))))

(DEFUN GINT-RANGE (LO HI)
   (COND [(> LO HI) ()]
         [T (CONS LO
                  (DELAY (GINT-RANGE (+ 1 LO) HI)))]))

(DEFUN GINF (N)
   (CONS (GINT N)
         (DELAY (GINF (+ 10 N))) ))

(DEFUN GTHREAD2 (S1 S2)
   (CONS (SCAR S1)
         (DELAY (GTHREAD2 S2 (SCDR S1)))))
```

Definitions of generators are very simple with the new approach. All we have to do is to write a function that produces a list corresponding to the stream and then put in delays at the appropriate places (usually the recursive function calls). Of course, when we are producing an infinite stream, the corresponding list-producing function is not well defined because it goes into an infinite recursion; however, it is still useful as a conceptual device.

A comparison of APPEND and the new GAPPEND using DELAY brings out another important point. Although both functions appear to be recursive, GAPPEND is not. A call made to GAPPEND does not result in a recursive call because DELAY

produces a recipe containing GAPPEND and returns. It is only later when the recipe is forced that call to GAPPEND is made, but then it is not recursive.

Streams can be viewed as coroutines, where one of the coroutines executes a little and then transfers control to another, which again executes a little before transferring control back or to another coroutine. In the example,

```
(GAPPEND (GINT-RANGE 21 23) (GINT-RANGE 35 36))
```

we can imagine there to be three coroutines. Two of them evaluate the application of GINT-RANGE to the arguments given above. The third one applies GAPPEND to the appropriate arguments. If we focus our attention on the control (on these three routines), we find the following: The first routine executes a little producing (21 ...), the second routine executes producing (35 ...), and then GAPPEND executes producing (21 ...). As the stream is traversed, control keeps switching between the routines just as in coroutines.

Exercise 9.5 Define GWEAVE described in Exercise 9.2 using DELAY.

Exercise 9.6 Define GREPEAT and GREPEAT-N described in Exercises 9.3 and 9.4 using DELAY.

Exercise 9.7 Define PICK-EVERY-MTH that takes a number M and a stream and picks the Mth element from it (counting from 1).

```
(PICK-EVERY-MTH 3 (GINT 1)) => (3 6 9 ...)
```

```
(PICK-EVERY-MTH 3 (GINT 0)) => (2 5 8 ...)
```

Exercise 9.8 Define GFILTER that takes a sieve and a stream, and returns a stream of those elements that pass through the sieve. For example,

```
(GFILTER #'(LAMBDA (N) (> N 35))
         (GAPPEND '(30 39 46 8)
                  '(5 20 50)))
   => a stream equivalent to (39 46 50)
```

Exercise 9.9 Using GFILTER, generate a stream of odd numbers.

Exercise 9.10 There is a way that a recursive call might result from GAPPEND. It occurs when one of its argument streams containing a recipe with GAPPEND is normalized. Show by using the trace (of function calls) that the following results in recursive calls on GAPPEND.

```
(GAPPEND T1 '(40 50))
```

where

```
T1 = (GAPPEND '(10 11 12) '(7 8))
```

9.5 APPLICATIONS OF STREAMS

Some situations in which streams can be used with advantage are given below.

9.5.1 Efficiency

Streams are particularly useful when all the data in them does not have to be accessed. For example, if we perform an operation on the first *n* elements of a stream resulting from GAPPEND (because, say, a given predicate happens to be true for the first *n* elements only), we need to force only the first *n* recipes of the stream. In contrast, if lists are used, the entire list has to be constructed first.

   Another advantage of delayed evaluation is that a large data structure need not be constructed and stored in memory all at once. Parts of it are constructed when necessary. Thus, the result of delayed appending of two lists or streams (using GAP-PEND given below) takes only a few additional cons cells at a time, as opposed to as many cons cells as the length of the first argument, if APPEND is used.

```
(DEFUN GAPPEND (S1 S2)
   (COND [(NULL S1) S2]
         [T (CONS (SCAR S1)
                  (DELAY (GAPPEND (SCDR S1) S2)) )]))
```

Thus, if we have two lists T1 and T2, we can form a stream by appending them

```
(GAPPEND T1 T2)
```

which results in the following:

```
(<first-elem-of-T1>
 . #S(RECIPE
       FUNC <closure-of-(LAMBDA () (GAPPEND (SCDR S1) S2))>
       ARGS ()))
```

However, there is a price to be paid too. Construction and evaluation of recipes takes time. If the entire stream is to be accessed anyway, it might be simpler and more time-efficient to construct the list first.

9.5.2 Uniform View of Diverse Data Structures

   Streams allow user-defined functions that operate on every element of a list to operate on elements belonging to an arbitrary data structure. For example, suppose we define a mapping function MAP-WHILE that performs an operation on each element of a list as long as a predicate applied to the elements is true. (Unlike FILTER it may not reach the end of a list because it gives up when the predicate yields false.)

```
(DEFUN MAP-WHILE (P   G   L)
;;; Applies operator G on each element of list L as long
;;;   as predicate P is true, and returns a list of results.
   (COND [(NULL L) ()]
         [(FUNCALL P (CAR L))
          (CONS (FUNCALL G (CAR L))
                (MAP-WHILE P G (CDR L)) )]
         [T   ()]))
```

To perform an operation OP on each member of two lists T1 and T2 while a predicate PRED is true, we have three alternatives:

1. Append the two lists and then apply MAP-WHILE:

```
(MAP-WHILE #'PRED #'OP (APPEND T1 T2))
```

2. Define a new function that applies the given operator first on the elements of T1 and then on the elements of T2, as long as the given predicate is true.

```
(MAP-WHILE-2 #'PRED #'OP T1 T2)

(DEFUN MAP-WHILE-2 (P G T1 T2)
   (COND [(NULL T1) (MAP-WHILE P G T2)]
         [(FUNCALL P (CAR T1))
          (CONS (FUNCALL G (CAR T1))
                (MAP-WHILE-2
                       P G (CDR T1) T2))]
         [T ()]))
```

3. Define SMAP-WHILE which is the same as MAP-WHILE except CARs have been replaced by SCARs, and CDRs by SCDRs; the recursive call remains as before. Now, apply SMAP-WHILE to the stream formed by appending T1 to T2:

```
(SMAP-WHILE #'PRED #'OP (GAPPEND T1 T2))
```

The first solution is simple but quite expensive because the lists are appended before the processing begins. Thus, even though the lists may not be traversed fully, the cost of appending them is incurred. The second solution, though efficient, requires rewriting of MAP-WHILE and is not extensible to other data structures (to the union of three lists, for example). The third solution is simple, efficient, and extensible. It can also yield streams by delaying the recursive call in MAP-WHILE.

The essence of the third solution is that diverse data structures can be viewed as a stream by defining an appropriate stream generator on them. Functions that operate on streams can then be made to work unchanged on the data.

The discussion in this section should not create the impression that streams remove the need for all other data structures. All that has been shown here is that at times we are interested in scanning the values in a data structure ignoring some parts of the structure. Then, streams are a handy tool to have. Special properties of a data structure that make certain operations efficient, for example, binary search in a tree, are lost when a stream is constructed from the data structure.

Exercise 9.11 We have a function MAP-SQUARE that takes a stream of numbers and generates a stream of their squares. Use it to generate a stream that squares every third number in a stream, dropping the rest. (*Hint*: Use PICK-EVERY-MTH.)

Exercise 9.12 Write a function that takes every third number larger than 35 in a stream of numbers and generates a stream of their squares, dropping the rest of the numbers. (*Hint*: Use GFILTER and SQUARE, together with PICK-EVERY-MTH.)

9.5.3   Infinite Structures

Streams allow infinite data structures to be defined. Finite parts of these data structures can be traversed when necessary. Thus, the algorithm that decides what part to traverse is made independent of the generation of the actual data structure.

To find prime factors of a given number, for example, we need to repeatedly divide it by successive prime numbers. PRIME-FACTORS takes a number N whose prime factors have to be found, FACTORS the factors found so far, and PRIMES the infinite stream of prime numbers that gets traversed to as much length as necessary.

```
(DEFUN PRIME-FACTORS (N PRIMES FACTORS)
   (COND [(= 1 N) FACTORS]
         [(= 0 (REM N (SCAR PRIMES))) ;Another factor
                                      ; found
          (PRIME-FACTORS
                (/ N (SCAR PRIMES))
                PRIMES   ;SCDR not taken to get multiple
                         ; factors, if any, of the
                         ; same prime
                (CONS (SCAR PRIMES) FACTORS) )]
         [T (PRIME-FACTORS N (SCDR PRIMES) FACTORS)]))
```

The only thing that remains to be done is to define a stream of prime numbers. We do it using sieves of Eratosthenes.

The sieves of Eratosthenes method was first introduced in Sec. 8.5 to find the successive prime numbers. Here, we use it to form the stream of prime numbers. GPRIMES is a generator for the stream of prime numbers. Thus,

```
(GPRIMES) => (2 . <recipe-for-the-rest-of-primes>)
```

GPRIMES is patterned after N-PRIMES of Sec. 8.5, except here no N is specified

because we want all the prime numbers. As before, NEXT-PRIME is used to generate the next prime, and GEN-NOT-DIVISIBLEP the sieves.

```
(DEFUN GPRIMES ()
   (CONS
    2                ;The first prime
    (GPRIMES-AUX '(2) (LIST (GEN-NOT-DIVISIBLEP 2)) 3)))

(DEFUN GPRIMES-AUX (PRIMES-SO-FAR SIEVES-SO-FAR NUM)
   (LET ([PRIME (NEXT-PRIME SIEVES-SO-FAR NUM)])
      (CONS PRIME
            (DELAY (GPRIMES-AUX
                    (CONS PRIME PRIMES-SO-FAR)
                    (CONS (GEN-NOT-DIVISIBLEP PRIME)
                          SIEVES-SO-FAR)
                    (+ 2 PRIME) )))))
```

Exercise 9.13 Generate a stream of numbers in ascending order that have 10 or more factors. (Unlike primes, these are numbers that are highly divisible.)

Exercise 9.14 Repeat Exercise 9.13 when there are 10 or more distinct factors.

9.5.4 Parallel Execution

Streams are ideal candidates for implementation on a parallel machine. DELAY can be interpreted as spawning a new process P1, say, to apply a given function to its arguments. FORCE or NORMALIZE of a delayed function application is to be interpreted as obtaining the result of process P1 (which in turn might have spawned other processes). The parallelism is hidden from the user, who continues writing programs as before, except they now execute faster.

Exercise 9.15 Let the node of a binary tree be represented as

```
(DEFSTRUCT (NODE (:CONSTRUCTOR CONS-NODE
                                (VALUE LEFT RIGHT))
                 (:TYPE LIST))
           VALUE
           LEFT
           RIGHT)
```

GTREE-NODES generates a stream of VALUEs in a given tree in left-to-right, in-order sequence. For example, for the tree shown in Fig. 9-3 represented as

```
(100   (35 ()
              (39 () ()))
       (132 (115 () ())
       (134 (133 () ()) ()) ))
```

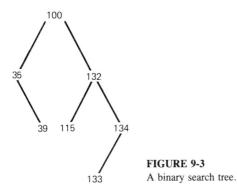

FIGURE 9-3
A binary search tree.

```
(35  39  100   115   132   133   134)
```

The above definition is useful in situations when we need to examine not all but only some of the VALUEs in the tree. For example, to check whether the in-order traversal of two trees is the same, all we have to do is write

```
(SEQUAL (GTREE-NODES T1)
        (GTREE-NODES T2) )
```

where SEQUAL is the same as EQUAL in which CARs and CDRs have been substituted by SCARs and SCDRs, respectively. In case T1 and T2 are not equal, the streams traversed are up to the first mismatch. Thus, in general, the entire tree need not be traversed.

Define GTREE-NODES.

Exercise 9.16 (Difficult) Try doing the above without streams and without first forming the two lists.

Exercise 9.17 We want to sum those VALUEs in an ordered tree which are less than 100. How can this be done without necessarily having to traverse the entire tree?

Exercise 9.18 If unnormalized streams (that is, streams which are recipes) are permitted, SCAR and SCDR have to be modified. They can no longer expect a normalized stream as their argument; at the same time they need not produce a normalized stream as their result. Give their new definitions.

Exercise 9.19 Redefine GAPPEND to work with unnormalized streams. Does your definition work on the following two arguments?

```
#S(RECIPE FUNC (LAMBDA () (GINT-RANGE 6 5)) ARGS ())    and
(3 . #S(RECIPE FUNC (LAMBDA () (GINT-RANGE 4 10)) ARGS()))?
```

Exercise 9.20 Unnormalized streams might have to be normalized repeatedly as in the following example where S is an unnormalized stream consisting of divisor and dividend:

```
(COND [(EQL (SCAR S) 0) 'INFINITY]
      [(EQL (SCAR S) 1) (SCAR (SCDR S))]
      [T (/ (SCAR (SCDR S)) (SCAR S))])
```

If S was normalized, its recipe would not be forced repeatedly. Hence normalized streams seem to be better. In most cases they are. However, there is a problem with their use. Whenever a stream is just a recipe, we force it to produce a normalized stream. This is done in anticipation that the recipe will have to be forced later. Rather than force it in every use we force it only once at the time the stream is created. Herein lies the flaw. If the recipe is not to be forced later, we have forced it unnecessarily. This flaw can be fatal when forcing a recipe that results in an infinite loop or nonterminating recursion. Infinite streams are quite legitimate, even desirable, as long as we traverse only a finite part of the stream. In our enthusiasm to force a recipe that is not yet needed, we end up with an undefined function. Thus, unnormalized streams are strictly more powerful than normalized ones: traversing a path (using SCAR and SCDR) in unnormalized streams might be well defined, whereas traversing the same path (using SCAR and SCDR) in normalized streams might not be.

Can you think of an application where the above would be true?

9.6 PIPES

It is possible to get the power of unnormalized streams with the efficiency of normalized streams. The trick is to substitute the recipe in place, after it is forced. Future traversals of the stream will not find the recipe, but instead, the result. In fact, the time efficiency of this scheme is better, in general, than that provided by normalized streams. For example, GUNION is extremely inefficient when its second argument is a stream.

```
(DEFUN GUNION (S1  S2)
    (COND  [(SNULL  S1)  S2]
           [(GMEMBER (SCAR  S1)  S2)
             (GUNION (SCDR  S1) S2) ]
           [T (CONS  (SCAR S1)
                        (DELAY (GUNION (SCDR S1) S2)))]))
```

The inefficiency arises because for each element of S1, the stream S2 is forced by GMEMBER (the membership testing function) by traversing S2 until an equal element is found or S2 is exhausted. In other words, we end up forcing S2, or parts of S2, repeatedly, as many times as the number of elements of S1.

The definitions PCAR and PCDR given below can be used instead of SCAR and SCDR, respectively, to avoid such repetitious computations. The implementation assumes a list representation of recipes.

```
(DEFSTRUCT (RECIPE (:CONSTRUCTOR MAKE-RECIPE (FUNC ARGS))
                   (:TYPE LIST)
                   (:NAMED))
            FUNC ARGS)

(DEFUN PCAR (S)  (CAR (PNORMALIZE S)) )

(DEFUN PCDR (S)  (CDR (PNORMALIZE S)) )
```

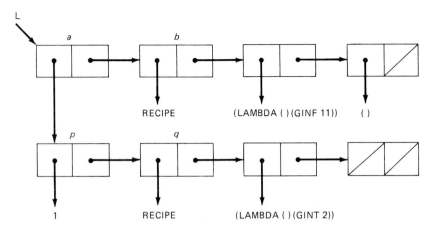

FIGURE 9-4

```
(DEFUN PNORMALIZE (S)
   (COND [(IS-RECIPE S)
         (LET ([X (APPLY (RECIPE-FUNC S)
                         (RECIPE-ARGS S))])
            (COND    [(NULL X)
                     ;; Construct a dummy recipe
                     ;; that evaluates to ().
                     (SETF (RECIPE-FUNC X) '(LAMBDA () ()))]
                     [T  (SETF (CAR S) (CAR X))
                         (SETF (CDR S) (CDR X))
                         (PNORMALIZE S)])])]
         [T S]))

(DEFUN PNULL (S)   (NULL (PNORMALIZE S)) )
```

PNORMALIZE forces the recipe in an unnormalized stream and substitutes the new stream in place in the recipe. There is one situation when this cannot be done: when the recipe results in (). This means that whenever a recipe evaluates to (), it will have to be evaluated each time it is traversed. If we wish to avoid this reevaluation because of efficiency (or worse because the generator has side effects), another recipe that generates () more efficiently is constructed and substituted in place.

To illustrate how PNORMALIZE works, let us consider an example. Suppose there is a function TEST that takes a stream as its argument,

```
(DEFUN TEST (L)
   (COND [(=  1 (PCAR (PCDR L)))    ...    ]
         [(=  6 (PCAR (PCDR L)))    ...    ]
         [(= 11 (PCAR (PCDR L)))    ...    ] ))
```

When it is applied to a stream of streams,

```
(TEST   (GINF 1))
```

L is bound to

```
((1 . #S(RECIPE FUNC (LAMBDA () (GINT 2)) ARGS ()))
 . #S(RECIPE FUNC (LAMBDA () (GINF 11)) ARGS ()))
```

Figure 9-4 shows the memory structure for the stream. The first time PCDR is applied to L, it yields,

```
#S(RECIPE FUNC (LAMBDA () (GINF 11)) ARGS ())
```

When PCAR is applied to it, it results in a call on PNORMALIZE with the argument #S(RECIPE FUNC (LAMBDA () (GINF 11)) ARGS ()). Figure 9-5 shows the memory structure of the argument of PNORMALIZE. Now, PNORMALIZE evaluates the recipe and substitutes in place (by modifying the contents of cons cell b) resulting in

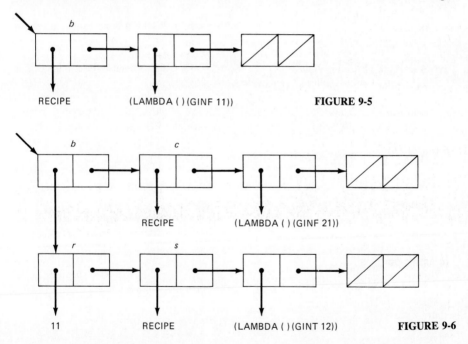

FIGURE 9-5

FIGURE 9-6

Fig. 9-6. Since the CDR pointer of cons cell a continues to point to cons cell b, L now has the value

```
((1 . #S(RECIPE FUNC (LAMBDA () (GINT 2)) ARGS ()))
 (11 . #S(RECIPE FUNC (LAMBDA () (GINT 12)) ARGS ()))
 . #S(RECIPE FUNC (LAMBDA () (GINF 21)) ARGS ()))
```

which is as shown in Fig. 9-7.

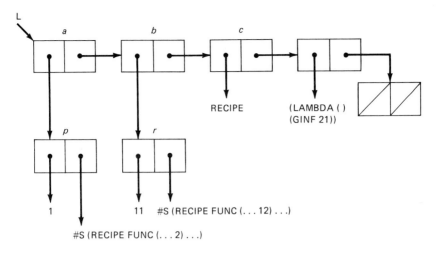

FIGURE 9-7

The next time PCDR is applied, it simply returns the tail which is no longer a recipe. When PCAR is taken, GINF does not need to be applied again.

> **Exercise 9.21** Define PFORCE-N that is similar to FORCE-N but uses PCAR and PCDR, etc. (*Note*: Handle unnormalized streams correctly.)

> **Exercise 9.22** Define GMEMBER using PCAR and PCDR so that its repeated application in GUNION is not inefficient. What happens when the following is evaluated?

```
(GUNION   (GINT-RANGE   21 22) (GINT-RANGE 19   21))
```

When recipes are substituted by their values in place in a stream, as shown above, the stream is called a *pipe*. Pipes are *memoryless*. No matter how many times PCAR or PCDR of the same pipe is taken, the respective results are the same. A pipe is memoryless irrespective of whether the generator in its recipe has side effects or not. This is unlike streams, where we require our generators to be side-effect free (for streams to be memoryless).

The following example establishes a pipe PF for reading from a file. GREAD, the generator, has side effects (namely, that it consumes the input), but the pipe PF is memoryless.

```
(DEFUN GREAD ()
    (CONS   (READ)
            (DELAY (GREAD)))))

(SETQ PF (GREAD))
```

Application of PCDR on PF many times yields the same pipe; in other words, PF is memoryless. PF would not be memoryless if SCAR and SCDR were applied to it.

This shows that if a generator used in producing a stream has side effects but the side effects do not affect other generators, functions, or streams (they only affect future application of this generator in this stream), then an appropriate pipe can be constructed.

> **Exercise 9.23** Show why PF is not memoryless if SCAR and SCDR are used to traverse it. Take an example that uses PF to illustrate the problems such a stream would have.

9.7 AN EXAMPLE—QUERY PROCESSOR WITH STREAMS

As an example, let us take the query processor discussed in Sec. 4.3 and make it generate streams. SIMP-QUERY-PROCESSOR takes a simple query, a database of facts, and an association list. It returns a list of new association lists. We will define GSIMP-QUERY-PROCESSOR that will, instead, return a stream of association lists. This is accomplished by introducing delay at appropriate places.

```
(DEFUN GSIMP-QUERY-PROCESSOR (Q DB ALIST)
;;; Returns a stream of ALISTS.
   (COND [(NULL DB) NIL]
         [T (LET ((MLIST (MATCH2 Q (CAR DB) ALIST)))
             (COND [(FAIL-P MLIST)
                    (GSIMP-QUERY-PROCESSOR
                      Q (CDR DB) ALIST)]
                   [T ;;MLIST is a new association list.
                    (CONS MLIST
                          (DELAY (GSIMP-QUERY-PROCESSOR
                                   Q (CDR DB) ALIST)))]
            ))]))
```

Thus the returned stream contains only one association list. The remaining are generated, if required, on demand.

> **Exercise 9.24** Define GTRAVERSE-DF which is similar to TRAVERSE-DF (Sec. 3.1.4) except that it generates a stream.

> **Exercise 9.25** Take the example tree in Fig. 3.1 and traverse it using GTRAVERSE-DF. (Assume that all nodes containing even numbers are goal nodes.) The result of the traversal is scanned for a state whose value is greater than 8. Identify the switching of control between the traverser and scanner.

> **Exercise 9.26** Implement QUERY-PROCESSOR described in Sec. 4.3 using streams.

> **Exercise 9.27** Suppose we want to generate not just the first but all possible solutions in INFER-AND (Sec. 6.1.3). Change it so that we get a stream of solutions. (*Hint*: First redefine the function so that it gives all solutions. Now introduce delays at appropriate places to get a stream.)

Exercise 9.28 Define GMATCH-TRIE-NODES as a lazy version of MATCH-TRIE-NODES (Sec. 7.4). Study its use in MATCH-ANTEC. (*Note*: This solution has been found not to be very effective in at least one case. [deKleer (1977) returned a stream of possibilities, while a later version deKleer (1978) returned a list.]

FURTHER READINGS

Streams were first proposed by Landin (1966). See Burge (1975) or Abelson and Sussman (1985) for an excellent discussion. SCHEME, a modern dialect of LISP, provides streams as a built-in facility [Rees (1986)].

CHAPTER
10

FUNCTIONAL PROGRAMMING

We have already seen the power of higher-order functions in Chap. 8. They were used to capture whole patterns of computation, and could be used with considerable power whenever the pattern recurred.

The approach presented in Chap. 8 was a limited one, however. A higher-order function could be used individually if it happened to match the problem. There was no proper framework within which higher-order functions could be combined together to solve a problem.

Take, for example, the problem of finding the prime factors of an integer. Solutions made use of higher-order functions like PASS-MULTI-SIEVES-P and FILTER-MULTI-SIEVES. Each of these is a powerful function. However, to put them together we have to make use of ordinary functions and conditionals. A higher-order function cannot be used to combine them. One of the reasons why this is so is because they return values instead of functions.

In this chapter, a framework of programming with higher-order functions is developed. The most important property of higher-order functions here shall be that they always return functions. Thus, for example, instead of MAPCAR we shall have FMAP which returns a function such that on applying it to an argument list we get the same result as by MAPCAR. This seemingly unimportant distinction is the key to the power of higher-order functions. Since the result of applying a higher-order function is a function, it can be the argument of another higher-order function. Finally, the

function returned by the appropriate combination of higher-order functions can be applied to actually solve the problem.

When dealing with higher-order functions, it is important to be clear about the types for functions as this can be a source of confusion. Hence, that is discussed first in the next section. Following it are a number of powerful higher-order functions. They are then discussed as part of a general framework. Finally, an example illustrates the power of the framework. Once a set of higher-order functions for the problem domain are defined, they can be combined resulting in concise and lucid programs.

10.1 TYPES FOR FUNCTIONS

Let us first introduce types for the domain and the range of higher-order functions. It will help us in understanding them better. As an example, let us consider EACH (same as in Sec. 8.1) or MAPCAR-1, which is a restricted form of MAPCAR that takes a monadic function as its first argument. In MAPCAR-1, suppose that the argument function (i.e., the first argument) maps from type Y to type Z [written as $(Y \rightarrow Z)$] and the second argument is a list of elements of type Y [written as list (Y)]; then it returns a list of elements of type Z:

```
MAPCAR-1: (Y->Z) x list(Y) -> list(Z)
```

Where list(Y) and list(Z) both include the null list as well. In the following example, the first argument of MAPCAR-1 maps from number to boolean; that is, type Y is number and Z is boolean.

```
(MAPCAR-1 #'EQ3 '(5 3 9)) => (NIL T NIL)
(DEFUN EQ3 (X) (EQL X 3))
```

We can find the types of expressions in the definition of MAPCAR-1 by identifying the types for arguments and the types of function applied to them.

```
(DEFUN MAPCAR-1 (F L)
   (COND [(NULL L) ()]
         [T  (CONS (FUNCALL F (CAR L))
                   (MAPCAR-1 F (CDR L)) )]))
```

To find the type of

```
(CONS  (FUNCALL F (CAR L))
       (MAPCAR-1 F (CDR L)) )
```

we construct the following table:

S-expr	Type
L	list(Y)
(CAR L)	Y
F	Y → Z
(FUNCALL F (CAR L))	Z
(CDR L)	list(Y)
(MAPCAR-1 F (CDR L))	list(Z)
(CONS (FUNCALL F (CAR L)) (MAPCAR-1 F (CDR L)))	list(Z)

Let us define a function called FMAP that takes a function that maps from type Y to Z, and returns a function that maps from the list of elements of type Y to the list of elements of type Z:

```
FMAP:  (Y -> Z)  ->  (list(Y) -> list(Z))
```

The resulting function when applied to a list has a result similar to MAPCAR-1. For example,

```
(FMAP #'EQ3)
```

evaluates to a function which when applied to a list of numbers, returns a list of booleans (obtained by applying EQ3 to each number). For example, when applied to (5 3 9), it yields (NIL T NIL):

```
(FUNCALL (FMAP #'EQ3) '(5 3 9)) => (NIL T NIL)
```

It is defined as

```
(DEFUN FMAP (F)
    #'(LAMBDA (L) (MAPCAR-1 F L)))     ;[1]
```

Now, when the following is evaluated, it results in the closure of a lambda expression:

---

[1]This definition requires that the LISP you are using supports lexical closure. Otherwise backquote must be used:

```
(DEFUN FMAP (F)
    `(LAMBDA (L) (MAPCAR-1 ',F L)))
```

```
(FMAP #'EQ3) -- evals-equivalent-to =>
     (LAMBDA (L)  (MAPCAR-1 #'EQ3 L))
```

Similarly, we have the following examples:

```
(FUNCALL (FMAP #'1+)  '(5 3 9)) => (6 4 10)

(FUNCALL (FMAP (FMAP #'1+))  '((5 1) (3) (9 4 )))
     => ((6 2)  (4)  (10 5))
```

Type analysis is helpful in understanding the last example which is perhaps not so obvious:

S-expr	Type
1+	number -> number
(FMAP #'1+)	list(number) -> list (number)
(FMAP (FMAP #'1+))	list(list(number)) -> list(list(number))

Exercise 10.1 What is the type of the following:

```
(FMAP (FMAP #'EQ3))
```

Exercise 10.2 What are the types of the following:

```
(FMAP #'FMAP)
(FUNCALL  (FMAP #'FMAP) '(1+))
(FUNCALL  (FMAP  #'FMAP)  '(1+  1-))
```

10.2 STRUCTURED FUNCTIONAL PROGRAMMING

In this section, we will define a number of higher-order functions. Rather than allow all kinds of higher-order functions, we shall restrict ourselves to those that return functions. These higher-order functions are called function-forming operators (FFOs).

To keep the complexity of programs under control, we maintain three distinct levels:

1. *Objects*: These are the data elements.
2. *Functions*: These map objects into objects.
3. *FFOs*: These map objects and functions into functions.

The objects are atoms or lists, as in LISP. All functions are monadic. Even the functions

that normally take more than one argument are monadic here; their arguments must be encapsulated in a list. For example, + ought to be applied to a single argument, namely, a list of length 2.

The FFOs need not be monadic. They, however, cannot be applied to FFOs but only to functions and objects. Such a system is called structured functional programming (SFP).

In SFP, one can either define a function or apply a function to an object by the following syntax:

```
@SFP(DEF <name> = <body>)
@SFP(<func> : <obj>)
```

where <name> is the name of the function being defined, <body> is a function name or an application of FFO to its arguments, and : indicates application of a function <func> to an object <obj>. Thus, <func> can be the name of a function or application of an FFO to appropriate arguments, and <obj> is either an object or the application of a function on appropriate objects. For example, using FMAP, we have

```
@SFP (DEF ADD1EACH  =  (FMAP 1+))
@SFP (ADD1EACH : (5   3   9))  =>  (6 4 10)
@SFP ((FMAP 1+) : (5 3 9)) => (6 4 10)
@SFP ((FMAP EQ3) : (5 3 9)) => (NIL T NIL)
@SFP ((FMAP (FMAP 1+)) : ((5 1) (3) (9 4)))
                 => ((6 2) (4) (10 5))
```

Let us first define the FFOs that are part of SFP. We have already seen FMAP.

The next FFO is called FCONS or construction. It takes a list of functions that take their argument over the same domain and returns a function which on being applied applies each of the functions in the list to the given argument and forms a list of the results. For example,

```
(FCONS 1+ EQ3)
```

is equal to a function that on being applied to a number N yields a list of length 2. The first element of the list is $(N + 1)$ and the second element T or NIL depending on whether N is 3 or not. The type of FCONS is

```
FCONS: (U->V1) ... (U->Vn) -> (U->(V1 ... Vn))
```

Thus,

```
@SFP((FCONS 1+ EQ3) : 4) => (5 NIL)
@SFP((FCONS 1+ EQ3) : 3) => (4 T)
@SFP((FMAP (FCONS  1+ EQ3)) : (5 3 9))
                 => ((6  NIL)  (4 T)  (10  NIL))
```

Another FFO called FCOMP takes two functions and produces their composition. Applying the composition is, as usual, equal to applying the second function and then the first one.

The conditional FFO FCOND takes a predicate and two functions:

```
(FCOND   P   F1   F2)
```

and it results in a function which on being applied to an object X first applies the predicate and, depending on the outcome, applies F1 or F2.

Similarly, the FFO FCONST when applied to an object, say *c*, produces a constant function. This constant function may be applied to any object, but it yields *c*.

For composition, conditional, and construction FFOs a simpler syntax will be used:

Old syntax	New syntax
(FCOMP <f1> <f2>)	<f1> * <f2>
(FCOND <pred> <f1> <f2>)	<pred> -> <f1> ; <f2>
(FCONS <f1> ... <fn>)	[<f1> ... <fn>]

In SFP, definitions of functions have no need for variables. For example, to define a function that tests whether the tail of an object is null, we write,

```
@SFP(DEF   NULLTAIL =   NULL*TAIL)
```

The definition above has no reference to the object variable. Unlike the above, the LISP definition is in terms of the object variable.

```
(DEFUN NULLTAIL (L)   (NULL (TAIL L)))
```

APPEND defined below appends two lists:

```
@SFP (DEF APPEND = NULL * FIRST -> SECOND;
                   CONS * [CAR*FIRST
                              APPEND*[CDR*FIRST SECOND]])
@SFP (DEF FIRST = CAR)
@SFP (DEF SECOND = CADR)
```

Note that FIRST and SECOND select the first list and the second list, respectively, from the argument.

Exercise 10.3 Define UNION and INTERSECTION in SFP. (See Sec. 1.5 for sets.)

Exercise 10.4 Define SUMPROD in SFP. (See Sec. 1.6 for description of SUMPROD.)

10.3 IMPLEMENTING FFOS IN LISP

The built-in FFOs in SFP have to be defined in LISP. We have already seen the definition of FMAP. The other FFOs can be defined in a similar way.

The following is the definition of FCONS and the result of applying it to a test example:

```
(DEFUN FCONS (&REST FUNS)
   #'(LAMBDA (ARG)
        (MAPCAR #'(LAMBDA (F) (FUNCALL F ARG))
              FUNS)))

(FCONS #'1+ #'EQ3) — evals-equivalent-to =>
  (LAMBDA (ARG) (MAPCAR #'(LAMBDA (F) (FUNCALL F ARG))
                        (LIST #'1+ #'EQ3)))

(DEFUN FCOMP (F1 F2)
  #'(LAMBDA (ARG) (FUNCALL F1 (FUNCALL F2 ARG))))

(DEFUN  FCOND (P F1 F2)
   #'(LAMBDA (ARG)
        (COND [(FUNCALL P ARG) (FUNCALL F1 ARG)]
              [T (FUNCALL F2 ARG)])))
```

Exercise 10.5 If your LISP does not have lexical closure, redefine the above FFOs using backquote.

Exercise 10.6 Define FREDUCE that takes a binary operation over a domain, its identity element, and returns a function which when applied to a list of elements of the domain left-reduces them like REDUCE. For example,

```
@SFP( (FREDUCE + 0) : (5  3  2)) => 10
@SFP( (FREDUCE TIMES 1) : (5  3  2)) => 30
```

where 0 is the identity for addition and 1 is the identity for multiplication.

Exercise 10.7 Just as we have defined FMAP instead of MAPCAR-1, define the corresponding FFO for FILTER (in Chap. 8). Use the FFOs defined so far to implement sieves of Eratosthenes for finding prime numbers.

Exercise 10.8 Define SFPPARSE that takes an SFP function definition or a function application, and parses the SFP expressions, inserting QUOTE and FUNCTION at appropriate places.

Exercise 10.9 Define a read macro for @ such that SFPPARSE is called automatically when @SFP is encountered.

10.4   AN EXAMPLE—PICTURE DEFINITIONS

We take an example now to illustrate the power of FFOs. The example is from the domain of pictures following Henderson (1980). We will discuss the domain in some detail. At first sight, it might appear unnecessary, but such a detailed discussion is necessary to arrive at a set of FFOs specific to the domain. Once such FFOs have been identified, the resulting programs are disarmingly simple. In particular, we will show how the FFOs can be used to specify complex picture patterns from skeleton patterns.

10.4.1   The Data Structure

Pictures are specified using vectors and line segments. *Vectors* represent displacement in space. Here we consider only the two-dimensional space of our paper or terminal screen. Vectors are with respect to a reference frame: an origin and the x and y axes. A vector can be specified either by its magnitude and direction (polar coordinates) or by its x and y components (cartesian coordinates). For example, a vector $\mathbf{V}$ can be represented by polar coordinates (L, θ) or by cartesian coordinates (x, y). (See Fig. 10-1.) Here we will use the cartesian coordinates.

Vectors can be added or subtracted. To add a vector $\mathbf{V}_2$ to vector $\mathbf{V}_1$, draw vector $\mathbf{V}_1$ and then draw vector $\mathbf{V}_2$ starting from the arrowhead of vector $\mathbf{V}_1$. (See Fig. 10-2.) Algebraically, if the vectors are

$$\mathbf{V}_1 = (x_1, y_1)$$
$$\mathbf{V}_2 = (x_2, y_2)$$

then,

$$\mathbf{V}_1 + \mathbf{V}_2 = (x_1 + x_2, y_1 + y_2)$$

Taking the negative of a vector involves keeping its magnitude the same but changing its direction by 180°. Thus, if

$$\mathbf{V} = (x, y)$$

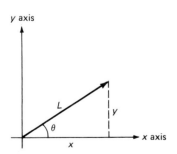

FIGURE 10-1

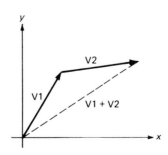

FIGURE 10-2

then,

$$-\mathbf{V} = (-x, -y)$$

Subtraction can be expressed in terms of addition and negative operation.

$$\mathbf{V}_1 - \mathbf{V}_2 = \mathbf{V}_1 + (-\mathbf{V}_2)$$

The null vector has zero magnitude and indeterminate direction. Therefore, both in polar and cartesian coordinates, we will write it as (0, 0).

A vector can be multiplied by a scalar constant.

$$\mathbf{V} = (x, y)$$
$$k\mathbf{V} = (kx, ky)$$

The following is the representation in cartesian coordinates of a vector in LISP:

```
(DEFSTRUCT (VEC (:CONSTRUCTOR MAKE-VEC (X Y)))
           X Y)
```

Functions for adding two vectors, taking the negative of a vector, scalar multiplication of a vector, and rotating a vector are given below:

```
(DEFUN VEC-+ (V1  V2)
   (MAKE-VEC  (+  (VEC-X  V1) (VEC-X  V2))
              (+  (VEC-Y  V1) (VEC-Y  V2)) ))


(DEFUN  VEC-NEG (V1)
   (MAKE-VEC  (-  (VEC-X  V1))
              (-  (VEC-Y  V1)) ))


(DEFUN  VEC-SMULT (V K)
   (MAKE-VEC  (*  K  (VEC-X  V1))
              (*  K  (VEC-Y  V2)) ))


(DEFUN VEC-ROT (V ANGLE)
;;; ANGLE — angle of rotation in radians.
   (LET ([L    (SQRT (SUMSQ (VEC-X V) (VEC-Y V)))]
         [ANG  (ATAN (/ (VEC-Y V)
                        (VEC-X V)))])
      (MAKE-VEC (* L (COS (+ ANG ANGLE)))
                (* L (SIN (+ ANG ANGLE))) )))
```

Exercise 10.10 Rewrite the above operations using the polar coordinate system.

Exercise 10.11 Define POLARVEC, a data type for vectors using polar coordinates, and define the various operations on such a data type in LISP.

Exercise 10.12 Define VECTOR-+, VECTOR-NEG, VECTOR-SMULT, and VECTOR-ROT as generic functions applicable to both VEC and POLARVEC. (*Hint*: VECTOR-+ must call the function VEC-+ or POLARVEC-+ depending on the type of its arguments.)

A *directed line segment* (simply called a *line segment*) is given by a pair of vectors (V_1, V_2); the first one gives the starting point of the line segment, and the second one if placed on the starting point gives the ending point of the line segment. (See Fig. 10-3.) (V_1, V_2) and $(V_1 + V_2, -V_2)$ represent different line segments because even though their endpoints are the same, their order is interchanged. The following is the representation of a line segment:

```
(DEFSTRUCT (LINE (:CONSTRUCTOR MAKE-LINE (ORG DIR)))
          ORG DIR)
```

Thus, vectors V_1 and V_2 and lines L_1 and L_2 are constructed as given below. (See Fig. 10-4.)

```
(LET*([V1  (MAKE-VEC  3   5)]
      [V2  (MAKE-VEC  5   3)]
      [L1  (MAKE-LINE  V1  V2)]
      [L2  (MAKE-LINE  V2  V1)])
      ... )
```

We define functions for translating a line segment, rotating it, and performing both the operations, together.

```
(DEFUN LINE-TRANS (L V)
    (MAKE-LINE (VEC-+ V (LINE-ORG L)) (LINE-DIR L)))
```

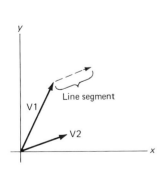

FIGURE 10-3

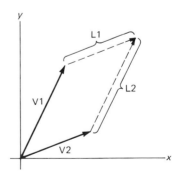

FIGURE 10-4

```
(DEFUN LINE-ROT (L ANG)
   (MAKE-LINE (LINE-ORG L) (VEC-ROT (LINE-DIR L) ANG)))

(DEFUN LINE-TRANSROT (L V ANG)
   (MAKE-LINE (VEC-+ V (LINE-ORG L))
              (VEC-ROT (LINE-DIR L) ANG)))
```

Similarly, the following perform scalar multiplication of the line segment and determine its length and slope.

```
(DEFUN LINE-SMULT (L K)
   (MAKE-LINE (LINE-ORG L)
              (VEC-SMULT (LINE-DIR L) K)))

(DEFUN LINE-LENGTH (L)
   (SQRT (+ (SQR (VEC-X (LINE-DIR L)))
            (SQR (VEC-Y (LINE-DIR L))) )))

(DEFUN LINE-SLOPE (L)
   (/ (VEC-Y (LINE-DIR L)) (VEC-X (LINE-DIR L)) ))

(DEFUN SQR (N) (* N N))
```

Now we are ready to define pictures. A *picture* consists of a list of line segments. We will use CONS-PIC instead of CONS to indicate that a list representing the picture is being constructed. For example, a picture consisting of two lines L_1 and L_2 is defined by the following data structure:

```
(CONS-PIC  L1  (CONS-PIC  L2  ()))
```

where CONS-PIC is defined as

```
(DEFUN CONS-PIC (E P)  (CONS E P))
```

The picture functions we will introduce in the rest of this chapter generate such data structures. It is assumed that a suitable DRAW command causes a picture to be drawn when given a picture data structure. When defining picture functions, we, at times, talk of producing a picture, but all that we mean is the generation of a picture data structure.

We will first define certain basic functions for drawing pictures, and FFOs for manipulating them. These will be defined in LISP and will act as the primitive functions and FFOs for SFP.

10.4.2 Picture Functions

We define below a function called REGULAR-CURVE which can be used to construct a regular polygon. It takes three arguments: number of edges, angle between edges, and a starting edge. For example,

```
(REGULAR-CURVE  4  (RADIAN 90)  '((1 1) (1 0)))
```

constructs a data structure for the square in Fig. 10-5. Line segment L_1 is specified by ((1 1) (1 0)). Line segment L_2 is constructed by computing the starting point as the sum of vectors (1 1) and (1 0) and then computing the displacement vector by rotating the vector (1 0) by 90°. Similarly, L_3 and L_4 are also constructed. Following is the definition of REGULAR-CURVE.

```
(DEFUN REGULAR-CURVE (N ANGLE EDGE)
   (COND [(EQL N 0) ()]
         [T (CONS-PIC
              EDGE
              (REGULAR-CURVE
                (1- N)
                ANGLE
                (LINE-TRANSROT
                  EDGE (LINE-DIR EDGE) ANGLE)))]))
```

Now, we can define TRIANGLE, SQUARE, HEXAGON, and OCTAGON—functions that take a starting edge and construct the corresponding regular polygon on the edge.

```
(DEFUN TRIANGLE (L) (REGULAR-CURVE  3 (RADIAN 120)  L))
(DEFUN SQUARE (L)   (REGULAR-CURVE  4 (RADIAN 90)   L))
(DEFUN HEXAGON (L)  (REGULAR-CURVE  6 (RADIAN 60)   L))
(DEFUN OCTAGON (L)  (REGULAR-CURVE 8 (RADIAN 45)    L))
```

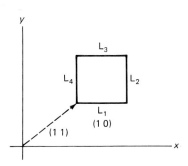

FIGURE 10-5
Square.

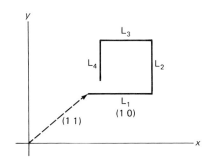

FIGURE 10-6
Spiral resembling a square.

```
(DEFUN RADIAN (ANGLE)
;;; Converts ANGLE in degrees into radians.
   (/ (* ANGLE PI) 180))
```

SPIRAL-CURVE can be defined similar to REGULAR-CURVE except that it takes a reduction factor as well by which the sizes of successive edges are reduced. For example,

```
(SPIRAL-CURVE   .9   4   (RADIAN 90)     '((1 1) (1 0)))
```

would construct a data structure for a spiral resembling a square as shown in Fig. 10-6. The starting line segment L_1 is given by ((1 1) (1 0)). The line segment L_2 is constructed by computing its origin and displacement vector as in REGULAR-CURVE except that the length of the displacement vector is 0.9. Similarly, the lengths of L_3 and L_4 are 0.81 and 0.729, respectively. The definition of SPIRAL-CURVE is left as an exercise. Clearly, SPIRAL-CURVE reduces to REGULAR-CURVE when its first argument is 1.

Using SP-SQUARE,

```
(DEFUN SP-SQUARE (K SPIRALS)
   #'(LAMBDA (EDGE)
       (SPIRAL-CURVE K (* 4 SPIRALS) (RADIAN 90) EDGE)))
```

a spiral of depth 3 shaped like a square can be drawn as follows (see Fig. 10-7):

```
(FUNCALL (SP-SQUARE .9 3)   '((1 1) (1 0)))
```

Exercise 10.13 Define SPIRAL-CURVE as described above.

Exercise 10.14 Use SP-SQUARE to generate a spiral that is clockwise. [*Hint*: What if the reduction factor (the first argument) is greater than 1?]

Exercise 10.15 In the definitions of REGULAR-CURVE and SPIRAL-CURVE, round-off errors in arithmetic (e.g., when VEC-ROT is applied) accumulate in the successive line segments. Redefine them so that such errors do not accumulate.

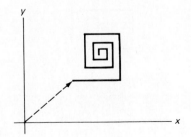

FIGURE 10-7

10.4.3   Picture FFOs

We shall be establishing a three-level hierarchy of SFP. At level 1 there are data structures for vectors, lines, and pictures. At level 2 are the picture functions which map objects to objects. Our picture functions take a line segment as their argument and produce (a data structure for) a picture, that is,

```
LINE -> PIC
```

or

```
VEC x VEC -> list (VEC x VEC)
```

We will denote it by the data type PF (for picture function type). We have already seen TRIANGLE, SQUARE, HEXAGON, OCTAGON, SP-SQUARE, etc., as examples. At level 3 are the FFOs that produce new picture functions of type PF from objects and other picture functions of type PF.

   We shall now be concerned with FFOs suitable for manipulating picture functions. We are, of course, free to use the FFOs defined in Sec. 10.2. For example,

```
(FMAP SQUARE)
```

generates a function that takes a list of line segments and constructs a square on each one of them (see Fig. 10-8).

```
@SFP ( (FMAP SQUARE) : (((1 1) (1 0))
                        ((2 1) (.75 0))
                        ((2.75 1)(.5 0)) ))
```

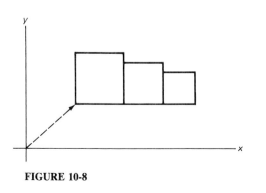

FIGURE 10-8

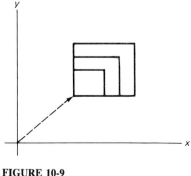

FIGURE 10-9

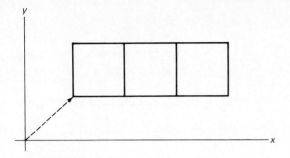

FIGURE 10-10

or (see Fig. 10-9)

```
@SFP ( (FMAP SQUARE) : (((1 1)(1 0))
                        ((1 1)(.75 0))
                        ((1 1)(.50 0)) ))
```

Let us now introduce new FFOs for the purpose of generating picture functions. All the picture functions are of type PF.

1. DISPLACEMENT FFOs. FFOs in this category are used for moving a picture by a specified amount. There are three FFOs in this category: XDISP, YDISP, and DDISP.

XDISP displaces pictures in the x direction. It takes a constant k and a picture function f and produces a new function that behaves like f, except that the picture is moved in the x direction. Its type is:

```
N x PF -> PF
```

where N is the domain of numbers.

The following function takes a line segment as its argument and produces three squares one after the other.

```
@SFP(DEF SQUARE3 = [SQUARE
                   (XDISP 1 SQUARE)
                   (XDISP 1 (XDISP 1 SQUARE))])
```

For example, the above applied to ((1 1)(1 0)) produces squares as shown in Fig. 10-10.

DDISP allows us to displace a picture in the direction of the line segment. In other words, it takes a constant k and a picture function f and returns a new function that when applied to a line segment L draws the same picture as f but displaced by k times the length of L along the direction of L.

```
@SFP ( [SQUARE (DDISP 1 SQUARE)] : ((1 2) (1 1)))
```

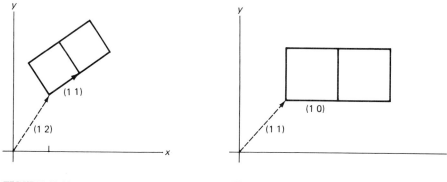

FIGURE 10-11   **FIGURE 10-12**

produces squares as shown in Fig. 10-11.

Exercise 10.16 What picture does the following produce?

```
@SFP( [SQUARE
       (DDISP 1 SQUARE)
       (DDISP 1 (DDISP 1 SQUARE))] : ((1 1)(1 1)) )
```

2. COPY FFOs. FFOs in this category are used to produce copies of a picture. XCOPY, YCOPY, and DCOPY belong to this class. XCOPY takes a number k and a picture function f and generates a new function that produces along the x direction k copies of the picture (each displaced in the x direction by an amount equal to the starting edge) that would have been generated by f. Its type is as follows:

```
XCOPY: N x PF -> PF
```

For example,

```
@SFP( (XCOPY 2 SQUARE) : ((1 1)(1 0)))
```

produces two copies of the square displaced in the x direction (see Fig. 10-12).
Similarly, YCOPY and DCOPY make k copies of a picture along the y direction and along the direction of the argument line segment, respectively.

3. SIZE FFO. This FFO allows us to change the size of a picture. SIZE takes a number k and a picture function and generates a new function that draws a picture whose size is k times that of the picture that would have been drawn by the argument function. Its type is as follows:

```
SIZE: N x PF -> PF
```

Thus,

```
(SIZE  .75 (XDISP 1 SQUARE))
```

on being applied produces a picture that is smaller in size by a factor of 0.75. The following

```
@SFP( [SQUARE (SIZE .75 (XDISP 1 SQUARE))] :
          ((1 1) (1 0)) )
```

produces squares as shown in Fig. 10-13.

> **Exercise 10.17** What picture does the following produce?
>
> ```
> @SFP( [SQUARE (SIZE .75 (DDISP 1 SQUARE))] :
>           ((1 1)(1 1)) )
> ```

4. ROTATION FFO. For rotating a picture we use another FFO called ROT. It takes an angle and a picture function and produces a new picture function that when applied produces the same picture as its argument function but rotated by the specified angle.

```
ROT: N x PF -> PF
```

10.4.4 Example Patterns

The picture functions and FFOs introduced above can be combined to yield powerful functions. To define new functions we will make use of the FFOs and picture functions defined so far. The following, for example, defines a function that draws a partitioned hexagon when applied to a line segment:

```
@SFP(DEF HIVE = (FMAP TRIANGLE) * HEXAGON)
```

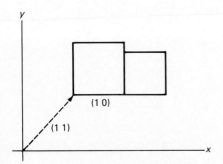

FIGURE 10-13

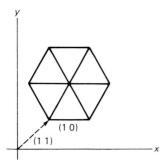

FIGURE 10-14
Hive.

Now,

`@SFP(HIVE : ((1 1) (1 0)))`

produces a data structure for the pattern in Fig. 10-14. HIVE can be combined again
using the FFOs yielding now a pattern of hives (see Fig. 10-15).

`@SFP(DEF BEEHIVE = (FMAP (DDISP 1) (SIZE .33 HIVE))))`

and

`@SFP (BEEHIVE : (HEXAGON : ((1 1)(1 0))))`

Exercise 10.18 Embed the beehives inside a hexagon similar to how the hives are
embedded.

Exercise 10.19 To avoid numerical errors use rational 1/3 rather than 0.3333. See what
difference it makes to the pictures of beehives.

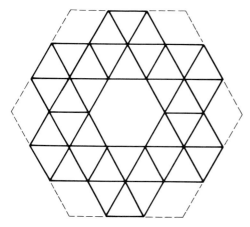

FIGURE 10-15
Beehive.

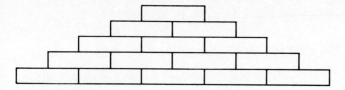

FIGURE 10-16

Exercise 10.20 Draw hives on the edges of a spiral hexagon.

Exercise 10.21 Define a function that draws a beehive without using higher-order functions. How does it compare with the definition given here?

Exercise 10.22 Generate the following pattern shown in Fig. 10-16 in SFP.

Exercise 10.23 Can you think of a set of FFOs for parsing of context-free grammars? If you find the right set, the parser will look just like the grammar.

10.4.5   Implementation of Picture FFOs

Here, without explanation, is the implementation of the picture displacement FFOs. The implementation is in LISP since no mechanism for defining FFOs in SFP has been described here.

```
(DEFUN XDISP (K F)
   #'(LAMBDA (L)
       (FUNCALL F
          (LINE-TRANS L (MAKE-VEC
                          (* K (VEC-X (LINE-DIR L)))
                          0))))))

(DEFUN DDISP (K F)
   #'(LAMBDA (L)
       (FUNCALL F (LINE-TRANS L (VEC-SMULT
                                  (LINE-DIR L) K)))))
```

The others can be defined similarly.

Exercise 10.24 Define YDISP which is like XDISP except that it allows us to displace a picture in the *y* direction.

Exercise 10.25 Define XCOPY, SIZE, and ROT FFOs.

Exercise 10.26 To what closure does the following expand?

```
(DDISP .3 #'SQUARE)
```

Show the lambda expression together with the relevant environment.

10.5   AN EXAMPLE—QUERY PROCESSOR

We saw an implementation of a query processor in Sec. 8.6 that makes use of higher-order functions like FILTER-XFORM. If we want to cast it in the SFP framework, we must identify the objects and define suitable functions and FFOs.

The objects are the patterns, items in the database, and association lists all represented as before (in Sec. 4.3). We next define an FFO called FFILTER-XFORM that is analogous to FILTER-XFORM. It takes a sieve function and produces a new function which if applied to a list would filter and transform its elements.

```
(DEFUN FFILTER-XFORM (SIEVE)
   #'(LAMBDA (L) (FILTER-XFORM SIEVE L)))
```

Now, the SIMP-QUERY-PROCESSOR that takes an argument list containing the query, the database, and an association list can be defined as follows:

```
@SFP(DEF SIMP-QUERY-PROCESSOR =
        (FFILTER-XFORM MATCH2 [FIRST THIRD SECOND]))
```

> **Exercise 10.27** (Difficult) Think of a set of FFOs useful in the domain of query processing. Using the FFOs, define QUERY-PROCESSOR (of Sec. 4.3).

> **Exercise 10.28** Study the power of the FFOs defined in the previous exercise by trying to implement other operators (of Exercises 4.2 and 4.3) using them. Compare the present implementation with that of Exercises 8.21 and 8.22.

> **Exercise 10.29** Think of a domain other than those already mentioned (e.g., pictures and context-free grammars) for which a set of FFOs can be fruitfully identified. Define the FFOs and illustrate their power by examples.

FURTHER READINGS

The SFP introduced here is based on FP [Backus (1978)]. It differs from it slightly in syntax. The syntax here is designed to be keyed in from the terminal and processed easily using LISP read macros.

Further extensions to FP are proposed in Backus (1981). To define new FFOs in SFP we have not shown any mechanism other than LISP. FFP described in Backus (1978) can be used to define higher-order functions (FFOs).

A much more elegant scheme for the definition of FFOs (in which algebraic axioms regarding the FFO can be systematically generated from the definition) is described in Srinivas (1985) and Srinivas and Sangal (1986). For its implementation in LISP see Roberts (1985).

For functional geometry see Henderson (1980). An interesting exercise in drawing one of Escher's pictures is shown in Henderson (1982).

PART
4

DATA-DRIVEN
PROGRAMMING

CHAPTER
11

DATA-DRIVEN PROGRAMMING

In data-driven programming, the data determines what function or program gets executed. There is no central program that decides on the operations and flow of control. One way of realizing a data-driven system is to attach functions to data or types of data and to invoke them when the data is encountered. Thus, the behavior of a data-driven system is determined not by a central program but by the collection of functions attached to the data. It is also an important modularity device.

In this chapter, we focus on the attachment of functions to types of data as a means of realizing data-driven programming. Two extended examples drive the point home.

11.1 ATTACHING FUNCTIONS TO DATA

When a program has to perform a large number of different actions depending on the type of data, there are two major ways of handling the situation:

1. The program body is defined to be a (large) case statement, having a case for each different type of data.
2. A function is defined for each different action to be performed and is attached to the appropriate type of data. The program is now nothing but a statement that retrieves the function attached to the type of data and applies it to the input data.

Take as an example the computable predicates in the expert systems shell in Sec. 6.2. When an atomic formula is a goal, a test is performed to determine whether

the predicate in the goal is a computable predicate or a database predicate. In case of the former, an appropriate function is applied. This function could be selected either by means of a COND form or simply by looking it up in a table (or property list). The latter approach was adopted in the implementation shown earlier.

Take SETF as another example. It takes an access form as its first parameter and applies an appropriate updating function depending on the access function. For example, given GET as the access function it uses an updating function (called PUT-PROP in some LISPs) to store a property, or given CAR it uses a function similar to RPLACA, etc. If we do not use data-driven programming, the program is nothing but a big case statement. To add a new access function we will have to modify the program. In contrast to this is the data-driven approach in which updating functions (called updaters in literature) are attached to the access functions. The main program now only needs to retrieve the attached function and apply it appropriately. Handling new access functions is now a simple matter; it does not entail a change in the program. (See DEFSETF in COMMON LISP.)

Similarly, in the case of a pretty printer, it is usually data-driven. Users can incorporate their own rules for pretty printing of new types of expressions. (Study the pretty printer in your LISP.)

There are two major advantages in this approach. First, it provides modularity. It is very easy to add a new type that can be handled by the program. All we have to do is to define an appropriate function and attach it to the type of data. Similarly, removing a type or making modifications is also easier because only a single function has to be changed. The second major reason is efficiency. By introducing efficient means of accessing the attached function, this approach is potentially more efficient than the case statement which involves a linear search.

In the next two sections we construct extended examples making use of data-driven programming. The first one deals with the implementation of generic functions and the second one with lexicon.

11.2 AN EXAMPLE—GENERIC FUNCTIONS

Generic functions perform different operations on their arguments depending on the data types of the arguments. For example, we can define a function called ADD that performs addition on real numbers and complex numbers and a union on sets of atoms.[1] To perform addition of real numbers ADD calls on +, to perform addition of complex numbers it calls COMPLEX-ADD, and to perform a union of two sets of atoms it calls SET-UNION-TAGGED. To call the correct function, the data type of the arguments has to be determined. Hence, manifest or discriminate data types (i.e., data types with tags) are used.

Let the representation of complex numbers include tags as follows:

---

[1]COMMON LISP has complex and rational data types as built-in types. Function + is already a generic function on them. They are used here for the purpose of illustration only.

```
(DEFSTRUCT (COMPLEX (:CONSTRUCTOR MAKE-COMPLEX (REAL IMAG))
                    (:TYPE     LIST)
                    (:NAMED))       ;Put tag
            REAL IMAG)
```

COMPLEX-P, a predicate for testing whether a given object is a complex number, is generated automatically.

Sets are represented by tagged lists. For example, a set containing RED, BLUE, and GREEN is represented by

```
(SET RED BLUE GREEN)
```

The following function tests whether a given object is a set:

```
(DEFUN SET-P (S) (EQ 'SET (CAR S)))
```

Numbers are built-in, and NUMBERP tests whether a given object is a number or not.

We are now ready to define ADD that uses COMPLEX-ADD, SET-UNION-TAGGED, etc.

```
(DEFUN ADD (N1 N2)
   (COND [(AND (NUMBERP N1) (NUMBERP N2)) (+ N1 N2)]
         [(AND (COMPLEX-P N1) (COMPLEX-P N2))
          (COMPLEX-ADD N1 N2)]
         [(AND (SET-P N1) (SET-P N2))
          (SET-UNION-TAGGED N1 N2)]
         [T (ERROR-MSG "Illegal operand type in ADD."
                       (LIST N1 N2))]))
```

```
(DEFUN COMPLEX-ADD (N1 N2)
   (MAKE-COMPLEX (+ (COMPLEX-REAL N1) (COMPLEX-REAL N2))
                 (+ (COMPLEX-IMAG N1) (COMPLEX-IMAG N2))))
```

```
(DEFUN SET-UNION-TAGGED (N1 N2)
;;; Return union of tagged representation of sets N1 and N2.
   (CONS 'SET (SET-UNION (CDR N1) (CDR N2))))
```

SET-UNION is described in Sec. 1.5.

Exercise 11.1 Define the generic functions called DIFF (for difference) and PRODUCT to work on numbers, complex numbers, and sets. For sets, PRODUCT should take their cartesian product.

If we wish to extend a set of generic functions to cover an additional data type, the definition of each of the functions must be changed. For example, if we want to

cover rational numbers, we must put appropriate function calls after checking the data type to be rational in ADD, DIFF, PRODUCT, etc. Thus, if rational numbers are represented by

```
(DEFSTRUCT (RAT (:CONSTRUCTOR MAKE-RAT (NUMER DENOM))
                (:TYPE   LIST)
                (:NAMED))
           NUMER DENOM)
```

and the functions RAT-ADD, RAT-DIFF, and RAT-PRODUCT are defined appropriately, then we must call these functions from ADD, DIFF, and PRODUCT (when their arguments are of type RAT).

Exercise 11.2 Extend ADD to cover rational numbers.

As described earlier, it is undesirable to modify the code of the generic functions because it is against the principle of modularity. Besides, the functions might be compiled and in a package, and changing and recompiling will be a time-consuming step. Moreover, as the number of data types covered by a generic function increases, the number of clauses in COND also goes up resulting in a longer testing time to determine the type of its arguments.

We can make a table of the generic functions and their associated data types in which the entries show the names of the function to be called by the generic function:

	Numbers	Complex numbers	Sets
ADD	+	COMPLEX-ADD	SET-UNION-TAGGED
DIFF	−	COMPLEX-DIFF	SET-DIFF
PRODUCT	*	COMPLEX-TIMES	SET-CARTPROD

Adding a new data type means adding a new column to the table. Similarly, to add a new generic function, a new row must be added.

In the data-driven approach, the above table can be stored explicitly, and when a generic function is called, it examines the table to decide what function to call. To extend a generic function to a new data type, a new column entry needs to be made in the table; the code for the generic function remains unchanged. Also since items can be looked up quite efficiently in the table, the generic function is more efficient.

Implementation of the table using property lists is shown below for ADD.

```
(SETF (GET 'ADD 'NUMBER) #'+)
(SETF (GET 'ADD 'COMPLEX) #'COMPLEX-ADD)
(SETF (GET 'ADD 'SET) #'SET-UNION-TAGGED)
```

ADD is defined below using OPERATE:

```
(DEFUN ADD (N1 N2)
   (OPERATE 'ADD (LIST N1 N2)))

(DEFUN OPERATE (OP L)
;;; Appropriate function is called depending on
;;; the generic function OP
;;;  and the data type of the first element from L.
   (APPLY (GET OP (TYPE-VAL (CAR L)))
            L ))
```

OPERATE takes the generic function name and the arguments on which the generic function is to be applied, and applies the correct function by looking it up in the table. A function called TYPE-VAL that determines the tag of its argument must be available:

```
(DEFUN TYPE-VAL (L)
   (COND [(NUMBERP L) 'NUMBER] [T (CAR L)]))
```

> **Exercise 11.3** Consider the alternative organization of tables in which the row and the column are interchanged, as illustrated by the following example:
>
> ```
> (SETF (GET 'COMPLEX 'ADD) #'COMPLEX-ADD)
> ```
>
> Compare its relative merits with the earlier method.

11.2.1   Coercion of Types

We have seen until now that whenever a generic function is applied, it calls an appropriate function depending on the types of the arguments. What happens when a generic function is applied to arguments of mixed types? Whether such an application is meaningful will, of course, depend on the domains and the generic function. Sometimes, the domains denoted by the types are related and the generic function denotes a related operation on the domains. For example, NUMBERs and COMPLEX numbers are obviously related and ADD operation for both stands for a related operation. In such situations, it is meaningful to talk about applying a generic function on mixed arguments (e.g., ADD applied to a COMPLEX number and a NUMBER). At other times, it might not be meaningful to talk about application of a generic function (e.g., ADD applied to a number and a set).

To define the application of a generic function on arguments of mixed data types, we can follow one of two approaches:

1. Define a special function to handle each case of mixed arguments.
2. Define data type conversion (or coercion) routines, and call them whenever the type of an argument is not proper. After the type coercion has taken place, one of the appropriate, already-defined functions for performing the operation can be called.

For example, to apply ADD to a COMPLEX number and a NUMBER, this is what we would do in the two approaches: In the first approach, there is a need to define COMPLEX-AND-NUMBER-ADD to perform addition in such situations. In the second approach, a coercion routine, say NUMBER-TO-COMPLEX, will be called to convert the number to a complex number. After the coercion, however, ADD-COMPLEX is all that needs to be called.[2]

To analyze the relative merits of the two approaches, let us consider a generic function of m arguments over n types ($m > 1$, $n > 1$). A different function is called by the generic function when all its arguments are of one of the n types. Now, to handle arguments of mixed types, in the first approach we will have to define

$$n^m - n$$

additional functions for each generic function, while in the second approach

$$n(n - 1)$$

different coercion functions have to be defined only once, independent of the number of generic functions. Clearly, the second approach is better.

Type coercion routines can again be stored in a table (using property lists, say) and data-directed programming can be used.

Exercise 11.4 Show that the above formulas for the number of functions needed are correct.

Exercise 11.5 For a generic function defined over n types with type coercions, compare the number of clauses in the COND form in the generic function when data-driven programming is used and when it is not. (*Hint*: Compare the two definitions of ADD where coercion takes place only over two types. Generalize.)

Exercise 11.6 If we have a generic dyadic function over n types and all possible coercions are allowed among the types, the number of coercion routines needed are

$$n(n - 1)$$

This number can be reduced if the types are structured. Coercion routines need not be defined for every pair of types. We can make use of the structure of the types in doing a sequence of coercions. All that is needed is coercion routines for adjacent pairs in the structure.

Consider, for example, that a generic function PRODUCT is defined over the types NATURAL, INTEGER, RATIONAL, REAL, and COMPLEX. These types can be arranged in a linear chain with COMPLEX at the top:

---

[2]Although numbers are a proper subset of complex numbers as we know from mathematics, coercion from NUMBER to COMPLEX is still necessary. This is because the representation of the two is different.

```
COMPLEX
   |
REAL
   |
RATIONAL
   |
INTEGER
   |
NATURAL
```

Coercions can take place upward in this chain.

Define a coercion routine which takes a value and a type and coerces the value to the specified type using the type chain. (*Hint*: Select a suitable representation for a type structure which is restricted to being just a linear chain.)

Exercise 11.7 Repeat the last exercise when the type structure is not limited to being a chain but could be a tree or a directed acyclic graph. (*Hint*: Use the search techniques in Chap. 3 to search the type structure.)

11.3 AN EXAMPLE—LEXICON

A *lexicon* is a dictionary of sorts in which a set of words together with their entries can be stored. It is an important component of natural language processing systems. Whenever there is a need to check whether a given word belongs to a lexical category (noun, verb, etc.) the lexicon is consulted and the entry or entries for the word are retrieved and checked. Similarly, other relevant information about a word can also be obtained from the lexicon.

In this section, we will see how different forms of a word can be generated from the lexicon using data-driven programming. For example, the word "taste" can take different forms like "tastes," "tasted," and "tasting." Each form has a different entry associated with it:

```
TASTE: (VERB (NUMBER PLURAL) (TENSE PRESENT)
                    ... (TRANSITIVITY T) )
TASTES: (VERB (NUMBER SINGULAR) (TENSE PRESENT)
                    ... (TRANSITIVITY T) )
TASTED: (VERB (TENSE PAST)
                    ... (TRANSITIVITY T) )
TASTING: (VERB (ASPECT CONTINUOUS)
                    ... (TRANSITIVITY T) )
```

Parts of the entries are common (relating to TRANSITIVITY, for example), while others are different (relating to NUMBER, TENSE, etc.). Our lexicon will store only the base form or common prefix; all the other forms will be generated by applying the function attached to the base form.

First we need to select a representation for the lexicon. Let us use discrimination tries (see Sec. 7.3) on characters of words. For example, a lexicon containing "boy," "tail," "tally," and "taste" would look as shown in Fig. 11-1. A * indicates that there is an entry. Similar to before, a trie node can be defined as follows:

```
(DEFSTRUCT (TRIE (:CONSTRUCTOR MAKE-TRIE
                                (CHAR ENTRY SONS)))
           CHAR ENTRY SONS)
```

Now, if we did not use data-driven programming and made separate entries for different forms of words, the lexicon will consume more space. For example, if different forms of the word "taste" are explicitly present, we will have the lexicon shown in Fig. 11-2. We would like instead to be able to associate a function with the base words to generate the different forms. For example, we could associate a function called NORMAL-VERB with the base word "tast" as shown in Fig. 11-3. This function on being applied would generate the other forms.

A design to accomplish the above is described below, but many other variations are possible. It assumes that the word to be searched is given as a list of characters.

With the base word, an entry of the following form is associated,

```
(BASE-WORD    (GENERATOR    <fn>)    ... )
```

where <fn> is either a lambda expression or the name of a function and "..." indicates the part that is common to all the different forms of the word. For the base word 'TAST' we shall have:

```
(BASE-WORD    (GENERATOR    NORMAL-VERB)
              (TRANSITIVITY    T))
```

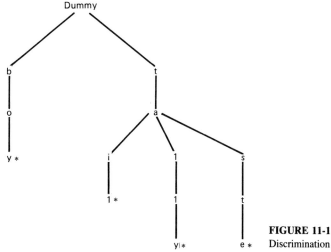

Dummy

b

o

y *

t

a

i

1 *

1

1

yı*

s

t

e *

FIGURE 11-1
Discrimination trie for lexicon.

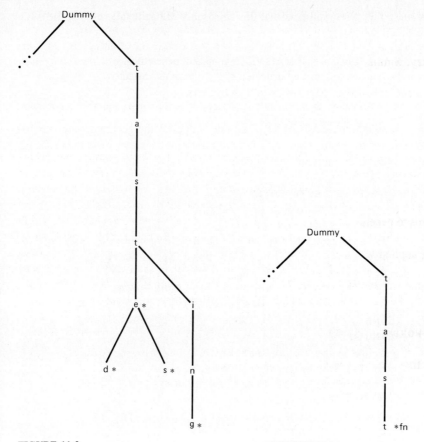

FIGURE 11-2
Lexicon with separate entries.

FIGURE 11-3
Lexicon with base forms and generators.

The attached function <fn> takes two arguments: (1) the remaining characters in the input word, and (2) the common part of the entries. We can now define NORMAL-VERB as an example:

```
(DEFUN NORMAL-VERB (REM-WORD COMMON)
 (COND [(NULL REM-WORD) ()]
       [(EQUAL '(E) REM-WORD)
         (APPEND '(VERB (NUMBER PLURAL) (TENSE PRESENT))
               COMMON)]
       [(EQUAL '(E S) REM-WORD)
         (APPEND '(VERB (NUMBER SINGULAR) (TENSE PRESENT))
               COMMON)]
       [(EQUAL '(E D) REM-WORD)
         (APPEND '(VERB (TENSE PAST)) COMMON)]
       [(EQUAL '(I N G) REM-WORD)
         (APPEND '(VERB (ASPECT CONTINUOUS)) COMMON)]))
```

An important point to remember is that this function will handle all verbs in the same class as TASTE.

Exercise 11.8 Redefine NORMAL-VERB to make it more efficient. (*Hint*: Use a private trie in the function to speed up matching of the remaining characters.)

Exercise 11.9 Identify the commonly occurring forms for nouns, and write a generator.

Let us now define SEARCH-TRIE so that it applies the generators. It searches for the presence of the word in the trie first. On failure, it backtracks and tries to apply generators if any, at the intermediate nodes.

```
(DEFUN SEARCH-TRIE (WORD TRIE)
   (COND
      [(NULL WORD) (TRIE-ENTRY TRIE)]
      [T ;; Using head of the WORD select a son trie, say X,
         ;; and continue search. In case of failure, try
         ;; the generator, if any.
       (LET ((X (ASSOC (CAR WORD) (TRIE-SONS TRIE)
                       :KEY #'TRIE-CHAR)))
          (COND
            [(NULL X)
             ;; Failure to select any of the son tries.
             ;; Try applying the generator.
             (COND [(IS-BASE (TRIE-ENTRY TRIE))
                    (FUNCALL
                       (GET-GENERATOR (TRIE-ENTRY TRIE))
                       WORD
                       (CDDR (TRIE-ENTRY TRIE)))]
                   [T NIL])]
            [T ;; A son trie selected. Pursue it and store
               ;; the result in Y.
             (LET ((Y (SEARCH-TRIE (CDR WORD) X)))
                (COND
                  [(NULL Y)
                   ;; Pursuing a son trie did not help.
                   ;; Try the generator.
                   (COND [(IS-BASE (TRIE-ENTRY TRIE))
                          (FUNCALL
                             (GET-GENERATOR (TRIE-ENTRY TRIE))
                             WORD
                             (CDDR (TRIE-ENTRY TRIE)))]
                         [T NIL])]
                  [T Y]))])))]))

(DEFUN IS-BASE (ENTRY) (EQ 'BASE-WORD (CAR ENTRY)))
```

```
(DEFUN GET-GENERATOR (ENTRY)
     (CADR (ASSOC 'GENERATOR (CDR ENTRY))))
```

Exercise 11.10 Develop an expander function for the generators. What it must do is to enter the generated entry explicitly in the trie structure so that the future search for the entry becomes faster. (*Note*: This will be at the cost of extra space.)

Exercise 11.11 Suppose we want to associate more than one entry with a word in the lexicon. Write SEARCH-TRIE so that all possible entries are returned. (*Note*: You must apply the generators even after one entry has been obtained.)

Exercise 11.12 Develop an alternative scheme for implementing generators.

FURTHER READINGS

Abelson and Sussman (1985) contains more details on the example given here on generic functions. For a variation of the lexicon described here see Sangal et al. (1988). Private tries are attached with base words for more efficient searches.

PART
5

OBJECT-
ORIENTED
PROGRAMMING

CHAPTER
12

OBJECT-ORIENTED PROGRAMMING

Object-oriented programming is based on objects, classes, and messages. To solve a problem in such a programming system, relevant objects or classes of objects are identified and defined. Objects contain state information and inherit properties along a hierarchy. They interact by means of messages, and this interaction produces the solution to the problem.

In this chapter we will first explore the power of inheritance hierarchy, and then we will see how such a system, called VASTU, can be built. An extended example from geometry follows it.

12.1 OBJECT, CLASS, METHOD, MESSAGE

In the last chapter, while discussing data-driven programming, we saw how procedures could be attached to data. In the example on generic functions, the addition functions for numbers, complex numbers, and sets were attached to the respective data types so that they could be applied when necessary. It is possible to view the above in terms of objects, classes, and operations on them. Individual numbers, complex numbers, and sets are objects. The individual numbers belong to the class of numbers, and so on.[1] Now, an appropriate addition function is attached to each of the different classes and is applied when objects of the class are encountered.

So far, the object-oriented view has provided us simply with a way of looking at what we have already achieved. It can be extended, however, to give us additional power. First, associate state information with the object used to model an entity in

---

[1] A class is like a type.

the real world or problem domain. For example, while simulating train wagons and train yards, an object might be defined for each wagon. The object would contain state information like its location, contents, model number, and date last inspected. [Note that in the earlier example the objects (numbers, etc.) were immutable and did not change.]

Second, a class is used to define a set of objects that share some common properties. Members or instances of a class are objects. Information common to the objects of a class need not be stored repeatedly with every object; instead it can be attached to the class and accessed when needed. For example, information about the required repairing frequency of a wagon of a particular model can be associated with the class defined for the model. It need not be stored along with each individual wagon.

Third, the classes may be arranged in a hierarchical manner. The relationship between two adjacent classes in the hierarchy is called IS-A or subset relationship. A class lower down in the hierarchy inherits properties from classes higher up. For example, a class of wagons with a particular model number is a subset of the class of wagons. The latter, in turn, is a subset of the class of rolling stock. Now, if we say for the wagon class that its members do not have an engine or motor, this is inherited by the subclasses of wagons (of different models) and, finally, by the individual wagon objects.

Finally, the objects interact by means of messages rather than by operations (similar to procedure calls). A message sent to an object can cause it to change state, to send messages to other objects, etc. The types of messages that an object can receive are determined by its class. Associated with a class are a fixed set of methods (similar to procedure definitions) each describing how to deal with a different type of message.

As another example, take the domain of a university. A student class is a subset of person class, and student-at-IITK is a subset of student class. Conversely, person and student are superclasses of student-at-IITK. S_1, S_2, and S_3 are instances of the class student-at-IITK (see Fig. 12-1). Each of the classes—person, student, and student-

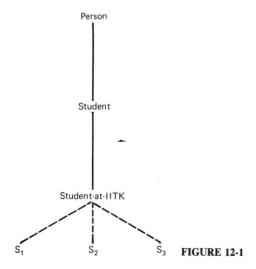

FIGURE 12-1

at-IITK—will have the common attributes name and age, while only the last two will have the attributes school, status, and year. Further, name of the school is the same for S_1, S_2, and S_3 and is associated with the class student-at-IITK. A syntax will be described shortly that allows us to express this.

12.2 VASTU—AN OBJECT-ORIENTED LANGUAGE

VASTU is an object-oriented language following SMALLTALK [Goldberg (1983)], FLAVORS [Weinberg (1983)], COMMONLOOPS [Bobrow (1985)], and SCOOPS [Srivastava (1986)].

A *class* is defined in VASTU using DEFCLASS. A class may have two types of variables: *class variables* and *instance variables*. The instance variables are associated with every instance of the class, while the class variables are associated with the class. Class variables are accessible, however, from its instances. Variables as usual in procedural programming are used to store values and references to objects. Superclasses and methods of a class are also defined when the class is defined.

Superclasses allow us to define a hierarchy of classes over which inheritance of variables and methods takes place. An instance of a class has as its *local* variables all the instance variables of its defining class and its superclasses. These are used to store the state of the object. The class variables of a class are accessible from its instances or the instances of its subclasses. They can be used to share data among the instances for storage efficiency (because such common data need not be copied in each of the instances), for communication, or to store aggregate information pertaining to the class. When an instance receives a message, it invokes an appropriate *method* defined in its class or its superclass. In other words, an object has accessible to it methods in its defining class or its superclasses.

Whenever there is a name conflict among the variables or among the methods, first the defining class is looked up followed by its superclasses in left-to-right, depth-first order.

Take for example the classes PERSON, STUDENT, and STUDENT-AT-IITK. PERSON has instance variables NAME and AGE. Its subclass STUDENT has the instance variables SCHOOL, YEAR, and STATUS. Thus an instance of STUDENT will have five instance variables. STUDENTS-AT-IITK is a subclass of STUDENT. It has the same instance variables, but it specifies the default (or initialization) value of SCHOOL as IITK. It also has a class variable that keeps count of instances, i.e., students at IITK.

```
(DEFCLASS PERSON
    (INSTVARS NAME AGE)
    (SUPERS CLASS)
      (METHODS   ...))


(DEFCLASS STUDENT
    (INSTVARS SCHOOL STATUS YEAR)
```

```
(SUPERS PERSON)
(METHODS    ...))

(DEFCLASS STUDENT-AT-IITK
    (CLASSVARS NUM-STUDENTS)
    (INSTVARS (SCHOOL 'IITK)) ;default value of variable.
    (SUPERS STUDENT)
    (METHODS...))
```

Let us now look at messages and methods. A *message* expression or simply a message has the following form:

```
(SEND <obj-parm> <message-type> <parm1>...<parmn>)
```

Where <message-type> must be an atom and <obj-parm> and <parm1> to <parmn> can be expressions. An *expression* is either a variable, a function application in LISP, or a message.

Evaluating a message means sending a message and receiving a response. To send the message, each of <obj-parm> and <parm1> to <parmn> are evaluated yielding, say, <obj> and <arg1> to <argn>, respectively. Now the message can be sent to the object <obj> with type <message-type> and arguments <arg1> to <argn>. The object <obj> on receiving the message applies the method <message-type> to the received arguments and returns the value. The returned value is received back from where the message was sent.

A *method* is a sequence of steps (somewhat like a procedure). A *step* might be an expression, an assignment statement, or a return statement. To *execute* or *evaluate a step,* the following rules are followed:

1. If it is a message (expression), it is sent to the appropriate object.
2. If it is a function application (expression), it is evaluated as usual by evaluating the parameters and applying the function with variables taking their values from the instance and classes.
3. If it is an assignment, the value of the variable is changed. It is written like in LISP using SETF.
4. If it is a return statement, the value is returned and the execution of the method terminates.

If the last step of the method is executed and it is not a return statement, reference to the object which had invoked the method is returned. Details of the messages, methods, and steps should become clear from examples below.

```
(DEFCLASS PERSON
    (INSTVARS NAME AGE)
    (SUPERS CLASS)
```

```
(METHODS
    (DEFMETHOD INCR-AGE ()
        (SETF AGE (SEND 1 + AGE))))))
```

INCR-AGE is a method that takes nil arguments. Its body contains an assignment statement which increments an instance variable. It contains a message expression.

```
(SEND 1 + AGE)
```

evaluates to a number one more than the current value of AGE. It is a message in which 1 is the object (of built-in class NUMBER) to which is sent the message (+ <value-of-AGE>). The correct number is received by the sender to its message. It could also have been written using function application expression

```
(DEFMETHOD INCR-AGE ()
    (SETF AGE (+ 1 AGE)))
```

The methods can refer to a variable called SELF which is bound to the object that has invoked the current method. This allows an object to send messages to itself.

There is a built-in message MAKE that when sent to a class returns a new instance of the class. The instance variables in the new instance have a value if the initialization is defined for the variable; otherwise they are undefined.

Exercise 12.1 Take the train wagons and train yards example, and use it to simulate wagon movement and repair. (*Hint*: Define suitable methods which cause a wagon object to change location from one city to another. For the time being ignore the wagon's placement on rails and intermediate locations.)

Exercise 12.2 Take your favorite domain (e.g., book, furniture, or robots in a blocks world) and identify classes, and instance and class variables.

Variables can be *active* in that procedures are invoked whenever the value of a variable is retrieved or updated. For example, ANGLES in the following is an active variable:

```
(DEFCLASS TRIANGLE ()
    (INSTVARS SIDES
            (NUM-SIDES 3)
            (ANGLES () #'GET-ANGLES #'SET-ANGLES))
    ...)
```

Whenever the value of ANGLES is retrieved, GET-ANGLES is called, and whatever it returns, that is the value returned. Similarly, if ANGLES is to be updated, SET-ANGLES is called. The syntax therefore is

```
(<var> <init> <get-fn> <set-fn>)
```

where <get-fn> and <set-fn> must be defined as methods. <init> is the initial value at the time an instance is created. Active values allow us to compute values on demand.

Finally, it should be mentioned that the COMMON LISP object system is being standardized and is expected to be available shortly. It is based on generic functions rather than messages.

12.3 AN EXAMPLE—GEOMETRIC FIGURES

The example we consider is from geometry. There are classes of polygonal figures each with certain properties. They fall naturally in a hierarchy. Figure 12-2 shows a hierarchy of quadrilaterals. The following are the descriptions of the figures:

1. **Polygon.** A closed rectilinear figure of an arbitrary number n of sides which has n internal angles
2. **Quadrilateral.** A polygon of 4 sides
3. **Trapezoid.** A quadrilateral at least one of whose pair of opposite sides are parallel
4. **Parallelogram.** A trapezoid both of whose opposite pairs of sides are parallel

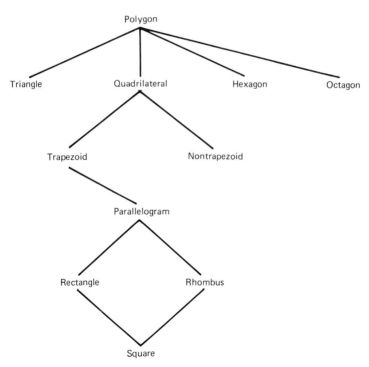

FIGURE 12-2
A hierarchy of quadrilaterals.

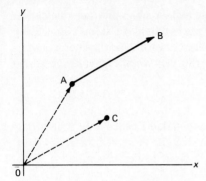

FIGURE 12-3

5. Rectangle. A parallelogram each of whose internal angles is a right angle
6. Rhombus. A parallelogram whose sides are all of equal length
7. Square. A rectangle and a rhombus

To define classes for the above figures, a representation has to be chosen. We decide to represent a polygon by a list of directed line segments representing its successive sides. A directed line segment is represented by a pair of vectors, and a vector by a pair of *x, y* coordinates as described in Sec. 10.4.1. For example, a directed line segment *AB,* shown in Fig. 12-3, is represented by the pair of vectors *OA* and *OC,* where *OA* gives the starting point of the segment and *OC* the direction and length. If the coordinates of *A* are (4, 3) and that of *C* (5, 2), then *AB* is represented as

```
((4 3) (5 2))
```

Exercise 12.3 Define vector and lines as classes. Each of them should have methods for returning values of all instance variables.

The following are the definitions of POLYGON and QUADRILATERAL:

```
(DEFCLASS POLYGON
    (INSTVARS NUM-SIDES SIDES)
    (CLASSVARS)
    (SUPERS   CLASS)
    (METHODS
      (DEFMETHOD PERIMETER ()
          (REDUCE #'+ (MAPCAR #'LINE-LENGTH SIDES)))
      (DEFMETHOD ANGLES ()
          (GET-ANGLES SIDES )) ))

(DEFCLASS QUADRILATERAL
    (INSTVARS (NUM-SIDES 4))
    (SUPERS POLYGON) )
```

With every instance of POLYGON there are two variables that store the number of sides it has and the directed line segments representing the sides, respectively. Moreover, two methods are defined that can find the perimeter and the internal angles. The QUADRILATERAL inherits all the above. It further specifies that the number of sides is 4 by default.

Similarly, we can define classes for TRAPEZOID and PARALLELOGRAM. In case of TRAPEZOID there is a method that determines which of the sides are parallel. The PARALLELOGRAM has an instance variable called TWO-SIDES that stores two adjacent sides, from which all the sides can be generated by GET-SIDES. SIDES is now an active variable whose value can be generated if needed.

```
(DEFCLASS TRAPEZOID
     (SUPERS QUADRILATERAL)
     (METHODS
        (DEFMETHOD PARALLEL-SIDES ()
           (COND [(= (LINE-SLOPE (CAR SIDES))
                     (LINE-SLOPE (CADDR SIDES)))
                  (LIST (CAR SIDES) (CADDR SIDES))]
                 [(= (LINE-SLOPE (CADR SIDES))
                     (LINE-SLOPE (CADDDR SIDES)))
                  (LIST (CADR SIDES)(CADDDR SIDES))]
                 [T (ERROR-MSG "No parallel sides" SIDES)
                  ()]))))


(DEFCLASS PARALLELOGRAM
     (INSTVARS TWO-SIDES (SIDES () #'GET-SIDES))
     (SUPERS TRAPEZOID)
     (METHODS
       (DEFMETHOD GET-SIDES ()
       ;;Generates all four sides given two adjacent sides.
         (COND [(NULL SIDES)
                (LET* ((FIRST (CAR TWO-SIDES))
                       (SECOND (CADR TWO-SIDES))
                       (THIRD (MAKE-LINE
                                 (VEC-+ (LINE-ORG SECOND)
                                        (LINE-DIR SECOND))
                                 (VEC-NEG
                                    (LINE-DIR FIRST)))))
                  (SETF SIDES
                     (LIST FIRST SECOND THIRD
                        (MAKE-LINE (VEC-+ (LINE-ORG THIRD)
                                          (LINE-DIR THIRD))
                                   (VEC-NEG
                                      (LINE-DIR SECOND))))))])
```

```
        [T SIDES]))
    (DEFMETHOD PERIMETER ()
        (* 2 (+ (LINE-LENGTH (CAR TWO-SIDES))
                (LINE-LENGTH (CADR TWO-SIDES)))))))))
```

The method PERIMETER defined for a parallelogram is more efficient than the one
defined for a general polygon. The RECTANGLE and SQUARE can be defined
similarly.

```
(DEFCLASS RECTANGLE
    (SUPERS PARALLELOGRAM)
    (METHODS
        (DEFMETHOD ANGLES ()
            (LIST 90 90 90 90))))

(DEFCLASS SQUARE
    (INSTVARS BASE
                (SIDES () #'GEN-SIDES))
    (SUPERS RECTANGLE RHOMBUS)
    (METHODS
      (DEFMETHOD GEN-SIDES ()
          (REGULAR-CURVE 4 90 BASE))
      (DEFMETHOD PERIMETER ()
          (* 4 (LINE-LENGTH BASE)))))
```

Exercise 12.4 Define a class for rhombus.

Exercise 12.5 Define a method for finding areas and internal angles in a polygon. Can
you make it more efficient for the parallelogram?

Exercise 12.6 Redefine the classes TRAPEZOID and PARALLELOGRAM so that they
make use of the classes for vectors and lines. (See Exercise 12.3.)

Exercise 12.7 Develop a hierarchical tree for TRIANGLE in Figure 12-2.

Exercise 12.8 In Figure 12-2, the classes are not structured in a tree form, but rather as
a directed acyclic graph (see rhombus). Suppose the following classes were available:

EQUI-ANGULAR   Polygonal figure whose external angles are all the same
EQUI-SIDES   Polygonal figure whose sides are all equal in length
REGULAR   Polygonal figure which is both EQUI-ANGULAR and
                EQUI-SIDES

Incorporate the above in a polygon hierarchy of classes in which, for example, SQUARE
and EQUILATERAL TRIANGLE inherit properties from REGULAR.

The above package can be used to draw pictures. Let us say our picture is made
of figures, and each figure is a set of polygons. By grouping polygons into figures

we can get more complex shapes and can perform operations like translation and rotation on the shape without worrying about the individual polygons. The class FIGURE is defined below with one instance variable POLYGONS whose value is a list of POLYGON objects.

```
(DEFCLASS FIGURE
   (INSTVARS POLYGONS)
   (METHODS
      (DEFMETHOD TRANSLATE (VEC)
         (SETF POLYGONS
               (TRANSLATE-AUX VEC POLYGONS)))
      (DEFMETHOD TRANSLATE-AUX (VEC POLYGONS)
         (COND [(NULL POLYGONS) ()]
               [T (SEND (CAR POLYGONS) MOVE VEC)
                  (TRANSLATE VEC (CDR POLYGONS))]))))
```

A message MOVE is sent to each of the polygon objects causing a translation.

Exercise 12.9 Define the MOVE method for polygons. (*Hint*: You will also have to define it for PARALLELOGRAM which uses a reduced representation of two sides instead of four, and similarly for SQUARE.)

Exercise 12.10 Define ROTATE for polygons.

Exercise 12.11 Take another domain, say that of courses and prerequisites, and model it in VASTU.

12.4   IMPLEMENTING VASTU

In this section, we see how an object-oriented language can be implemented. The implementation relies on lexical closure. For pedagogical reasons, the implementation we consider first does not handle class variables.

12.4.1   Storing Class Definitions and Hierarchy

Since we will be needing the class definitions, particularly information about the class hierarchy, we need to store them. While storing the class definitions, we store both the SUPERS as well as SUBS hierarchy. Given a class definition

```
(DEFCLASS <name>
   (INSTVARS        <i1> ... <im>)
   (CLASSVARS       <c1> ... <cn>)
   (SUPERS          <cl1>... <clk>)
   (METHODS         <m1> ... <mp>))
```

we store the following under various attributes of <name>:

Attribute	Value
CLASS	((INSTVARS ...)
	(CLASSVARS ...)
	(SUPERS ...)
	(METHODS ...)
INSTVARS	($<i1>$ ... $<im>$)
CLASSVARS	($<c1>$ ... $<cn>$)
SUPERS	($<cl1>$... $<clk>$)
METHODS	($<m1>$ ... $<mp>$)
SUBS	...

The value under attribute CLASS is for documentation purposes only. Values under other attributes may be changed during execution. The value under SUBS is the reverse hierarchy of SUPERS and is obtained by traversing the SUPERS hierarchy in the reverse direction. The following implements the above.

```
(DEFMACRO DEFCLASS (NAME &REST DEF)
   (SETF (GET NAME 'CLASS) DEF)
   (SETF (GET NAME 'INSTVARS)
         (CONV-FORM (CDR (ASSOC 'INSTVARS DEF))))
   (SETF (GET NAME 'CLASSVARS)
         (CONV-FORM (CDR (ASSOC 'CLASSVARS DEF))))
   (SETF (GET NAME 'METHODS)
         (CDR (ASSOC 'METHODS DEF)))
   (LET ((SUPERS (CDR (ASSOC 'SUPERS DEF))))
      (SETF (GET NAME 'SUPERS) SUPERS)
      (STORE-SUB SUPERS NAME))
   (LIST 'QUOTE NAME))


(DEFUN CONV-FORM (VARS)
;;;Takes a list of instance or class VARS
;;;as given in the definition of a class.
;;;If any element of VARS is an atom, it puts it
;;;into a list. This will be used later as part of LET.
   (COND [(NULL VARS) ()]
         [(ATOM (CAR VARS)) (CONS (LIST (CAR VARS))
                                  (CONV-FORM (CDR VARS)))]
         [T (CONS (CAR VARS) (CONV-FORM (CDR VARS)))]))


(DEFUN STORE-SUB (SUPERS NAME)
;;;Store the NAME as a subclass of each of the classes
;;;in SUPERS.
   (COND [(NULL SUPERS) ()]
```

```
[T (SETF (GET (CAR SUPERS) 'SUBS)
          (CONS NAME (GET (CAR SUPERS) 'SUBS)))
   (STORE-SUB (CDR SUPERS) NAME)]))
```

12.4.2   Handling Instance Variables

For simplicity of implementation, let us assume that we will be dealing only with a tree of classes (and not a general directed acyclic graph) and that none of the classes have any class variables. The first assumption simplifies the search and the second one assures us that there will be no shared variables among the instances of classes.

The approach we describe here is based on taking lexical closure. If a class has some instance variables $<i1>$ to $<im>$ and methods $<m1>$ to $<mp>$, then to create an instance we evaluate the following:

```
(LET ((SELF (GENSYM))
      <i1>
        .
        .
        .
      <im>)
  (SETF (GET SELF '<m1>) #'<lambda-for-m1>)
        .
        .
        .
  (SETF (GET SELF '<mp>) #'<lambda-for-mp>)
  SELF)
```

where $<lambda\text{-}for\text{-}m1>$ is the lambda expression corresponding to the method $<m1>$, and so on.

When the above is evaluated, GENSYM generates a symbol that gets bound to SELF. This will denote the instance being created. The methods are installed on the property list of the symbol. To install the methods, closures of the functions (for methods) are taken in the environment in which SELF is bound to the symbol, and the instance variables are bound to the initial values, if any. SELF and the instance variables are local to the LET form containing the SETF form and are not accessible from any function other than the particular methods.

SEND is a macro that expands its form

```
(SEND <instance> <method> <p1> ... <pn>)
```

to

```
(FUNCALL (GET <instance> '<method>) <p1> ... <pn>)
```

in case the $<instance>$ belongs to a user-defined class and to

```
(FUNCALL '<method> <instance> <p1> ... <pn>)
```

in case the <instance> is of a built-in type.

Thus, sending a message to an instance becomes applying the closure of the method for the instance to the given arguments. Since it is a closure taken as described earlier, free variables in the method referring to the instance variables are resolved correctly.

```
(DEFMACRO SEND (INST METHOD &REST PARMS)
  `(COND [(BUILT-IN-TYPE ',INST)
          (FUNCALL ',METHOD ',INST ,@PARMS)]
         [T (FUNCALL (GET ',INST ',METHOD) ,@PARMS)]))
```

The LET form described earlier can be put in a nil-adic lambda expression

```
(LAMBDA ()
        ... ; LET form earlier
        )
```

and installed as the MAKE function of the class. Whenever it is called and its body evaluated, a new symbol is generated and its methods with private local variables installed.

In the LET form earlier, all the instance variables of the class must be determined. Thus, the instance variables need to be inherited from its superclasses. The implementation shown below does not perform the inheritance separately but as part of the generation of MAKE function for all the classes in a tree. It takes as its arguments a class name and the names of instance variables in its superclasses. Initially, it is given the root class and ().

```
(DEFUN GEN-MAKES (CLASS INSTVARS)
;;; Generates a lambda containing the LET form as above
;;; and stores it as the MAKE function of the class.
  (LET ((NEWINSTVARS
          (APPEND INSTVARS
                  (GET CLASS 'INSTVARS))))
    (SETF (GET CLASS 'MAKE)
          `(LAMBDA ()
             (LET ((SELF (GENSYM))
                   ,@NEW-INSTVARS)
               ,@(GEN-INSTALLATION (GET CLASS 'METHODS))
               )))
    (GEN-MAKES-LIST (GET CLASS 'SUBS) NEW-INSTVARS)))

(DEFUN GEN-INSTALLATION (METHODS)
;;; Generates expressions for taking closure of the methods
;;; and installing them.
```

```
(COND [(NULL METHODS) ()]
      [T (CONS
           `(SETF (GET SELF ',(CADAR METHODS))
                  #'(LAMBDA ,@(CDDAR METHODS)))
           (GEN-INSTALLATION (CDR METHODS)))]))

(DEFUN GEN-MAKES-LIST (CLASSES INSTVARS)
   (COND [(NULL CLASSES) ()]
         [T (GEN-MAKES (CAR CLASSES) INSTVARS)
            (GEN-MAKES-LIST (CDR CLASSES) INSTVARS)]))
```

Exercise 12.12 There are other ways of implementing object-oriented languages. Two alternatives are given below:

1. If your implementation of LISP allows you to bind the environment to a variable (as in SCHEME), then for each instance of a class the environment can be bound to the instance. Now, when a message is sent to the instance, the appropriate method can be obtained from its class and applied under the environment to the arguments in the message.
2. If your LISP does not have closure facility, the values of the instance variables can be stored on the property list of the symbol for "instance." However, the methods will have to be transformed so that they access the instance variables appropriately.

Try implementing these alternatives, and compare their relative efficiency.

12.4.3 Handling Class Variables

In this section, we show how class variables can be handled. Again, closures are used for the implementation. The class variables are accessible from the instances. The classes must be structured as a tree for this implementation to work.

Let us understand the principles first. Let there be the tree structure shown in Fig. 12-4 among the classes CL1 to CL4. Pairs $(\overline{Ci}, \overline{Ii})$ are the class variables and instance variables, respectively, for the ith class.

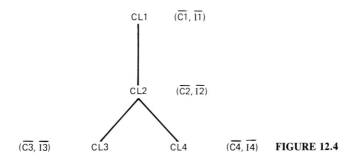

FIGURE 12.4

The MAKE function for instances of classes looks the same as before; however, its closure must be taken in the environment such that the class variables are shared. The following on evaluation generates the MAKE function for instances of each of the four classes CL1 to CL4.

```
(LET (C1)
 (LET (C2)
  (LET (C3)
   (SETF (GET 'CL3 'MAKE)
     #'(LAMBDA ()
         (LET ((SELF (GENSYM))
               UI3)
           (SETF (GET SELF '<m1>) #'<lambda-for-m1>)
             .
             .
             .
           SELF))))
  (LET (C4)
    (SETF (GET 'CL4 'MAKE) ...))
  (SETF (GET 'CL2 'MAKE) ...))
 (SETF (GET 'CL1 'MAKE) ...))
```

Where UI3 are the instance variables of CL3 after inheritance.

Function GEN-MAKES2 implements the above. (Compare with GEN-MAKES in the previous section.)

```
(DEFMACRO GEN-MAKES2 (CLASS)
   `(GEN-FORM-FOR-MAKES ',CLASS ()))

(DEFUN GEN-FORM-FOR-MAKES (CLASS INSTVARS)
;;; Generates a form which on evaluation produces the MAKE
;;; functions for each of the subclasses of CLASS including
;;; the latter.
   (LET ((NEW (APPEND INSTVARS
                      (GET CLASS 'INSTVARS))))
      `(LET (,@(GET CLASS 'CLASSVARS))
         ,@(GEN-FORMS-FOR-MAKES-LIST
                 (GET CLASS 'SUBS)
                 NEW)
         (SETF (GET ',CLASS 'MAKE)
               #'(LAMBDA ()
           (LET ((SELF (GENSYM))
                 ,@ NEW)
             ,@(GEN-INSTALLATION
                    (GET CLASS 'METHODS))
           ))))))
```

```
(DEFUN GEN-FORM-FOR-MAKES-LIST (CLASSES INSTVAR)
    (COND [(NULL CLASSES) ()]
          [T (CONS (GEN-FORM-FOR-MAKES
                        (CAR CLASSES) INSTVAR)
                   (GEN-FORM-FOR-MAKES-LIST
                        (CDR CLASSES) INSTVAR))]))
```

Exercise 12.13 The implementation shown does not handle active variables. To take care of active variables in a method, process the definition of the method replacing the occurrences of the active variables by appropriate get and put functions.

Exercise 12.14 Repeat Exercise 12.12 to handle class variables as well.

FURTHER READINGS

SMALLTALK is a language based exclusively on the paradigm of object-oriented programming. Read Ingalls (1981) for the philosophy and design principles behind SMALLTALK. Goldberg (1983) and (1984) describes the SMALLTALK language and its implementation.

FLAVORS and LOOPS [Bobrow and Stefik (1983)] are object-oriented systems in LISP. SCOOPS [Srivastava (1986)] describes an implementation on which the present one is based.

CHAPTER
13

FRAME-BASED
SYSTEM

In this chapter we introduce the idea of frames by means of a particular frame-based system. It combines the notion of inheritance from object-oriented programming with a logic-based specification language.

13.1 FRAME, SLOT, ASPECT, AND DESCRIPTOR

We have seen and used property lists extensively. They can be used to associate values under attributes for atoms. Frames can be thought of as generalized property lists in which an atom (naming a frame) can have not just values but specifications under attributes (called slots). Inheritance can also take place across frames. Frames can be used to represent entities, actions, situations, or their classes.

A *frame* is a data structure which has a name, slots, and fillers. A *filler* of a slot is a pair: an *aspect* and a *value*. The value might be a number or the name of a frame, but more generally, it can be a *descriptor*. When the aspect is equality and the value is a number or the name of a frame, the filler of the slot is referred to as the value of the slot. A slot can have more than one filler at a time. We illustrate these by examples. The sentence

Ram gave the book to Mohan.

might be represented as

```
(DEFFRAME GIVE-1
    (BELONGS-TO = GIVE)
    (SUBJ       = RAM)
    (OBJ        = BOOK-1)
    (RECIP      = MOHAN))
```

This frame has four slots: BELONGS-TO, SUBJ, OBJ, AND RECIP. Each of the slots has = as the aspect and an atom as a value. On the other hand, if we had the following action to represent:

> Ram gave a book written by the same author who
> wrote *Meghdoot* to the boy who came yesterday.

we will have general descriptors instead of just atoms.

```
(DEFFRAME GIVE-2
    (BELONGS-TO = GIVE)
    (SUBJ      = RAM)
    (OBJ       = <book-by-the-author-of-Meghdoot>)
    (RECIP     = <subj-of-coming-yesterday>))
```

where the filler of the OBJ and RECIP slots contains a descriptor. (The syntax for descriptors will be introduced in the next section.)

Inheritance takes place over a hierarchy established by BELONGS TO and SUPERS. For example, we can define GIVE-BOOK as a class of actions in which the object of the giving action is a book. All the instances of the class then automatically inherit this property. For example,

```
(DEFFRAME GIVE-BOOK
    (SUPERS = GIVE)
    (INSTSLOTS
        (OBJ = <a-book>) ))

(DEFFRAME GIVE-3
    (BELONGS-TO = GIVE-BOOK)
    (SUBJ      = MOHAN)
    (RECIP     = SITA))
```

GIVE-3 belongs to the class GIVE-BOOK; i.e., GIVE-3 is an instance of GIVE-BOOK. The slot OBJ of GIVE-3 inherits the specifications of OBJ from GIVE-BOOK.

GIVE is a superclass of GIVE-BOOK.

```
(DEFFRAME GIVE
    (SUPERS = ACTION)
    (INSTSLOTS
        (PRECOND = <SUBJ-should-possess-the-OBJ>)
        (POSTCOND = <RECIP-should-possess-the-OBJ>) ))
```

Hence, the instances of GIVE-BOOK are also the instances of GIVE. As a consequence, GIVE-3 inherits the PRECOND and POSTCOND from GIVE (see Fig. 13-1). Note that INSTSLOTS is followed by slots and fillers, which hold not for the frame in which they occur but its instances. They are somewhat like the instance variables of objects (Chap. 12) and are called instance slots.

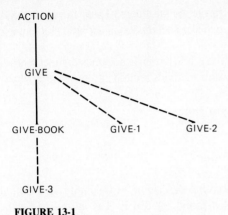

FIGURE 13-1

Having seen frames informally, let us look at their definitions more formally. In particular, let us see the specification language.

13.2 VIDYA—A KNOWLEDGE REPRESENTATION SYSTEM

VIDYA is a frame-based knowledge representation system. The syntax for defining frames in VIDYA is as follows:

```
(DEFFRAME <frame-name>
    (<slotname> <aspect> <descr>)
        .
        .
        .
    (<slotname> <aspect> <descr>)
    (INSTSLOTS
        (<slotname> <aspect> <descr>)
            .
            .
            .
        ))
```

where <framename> and <slotname>s are atoms that name the frame and its slots, respectively. <aspect> is one of =, <, >, etc., and <descr> is a descriptor to be defined shortly. Slot name SUPERS helps establish the class hierarchy, and BE-LONGS-TO establishes the instance relationship between two frames. They both take = as their aspect and an atom as the descriptor. The two together, <aspect> and <descr>, are called the filler of the slot. The three together, <slotname>, <aspect>, and <descr>, are called the slot specification. If a slot name has two fillers, the slot

name appears twice as <slotname> each with one of the fillers. Thus, for example, if a frame has two superclasses, there will be two slot specifications with the slot name SUPERS.

We next consider descriptors. After all, that is what makes frames distinct from usual object-oriented programming. It also makes methods redundant, and that is why there are no separate methods in VIDYA.

13.2.1 Descriptors

A *descriptor* can take any of the following forms:

1. *Atomic descriptor.* This is the simplest possible descriptor. It is simply an atom. The atom can be a number, the name of a frame, or SELF. The atom SELF is always equal to the current frame.
2. *Slot access descriptor.* A slot name followed by a : followed by a descriptor is called the slot access descriptor. It is like applying a function denoted by the slot name to an object denoted by the descriptor.

```
<slotname> : <descr>
```

For example,

```
SUBJ : GIVE-1
POSSESSOR : (OBJ : GIVE-2)
```

It yields the filler of a slot in a frame with appropriate inheritances taking place.
3. *Restriction descriptor.* A frame name followed by || followed by its slot specifications is the restriction descriptor:

```
(<framename> || <slotname> <aspect> <descr>
                      .
                      .
                      .
              || <slotname> <aspect> <descr>)
```

It denotes a subclass of the class named by <framename>, such that the given slot specifications are satisfied. For example,

```
(GIVE || SUBJ = RAM)
```

denotes the class of giving actions in which the subject is Ram. Similarly,

```
(READ || OBJ = (BOOK || AUTHOR = KALIDASA))
```

denotes the reading actions involving all the books that are written by Kalidasa.

4. *Arbitrary element.* A ? followed by a descriptor denoting a class specifies an element of the class

```
?<descr>
```

For example,

```
?(BOOK ‖ AUTHOR = KALIDASA)
```

denotes a book written by Kalidasa. Thus, the following denotes reading actions involving reading of a book written by Kalidasa:

```
(READ ‖ OBJ = ?(BOOK ‖ AUTHOR = KALIDASA))
```

5. *Propositional descriptor.* A propositional descriptor is a pair of descriptors separated by a relational operator

```
(<descr> <relop> <descr>)
```

For example,

```
(SUBJ : GIVE-1 = RAM)
```

is a proposition that on evaluation yields true or false. The relational operator can be one of $=$, $<$, $>$, etc., just like aspects.

6. *Procedural descriptor.* A procedural descriptor is of the form:

```
(LISPFUNC <procname> <descr1> ... <descrn>)
```

where $<$procname$>$ is the name of a LISP function. When it is evaluated, the named function is applied to the arguments $<$descr1$>$ to $<$descrn$>$. This allows procedures to be attached to the slots, or in fact, anywhere in the frames.
We can now write GIVE-2 and COME-1 as described earlier, in full.

```
(DEFFRAME GIVE-2
     (BELONGS-TO = GIVE)
     (SUBJ       = RAM)
     (OBJ        = ?(BOOK‖AUTHOR = AUTHOR: ?(BOOK ‖ TITLE
                                                 =MEGHDOOT))
                 ;; A book whose author is the same as
                 ;; the author of Meghdoot.
      )
     (RECIP      = SUBJ : ?(COME ‖ TIME = 15-AUG)
                 ;;A person who came on Aug. 15.
     ))
```

```
(DEFFRAME COME-1
    (BELONGS-TO = COME)
    (SUBJ      = MOHAN)
    (TIME      = 15-AUG))
```

If we look at the filler of OBJ in GIVE-2, we have the following descriptors with their meanings:

(BOOK ‖ TITLE = MEGHDOOT). Set of books with the title *Meghdoot*

?(BOOK ‖ TITLE = MEGHDOOT). A book whose title is *Meghdoot*

(BOOK ‖ AUTHOR = AUTHOR : ?(BOOK ‖ TITLE = MEGHDOOT)). Class of books such that their author is the same as that for *Meghdoot*, in other words, books written by the author of *Meghdoot*

?(BOOK ‖ AUTHOR = AUTHOR : ?(BOOK ‖ TITLE = MEGHDOOT)). A book written by the author of *Meghdoot* (including *Meghdoot*)

Similarly, the classes GIVE-BOOK and GIVE are shown below.

```
(DEFFRAME GIVE-BOOK
    (SUPERS = GIVE)
    (INSTSLOTS
       (OBJ = ?BOOK)))

(DEFFRAME GIVE
    (SUPERS = ACTION)
    (INSTSLOTS
       (PRECOND = (POSSESSOR : OBJ : SELF = SUBJ : SELF))
       (POSTCOND = (POSSESSOR : OBJ : SELF = RECIP : SELF))
    ))
```

13.3   IMPLEMENTING VIDYA

In implementing VIDYA, the first question, as usual, is that of representation. How should the frames be represented? How should the descriptors be stored?

13.3.1   Representation of Descriptors and Frames

The descriptors are represented as follows, where <framename>, <aspect>, and <slotname> are appropriate atoms and <descr> is the representation of the concerned descriptor:

1. Atomic descriptor. Represented as the atom.
2. Slot access descriptor.

```
($SLOTACCESS <slotname> <descr>)
```

3. Restriction.

```
($RESTR <framename>
        <slotspec> ... <slotspec>)
```

where <framename> is the name of a frame, and <slotspec> is

```
(<slotname> <aspect> <descr>)
```

4. Arbitrary element.

```
(? <descr>)
```

5. Proposition.

```
(<relop> <descr> <descr>)
```

6. Procedural.

```
(LISPFUNC <proc> <descr> ... <descr>)
```

A frame is stored using property lists of the atom naming the frame. Following are the relevant attributes and their values for inheritance for a frame F.

Attribute	Value
SUPERS	List of names of frames that denote superclasses of F.
SUBS	List of names of frames that denote subclasses of F.
BELONGS-TO	List containing the name of the frames to whose classes F belongs.
INSTS	List of names of frames that are instances of F.

A frame that denotes a class will normally have values for SUPERS, SUBS, and INSTS. A frame denoting an instance, on the other hand, will have values for BE-LONGS-TO. Of course, a frame may have values for all four. That, however, will occur only when we are dealing with a set of sets.

Values of INSTSLOTS are stored under the attribute INSTSLOTS, and fillers of a slot are stored under the slot name.

```
(DEFMACRO DEFFRAME (&WHOLE L)
    (STORE (CADR L) (CDDR L))
    `,(CADR L))
```

```
(DEFUN STORE (FRAME SLOTSPECS)
;;; Store the SLOTSPECS under suitable properties of FRAME.
    (COND [(NULL SLOTSPECS) NIL]
          [(EQ 'SUPERS (CAAR SLOTSPECS))
           (SETF (GET FRAME 'SUPERS)
                 (APPEND (GET FRAME 'SUPERS)
                         (CDDAR SLOTSPECS)))
           (STORE-LIST (CDDAR SLOTSPECS) 'SUBS FRAME)]
          [(EQ 'SUBS (CAAR SLOTSPECS))
           (SETF (GET FRAME 'SUBS)
                 (APPEND (GET FRAME 'SUBS)
                         (CDDAR SLOTSPECS)))
           (STORE-LIST (CDDAR SLOTSPECS) 'SUPERS FRAME)]
          [(EQ 'BELONGS-TO (CAAR SLOTSPECS))
           (SETF (GET FRAME 'BELONGS-TO)
                 (APPEND (GET FRAME 'BELONGS-TO)
                         (CDDAR SLOTSPECS)))
           (STORE-LIST (CDDAR SLOTSPECS) 'INSTS FRAME)]
          [(EQ 'INSTS (CAAR SLOTSPECS))
           (SETF (GET FRAME 'INSTS)
                 (APPEND (GET FRAME 'INSTS)
                         (CDDAR SLOTSPECS)))
           (STORE-LIST (CDDAR SLOTSPECS)
                       'BELONGS-TO
                       FRAME)]
          [(EQ 'INSTSLOTS (CAAR SLOTSPECS))
           (SETF (GET FRAME 'INSTSLOTS)
                 (CDDAR SLOTSPECS))]
          [T (SETF (GET FRAME (CAAR SLOTSPECS))
                   (APPEND (GET FRAME (CAAR SLOTSPECS))
                           (CDDAR SLOTSPECS)))])
          (COND [(NULL SLOTSPECS) ()]
                [T (STORE FRAME (CDR SLOTSPECS))]))

(DEFUN STORE-LIST (FRAMES PROP VAL)
;;; Store VAL under attribute PROP in the property list
;;; of each of the FRAMES.
    (COND [(NULL FRAMES) NIL]
          [T (SETF (GET (CAR FRAMES) PROP)
                   (CONS VAL (GET (CAR FRAMES) PROP)))
             (STORE-LIST (CDR FRAMES) PROP VAL)]))
```

Exercise 13.1 Define MAKE-DESCR that takes a descriptor as its parameter and returns its representation. Try your function on the following:

```
(BOOK ‖ TITLE =MEGHDOOT)
(AUTHOR : ?(BOOK ‖ TITLE = MEGHDOOT))
(AUTHOR : BOOK-1 = KALIDASA)
```

The precedence of operators in decreasing order is ?, aspects, :, ‖, and relational operators.

Exercise 13.2 Using read macros,

```
@D(<descr>)
```

should be read as

```
(MAKE-DESCR <descr>)
```

Define @ as a read macro character.

13.3.2 Matching Descriptors

To access a slot in a frame F, there are two cases which might yield a filler:

1. The slot might have a filler in F itself.
2. The slot might not have a filler in F, but it may be possible to inherit a value for the slot by considering frames of which F is an instance.

But this is only part of the story. In general, the filler might be a descriptor. It is necessary, therefore, to try to "simplify" or "match" the filler.

Matching is a process by which a descriptor is simplified, possibly leading to a number or the name of a frame. The following is a sketch of the rules for different kinds of descriptors.

1. Atomic descriptor terminates matching, and the same atomic descriptor is returned.
2. Slot access descriptor (s:d). Match the descriptor d resulting in, say, e. Get the filler of the slot s in e and match the filler. If no filler is found, then return the descriptor (s:e).
3. Restriction descriptor (f‖...). Using the frame name f identify an already existing subclass such that the restrictions in the descriptor are exactly satisfied by the class. Return the frame if found, otherwise the same restriction descriptor is returned.
4. Arbitrary element (?d). The descriptor d is matched. If it yields a frame containing exactly one instance, the instance frame is returned. Otherwise ? followed by the new frame is returned.
5. Propositional descriptor. Both the left- and the right-hand sides are matched and are returned after forming their proposition.
6. Procedural descriptor. The arguments are matched, and the function is called with them.

The above rules can be worked out in more detail. Here, we present a matching algorithm that deals only with atoms and slot access descriptors. MATCH-SLOTAC-CESS takes as its arguments a slot name s, and a descriptor d, to which the slot name is to be applied. It first simplifies d, by calling MATCH-DESCR.

The simplification results, hopefully, in a frame name. If it has a slot s, its filler is returned. If not, inheritance is tried by retrieving the frames to which it belongs and their superclasses, and looking for a filler of the slot s under property INSTSLOTS. INHERIT-INST takes a slot name and a list of frames representing the superclass, and performs the above inheritance.

```
(DEFUN TOP-MATCH (DESCR)
    (LET ((X (MATCH-DESCR DESCR)))
        (COND [(FAIL-P X) DESCR]
              [T X])))


(DEFUN MATCH-DESCR (DESCR)
;;; Simplifies the DESCR if possible.
    (COND [(ATOM DESCR) DESCR]
          [(SLOTACCESS-P DESCR) (MATCH-SLOTACCESS DESCR)]
          [T (ERROR-MSG "Cannot handle other types."
                        DESCR)
             '$FAIL]))


(DEFUN SLOTACCESS-P (L) (EQ '$SLOTACCESS (CAR L)))


(DEFUN FAIL-P (D) (EQ '$FAIL D))


(DEFUN MATCH-SLOTACCESS (DESCR)
;;; See description in text above.
    (LET ((FRAME (MATCH-DESCR (CADDR DESCR)))
          (SLOT (CADR DESCR)))
        (COND [(FAIL-P FRAME) DESCR]
              [(ATOM FRAME)
               (LET ((FILLER (GET FRAME SLOT)))
                   (COND [(NULL FILLER)
                          ;; Slot not found. Try inheriting
                          ;; from a super.
                          (MATCH-DESCR
                              (INHERIT-INST SLOT
                                      (GET FRAME
                                           'BELONGS-TO)))]
                         [(ATOM FILLER) FILLER]
                         [(EQL '= (CAR FILLER))
                          (MATCH-DESCR (CADR FILLER))]
                         [T (MATCH-DESCR FILLER)])))]
```

```
          [T (ERROR-MSG "Cannot handle other types."
                        FRAME)
              '$FAIL])))

(DEFUN INHERIT-INST (SLOT FRAMES)
;;; Left-to-right, depth-first search for an instance
;;; slot called SLOT in FRAMES or their supers.
    (DO ((SUPERS FRAMES (CDR SUPERS)))
        ((NULL SUPERS) '$FAIL)
      (LET ((VAL (SLOTACCESS-INST SLOT (CAR SUPERS))))
        (COND [VAL (RETURN VAL)]))))

(DEFUN SLOTACCESS-INST (SLOT FRAME)
;;; Look for instance slot called SLOT in the FRAME
;;; or its supers.
    (LET ((INSTSLOTS (GET FRAME 'INSTSLOTS)))
      (COND [(NULL INSTSLOTS)
              ;; INSTSLOTS empty. Try inheritance.
              (INHERIT-INST SLOT (GET FRAME 'SUPERS))]
            [T (LET ((VAL (ASSOC SLOT INSTSLOTS)))
                 (COND [(NULL VAL)
                        ;; Required INSTSLOT not found.
                        (INHERIT-INST SLOT
                                      (GET FRAME
                                           'SUPERS))]
                       [T VAL]))])))
```

Exercise 13.3 Work out the rules sketched in this section for a general matcher including all the descriptors.

Exercise 13.4 How will you handle SELF while matching?

Exercise 13.5 Implement the rules worked out in Exercise 13.3 together with the correct handling of SELF.

FURTHER READINGS

VIDYA has been described in Sangal and Roy (1987). Its design has been influenced by KRL [Bobrow and Winograd (1977)] and PREP [Hawkinson (1981)].

There are many knowledge representation systems around. For example, semantic networks [Hendrix (1979) and Shapiro (1979)], frame-based system [Roberts and Goldstein (1977)] and Bobrow (1977)], conceptual graphs [Sowa (1984)], and others [Brachman (1979)]. [Findler (1979)] is a collection of papers describing several knowledge representation systems developed in the 1970s.

APPENDIX

GLOSSARY OF COMMONLY USED FUNCTIONS

Commonly used functions in this book are listed below in alphabetical order. The format is:

`function-name: arg1....argn`

where arg1 to argn are arguments of the function called function-name. The arguments are objects that are obtained after evaluation of the parameters in the function call. The commonly used abbreviations are ⟨symbol⟩ or ⟨name⟩ for symbol, ⟨expr⟩ for S-expr, ⟨list⟩ for list, ⟨fn⟩ for function, etc. These may be subscripted. The optional arguments follow &OPTIONAL, and keyword arguments follow &KEY after the argument (arg1 to argn above). They are indicated but not described.

    Special forms and macros are shown as

`name:parm1...parmn`   [macro or special form]:

where name is the macro name or special form, and parm1 to parmn are actual parameters (not arguments). They are evaluated as per description. &OPTIONAL and &KEY are as before.

`AND: ⟨expr1⟩...⟨exprn⟩`   [macro]

    Each of the parameters ⟨expri⟩s is evaluated from left to right until one returns NIL, or all parameters have been evaluated. Returns the value of the last parameter evaluated.

APPEND: ⟨list⟩...⟨listn⟩

Returns the list formed by joining the argument lists in the given order.

APPLY: ⟨fn⟩ ⟨args⟩

Applies the first argument which must be a function (given by function name, a lambda expression, or a closure) to the second argument which must be a list containing arguments of the function. Result of the application is returned.

AREF: ⟨array⟩ ⟨ind1⟩...⟨indn⟩

Returns an element of an n-dimensional ⟨array⟩ given by the indices ⟨ind1⟩ to ⟨indn⟩.

ASSOC: ⟨key⟩ ⟨alist⟩ &KEY :TEST :KEY

Returns the sublist in ⟨alist⟩ whose first element is EQL to ⟨key⟩.

ATOM: ⟨S-expr⟩

Returns true if ⟨S-expr⟩ is an atom, otherwise returns NIL.

BOUNDP: ⟨symbol⟩

Returns true if dynamic (special) variable ⟨symbol⟩ has a value, otherwise returns NIL.

CxxxxR: ⟨list⟩

Each x must be A or D. the sequence of A's and D's indicates the sequence of CAR or CDR operations to be performed on the ⟨list⟩. For example, (CADAAR L) is equivalent to (CAR(CDR(CAR(CAR L)))). Sequences of xs of length 1 to 3 are also permitted.

CATCH: ⟨tag⟩ ⟨form1⟩...⟨formm⟩   [special form]

The parameters are evaluated from left to right. While evaluating a ⟨formn⟩, if a THROW-form is evaluated with the same tag as the value of ⟨tag⟩, the result specified by THROW is immediately returned.

CLOSE: ⟨io-stream⟩ &KEY :ABORT

The argument stream is closed.

COND: (⟨test1⟩ ⟨expr⟩...⟨expr⟩) ... (⟨testn⟩ ⟨expr⟩ ... ⟨expr⟩)
                    [special form]

COND is the case statement. First ⟨test-1⟩ is evaluated. If it evaluates to non-null, each of the ⟨expr⟩s following the ⟨test1⟩ is evaluated, and the value of the last form is returned. If ⟨test-1⟩ evaluates to NIL, ⟨test2⟩ is evaluated and similar procedure is followed. If none of the tests evaluate to true, NIL is returned.

CONS: ⟨expr1⟩ ⟨expr2⟩

Returns a list whose head is ⟨expr1⟩ and tail is ⟨expr2⟩.

CONSP: ⟨expr⟩

Returns true if its argument is a non-null list.

DECLARE: (SPECIAL ⟨var⟩...⟨var⟩**)** [special form]

Declares each of the ⟨var⟩s as special.

DEFMACRO: ⟨name⟩ ⟨formals⟩ ⟨form1⟩...⟨formn⟩ [macro]

This is used for defining a macro called ⟨name⟩ having formal parameters ⟨formals⟩ with body consisting of ⟨form1⟩ to ⟨formn⟩.

DEFSTRUCT: ⟨name⟩ ⟨slot1⟩...⟨slotk⟩ [macro]

Defines a structure called ⟨name⟩ having ⟨sloti⟩s as slots. It generates the keyword constructor called MAKE-⟨name⟩, and the selector functions as ⟨name⟩-⟨sloti⟩s.

DEFUN: ⟨name⟩ ⟨formals⟩ ⟨form1⟩...⟨formn⟩ [special form]

This defines a function called ⟨name⟩ having formal parameters ⟨formals⟩ with body consisting of ⟨form1⟩ to ⟨formn⟩.

DEFVAR: ⟨name⟩ **&OPTIONAL** ⟨init-value⟩ ⟨doc⟩ [macro]

This declares ⟨name⟩ as a global variable with optionally an initial value given by evaluation of ⟨init-value⟩. Comments are optionally given in ⟨doc⟩.

DO: ((⟨var1⟩ ⟨init1⟩ ⟨val1⟩'
            . . .
       (⟨varn⟩ ⟨initn⟩ ⟨valn⟩))
      (⟨test⟩ ⟨res1⟩...⟨resm⟩)
         ⟨expr1⟩...⟨exprk⟩ [macro]

⟨vari⟩s are local variables that get initialized to the respective values of ⟨initi⟩s. If ⟨test⟩ evaluates to true, ⟨resi⟩s are evaluated, and the value of the last expression is returned. If the test evaluates to NIL, each of ⟨expr1⟩ to ⟨exprk⟩ are evaluated, and the above repeats after evaluation of all the ⟨vali⟩s and setting the respective ⟨vari⟩s to their values.

DO*

DO* is also an iteration construct. It has the same relation to DO, as LET* has to LET.

EQ: ⟨expr1⟩ ⟨expr2⟩

Returns true if the first and second arguments are identical objects, otherwise returns NIL.

EQL: ⟨expr1⟩ ⟨expr2⟩

Returns true if the first and second arguments are identical objects or are equal numbers of same type, otherwise returns NIL.

EQUAL: ⟨expr1⟩ ⟨expr2⟩

Returns true if arguments are structurally similar, otherwise returns NIL.

FUNCALL: ⟨fn⟩ ⟨arg1⟩...⟨argn⟩

Applies the function in its first argument to the remaining arguments treating them as the function's arguments, and returns the value.

FUNCTION: ⟨fn⟩   [special form]

If ⟨fn⟩ is a symbol, returns the function associated with the symbol. If ⟨fn⟩ is a lambda expression, returns its closure.

FUNCTIONP: ⟨object⟩

Returns true if ⟨object⟩ is such that it can be applied using APPLY or FUNCALL.

GENSYM:

Returns an uninterned unique symbol.

GET: ⟨symbol⟩ ⟨attribute⟩

Returns the value on property list associated with ⟨symbol⟩ with attribute ⟨attribute⟩.

LENGTH: ⟨sequence⟩

⟨sequence⟩ can be a one-dimensional array or a list. Returns the number of elements in ⟨sequence⟩.

LET: ((var1) ⟨val1⟩)...((varn) ⟨valn⟩))
         ⟨form1⟩...⟨formn⟩   [special form]

Allows local variables ⟨vari⟩s to be introduced. Each of ⟨val1⟩ to ⟨valn⟩ are evaluated in sequence. After all the ⟨vali⟩s have been evaluated, respective local variables are bound to the evaluated values. In this new environment, ⟨form1⟩ to ⟨form⟩ in the body are evaluated and the value of the last form is returned.

LET*

Same as LET except ⟨val1⟩ is evaluated and ⟨var1⟩ is bound to its value, and so on, until ⟨varn⟩ is bound. Note that unlike LET, evaluation of each ⟨vali⟩ takes place in different environments. Following this the body is evaluated.

LOAD: ⟨filename⟩

Loads the contents of the file whose name is given by the string ⟨filename⟩ into LISP environment.

MAKE-ARRAY: ⟨dim-list⟩ &KEY :ELEMENT-TYPE

Creates an array whose rank is equal to the LENGTH of ⟨dim-list⟩ with the dimensions given by numbers in the list ⟨dim-list⟩.

MAPCAR: ⟨fn⟩ ⟨list1⟩...⟨listn⟩

Applies n-adic function ⟨fn⟩ to the first elements of ⟨list1⟩ to ⟨listn⟩, then to the second elements, and so on. The results are put in a list and returned.

MEMBER: ⟨item⟩ ⟨list⟩ &KEY :TEST :KEY

Tests for EQL equality between ⟨item⟩ and successive elements of ⟨list⟩. If successful, returns a tail of ⟨list⟩ that begins with the matched element.

NCONC: ⟨list1⟩...⟨listn⟩

Joins the ⟨listi⟩s by destructively changing the tail pointer in last cons cell of each of the first (n-1) ⟨listi⟩s.

NTH: ⟨n⟩ ⟨list⟩

Returns the (⟨n⟩ − 1)st element of ⟨list⟩ counting first element as first.

NULL: ⟨object⟩

Returns true if ⟨object⟩ is NIL, otherwise returns NIL.

NUMBERP: ⟨S-expr⟩

Returns true if ⟨S-expr⟩ is a number.

OPEN: ⟨filename⟩ &KEY :DIRECTION

Opens a file called ⟨filename⟩ for input-output and returns a stream object.

OR: ⟨expr1⟩...⟨exprn⟩   [macro]

Evaluates its parameters in turn until one evaluates to true. Returns the value of the last expression evaluated.

PAIRLIS: ⟨keys⟩ ⟨vals⟩ ⟨alist⟩

Forms pairs between keys in ⟨keys⟩ with respective values in ⟨vals⟩ and adds them to the association list ⟨alist⟩. Returns the new association list.

PRIN1: ⟨object⟩ &OPTIONAL ⟨output-stream⟩

Outputs the printed representation of ⟨object⟩ on a stream given by the value of *STAN-DARD-OUTPUT* or ⟨output-stream⟩ if specified. Roughly the output of PRIN1 is suitable for being read by READ. Returns ⟨object⟩.

PRINC

Same as PRIN1 except escape characters are not put. Roughly, its output is suitable for humans, not for READ.

PRINT: ⟨object⟩

Same as PRIN1 except puts out a new line first.

QUOTE: ⟨expr⟩   [special form]

Returns ⟨expr⟩ unevaluated.

READ: &OPTIONAL ⟨input-stream⟩ ⟨eof-error-p⟩

Reads the printed representation of a LISP object from a stream given by the value of *STANDARD-INPUT* or ⟨input-stream⟩ if specified, and builds the corresponding object.

REMPROP: ⟨symbol⟩ ⟨attribute⟩

Removes the value under ⟨attribute⟩ from the property list of ⟨symbol⟩.

RETURN: ⟨form⟩   [macro]

Evaluates ⟨form⟩ and returns the value from the lexically enclosing block such as DO, DO*.

SET: ⟨symbol⟩ ⟨value⟩

Assigns the ⟨value⟩ to special ⟨dynamic⟩ variable ⟨symbol⟩.

SETF: ⟨access-form⟩ ⟨val⟩   [macro]

Makes appropriate changes such that if the ⟨access-form⟩ were to be evaluated after SETF-expression, ⟨val⟩ would result. This can be used for setting values of lexical variables, fields in structures, array elements, list elements, parts of structure, and so on.

SETQ: ⟨symbol⟩ ⟨val⟩   [special form]

Evaluates its second parameter and assigns its value to ⟨symbol⟩.

SUBST: ⟨new⟩ ⟨old⟩ ⟨tree⟩ &OPTIONAL :TEST

Makes a copy of ⟨tree⟩ substituting every occurrence of ⟨old⟩ with ⟨new⟩. EQL is used by default to check equality of occurrence.

SYMBOL-FUNCTION: ⟨symbol⟩

Returns the current global function definition (if any) associated with ⟨symbol⟩, otherwise error.

SYMBOL-PLIST: ⟨symbol⟩

Returns the list containing attribute-value pairs associated with ⟨symbol⟩.

SYMBOL-VALUE: ⟨symbol⟩

Returns the current value of the dynamic (special) variable ⟨symbol⟩.

SYMBOLP: ⟨object⟩

Return true if ⟨object⟩ is a symbol.

TERPRI: &OPTIONAL ⟨output-stream⟩

Puts out a carriage return and a new line in the stream given by *STANDARD-OUTPUT* or ⟨output-stream⟩, if specified.

THROW: ⟨tag⟩ ⟨expr⟩   [macro]

Evaluates each of the two parameters and returns the value of ⟨expr⟩ to the CATCH-expression that has the named ⟨tag⟩.

+,−,*,/ : ⟨num1⟩ ⟨num2⟩

These functions perform the arithmetic operation as evident from the function name, or ⟨num1⟩ and ⟨num2⟩, and return the value.

=,⟨,⟨=,⟩,⟩=,/= : ⟨num1⟩, ⟨num2⟩

These functions return true or NIL if the arguments satisfy the condition as evident from the rational symbol.

REFERENCES

Abelson, H. A. and G. J. Sussman, *Structure and Interpretation of Computer Programs*, MIT Press, Cambridge, 1985.

Agarwal, Sanjay, Keshav Kant, and Rajeev Sangal, "Exhed: Expert System for Shell and Tube Condenser Design," *Int. Conf. on AI in Industry and Govt.*, E. Balaguruswamy (ed.), Macmillan India, New Delhi, 1989, pp. 88–102.

Backus, J., "Can Programming Be Liberated from the Von Neumann Style? A Functional Style and Its Algebra of Programs," *Communications of ACM*, vol. 21, no. 8, 1978.

Backus, J., "The Algebra of Functional Programs: Function Level Reasoning, Linear Equations, and Extended Definitions," *Formalization of Programming Concepts*, LNCS vol. 107, Springer-Verlag, Heidelberg, 1981.

Bhaskare, A. C., *Expert System for the Design of Shell and Tube Heat Exchanger without Phase Change*, M. Tech. thesis, Dept. of Mechanical Engg., I.I.T. Kanpur, India, 1986.

Bobrow, D. G., and T. Winograd, "An Overview of KRL, A Knowledge Representation Language," *Cognitive Science*, vol. 1, no. 1, 1977.

Bobrow, D. G., and M. Stefik, *The LOOPS Manual*, Xerox PARC, Palo Alto, CA, 1983.

Boyer, R. S., and J. S. Moore, "The Sharing of Structure in Theorem Proving Programs," *Machine Intelligence* 7, B. Meltzer and D. Michie (eds.), John Wiley, New York, 1972.

Brachman, Ronald J., "On the Epistemological Status of Semantic Networks," *Associative Networks: Representation and Use of Knowledge by Computers*," N. V. Findler (ed.), Academic Press, New York, 1979.

Brooks, Rodney A., *Programming in COMMON LISP*, John Wiley, New York, 1985.

Brownston, L., R. Farrel, E. Kant, and N. Martin, *Programming Expert Systems in OPS5*, Addison-Wesley, Reading, MA, 1985.

Burge, William H., *Recursive Programming Techniques*, Addison-Wesley, Reading, MA, 1975.

Chang, C. L. and R. C. T. Lee, *Symbolic Logic and Mechanical Theorem Proving*, Academic Press, New York, 1972.

Charniak, Eugene, Christopher K. Riebeck, and Drew V. McDermott, *Artificial Intelligence Programming*, Lawrence Earlbaum Associates, Hillsdale, NJ, 1980.

Clocksin, W. and C. Mellish, *Programming in Prolog*, Springer-Verlag, New York, 1981.

Dashora, V. K., *Meta Control and Functional Relations in Logic Programming*, M. Tech. thesis, Dept. of Computer Sc. and Engg., I.I.T. Kanpur, India, 1988.

Dashora, V. K., H. Karnick, T. V. Prabhakar, and R. Sangal, *Logic Programming with Functional Dependency,* Tech. Report TRCS-88-57, Dept. of Computer Sc. and Engg., I.I.T. Kanpur, India, 1988.

Date, C. J., *An Introduction to Database Systems, Vol. 1,* 4th ed., Addison-Wesley, Reading, MA, 1986.

Davis, R., and J. J. King, "An Overview of Production Systems," *Machine Intelligence* 8, Elcock and D. Michie (eds.), John Wiley, New York, 1977, pp. 300–334.

deKleer, Johan, Guy L. Steele, and Gerald J. Sussman, "AMORD: Explicit Control of Reasoning," *SIGPLAN Notices,* vol. 12, no. 8, Aug. 1977.

de Kleer, Johan, Jon Doyle, Guy L. Steele, and Gerald J. Sussman, *AMORD: A Deductive Procedure System,* AI Lab. memo. 435, M.I.T., Cambridge, MA, 1978.

Diwan, Deepak, *Rulesets: A Systems to Build Rule-Based Systems with Examples,* M. Tech. thesis, Dept. of Computer Sc. and Engg., I.I.T. Kanpur, India, 1986.

Enderton, Herbert B., *A Mathematical Introduction to Logic,* Academic Press, New York, 1972.

Findler, N. V. (ed.), *Associative Networks: Representation and Use of Knowledge by Computers,* Academic Press, New York, 1979.

Gallier, Jean H., *Logic for Computer Science,* John Wiley, New York, 1987.

Goldberg, A. and D. Robson, *Smalltalk-80: The Language and Its Implementation,* Addison-Wesley, Reading, MA, 1983.

Goldberg, A., *Smalltalk-80: The Interactive Environment,* Addison-Wesley, Reading, MA, 1984.

Hawkinson, L., *PREP: A Knowledge Representation Language,* MIT, Cambridge, unpublished, 1981.

Henderson, P., *Functional Programming, Applications and Implementation,* Prentice Hall, Englewood Cliffs, NJ, 1980.

Henderson, P., "Functional Geometry," *ACM Symposium on LISP and Functional Programming,* ACM, New York, 1982, pp. 179–187.

Hendrix, G. G., "Partitioned Semantic Networks," *Associative Networks: Representation and Use of Knowledge by Computers,* N. V. Findler (ed.), Academic Press, New York, 1979.

Hopcroft, John E. and J. D. Ullman, *Introduction to Automata Theory, Languages and Computation,* Addison-Wesley, Reading, MA, 1979.

Horowitz, Ellis and Sartaj Sahni, *Fundamentals of Computer Algorithms,* Computer Science Press, Rockville, MD, 1978.

Ingalls, D., "Smalltalk-76 Programming System Design and Implementation," *Proc. of 5th ACM Principles of Programming Languages,* ACM, New York, 1978, pp. 9–15.

Ingalls, Daniel H. H., "Design Principles Behind Smalltalk," *Byte,* August 1981.

Kapur, Deepak, M. S. Krishnamoorthy, and P. Narendran, "A New Linear Algorithm for Unification," *General Electric Report no. 82CRD-100,* Schenectady, NY, 1982.

Knuth, D. E., *Fundamental Algorithms,* Addison-Wesley, New York, 1973.

Kowalski, Robert A., *Logic for Problem Solving,* Elsevier North-Holland, Amsterdam, 1979.

Kumar, Ashok, and V. M. Malhotra, *A New Computation Rule for PROLOG,* Tech. Report TRCS-87-43, Dept. of Computer Sc. and Engg., I.I.T. Kanpur, India, 1987.

Kumar, G. Ravi, *An Expert System for the Design of Cooling Towers,* M. Tech. thesis, Dept. of Mechanical Engg., I.I.T., Kanpur, India, 1986.

Landin, P. J., "The Next 700 Programming Languages," *Comm. ACM,* vol. 9, no. 3, 1966, pp. 157–164.

Lloyd, J. W., *Foundations of Logic Programming,* Springer-Verlag, Heidelberg 1984.

Malhotra, V. M., *Accelerating a Prolog Interpreter by Preserving Its Execution History,* Tech. Report TRCS-87-41, Dept. of Computer Sc. and Engg., I.I.T. Kanpur, India, 1987.

Martelli, A. and U. Montaneri, "An Efficient Unification Algorithm," *TOPLAS,* vol. 4, no. 2, Apr. 1982.

Mukherjee, K. C., *A Temporal Logic-Programming System,* M. Tech. thesis, Dept. of Computer Sc. and Engg., I.I.T. Kanpur, India, 1988.

Newell, A., and H. A. Simon, *Human Problem Solving,* Prentice-Hall, Englewood Cliffs, NJ, 1972.

Nilsson, Nils J., *Principles of Artificial Intelligence,* Tioga, Palo Alto, CA, 1980.

Pearl, Judea, *Heuristics: Intelligent Search Strategies for Computer Problem Solving,* Addison-Wesley, Reading, MA, 1984.

Rees, Jonathan, and William Clinger (eds.), "Revised Report on the Algorithmic Language Scheme," *SIGPLAN Notices,* vol. 21, no. 12, Dec. 1986, pp. 37–79.

Rich, Elaine, *Artificial Intelligence,* McGraw-Hill, New York, 1983.

Roberts, Nirmal, *An Implementation of Higher-Order Functions in FP,* M. Tech. thesis, Dept. of Computer Science and Engg., I.I.T. Kanpur, 1985.

Roberts, R. B., and Ira B. Goldstein, *The FRL Manual,* AI Lab. Memo. 409, MIT, Cambridge, 1977.

Robinson, J. A. and E. E. Sibert, "LOGLISP: An Alternative to Prolog," *Machine Intelligence* 10, J. E. Hayes, D. Michie, and Y. H. Pao (eds.), John Wiley, New York, 1982.

Sangal, Rajeev, *VIDHI—An Expert Systems Shell,* Tech. Report TRCS-86-30, Dept. of Computer Sc. and Engg., I.I.T. Kanpur, India, 1986.

Sangal, Rajeev, and Subrata Roy, "KRS — A Knowledge Representation System," *Electro-Technology,* special issue on AI, Sept.–Dec. 1987, pp. 67–80.

Sangal, Rajeev, V. Chaitanya, and H. Karnick, *An Approach to Machine Translation in Indian Languages,* Tech. Report TRCS-88-53, Dept. of Computer Sc. and Engg., I.I.T. Kanpur, India, 1988.

Sell, Peter, *Expert Systems—A Practical Introduction,* Macmillan, London, 1985.

Shapiro, S. C., "The SNePS Semantic Network Processing System," *Associative Networks: Representation and Use of Knowledge by Computers,* N. V. Findler (ed.), Academic Press, New York, 1979, pp. 179–203.

Shortliff, Edward H., *Computer-Based Medical Consultation: MYCIN,* American Elsevier, New York, 1976.

Smullyan, R. M., *First-Order Logic,* Springer-Verlag, Berlin, 1968.

Sowa, John F. *Conceptual Structures,* Addison-Wesley, Reading, MA 1984.

Srinivas, K., Rajeev Sangal, and P. R. K. Rao, "COOL: An Expert System for Selection and Design of Heat Exchange Equipment," *WESTEX* 87, IEEE Expert Systems Conference, 1987.

Srinivas, Y. V., *A Framework for Functional Programming Based on Backus' FP,* M. Tech. thesis, Dept. of Computer Sc. and Engg., I.I.T. Kanpur, India, 1985.

Srinivas, Y. V. and Rajeev Sangal, "A Generalization of Backus' FP," *Proc. of 6FSTTCS, LNCS 241,* Springer-Verlag, Heidelberg, 1986.

Srivastava, A., *Implementing Object-Oriented Programming Systems Using First-Class Environments,* Texas Instruments, unpublished, 1986.

Steele, Guy L., *COMMON LISP: The Language,* Digital Press, Burlington, MA, 1984.

Ullman. J. D., *Principles of Database Systems,* 2d ed., Computer Science Press, Rockville, MD, 1983.

Warren, D. H. D., L. M. Pereira, and F. Pereira, "PROLOG—The Language and Its Implementation Compared with LISP," *SIGPLAN Notices,* vol. 12, no. 8, Aug. 1977.

Waterman, D. A., and F. Hayes-Roth, *Pattern Directed Inference Systems,* Academic Press, New York, 1978.

Weizenbaum, J., *Computer Power and Human Reason,* Freeman, San Francisco, CA, 1976.

Wilensky, Robert, *COMMON LISPcraft,* Norton, New York, 1987.

Winograd, Terry, *Language as a Cognitive Process, Vol. I: Syntax,* Addison-Wesley, Reading, MA, 1983.

Winston, Patrick H, and B. K. P. Horn, *LISP,* 2d ed., Addison-Wesley, Reading, MA, 1985.

INDEX

INDEX

DATE DUE / DATE DE RETOUR

MAR 2 0 1992		FEB 1 3 1995
		JUN 1 4 1999
APR 0 6 1992		JUN 1 4 1999
APR 1 2 1993		AUG 2 9 2000
APR 2 7 1993		AUG 2 9 2000
APR 2 4 1993		DEC 1 1 2001
OCT 1 5 1993		JAN 0 9 2002
OCT 2 8 1993		DEC 2 0 2001
OCT 2 6 1993		AUG 2 7 2007
JAN 1 2 1994		AUG 2 0 2007
JAN 2 7 1994		
JAN 3 1 1994		
FEB 0 9 1995		

38-297